P9-BZR-025

A Fantastic Ride

Bob Rohrman

A Fantastic Ride

A Patoka Press Publication

A Bob Rohrman Production

Distributed by Orange Media Group, Inc.
900 National Parkway, Suite 490
Schaumburg, IL 60173
Phone: 1-847-330-2946
Fax: 1-847-330-2947
http://omgorange.com/

ISBN: 978-0-9963247-2-4

Packaged by Blue River Press
Indianapolis, Indiana
www.brpbooks.com

Cover Design: Phil Velikan
Editor: Morgan Sears
Book Design: Dave Reed

Photos Courtesy of the Rohrman Family
Back Cover Photo Courtesy of Ashley Summers Photography

Printed in the United States of America

Dedication

This book - the story of my life - is dedicated with pride to my loving family, my dear friends and peers, my loyal, hard-working employees and all of our satisfied customers who have been frequent visitors to our dealerships and who have purchased vehicles from our trustworthy sales staffs throughout Indiana, Illinois and Wisconsin. I frequently have told family members, employees and customers that for me, selling automobiles is a labor of love - my hobby - and not a job. I hope you enjoy the story of my life, as well as the recollections of me as told by those who know me best. For sure, my life has been, is and will continue to be "A Fantastic Ride."

Contents

Foreword

After several years of thinking about this project, automobile legend Bob Rohrman, who celebrated his 82nd birthday in 2015, decided in July, 2014 to tell his fascinating and intriguing story in book form, an in-depth look at the life of a man who was born in a log cabin and rose to amass one of the nation's largest automotive empires.

One of eleven children, Rohrman was raised in a humble setting, living in Lafayette, IN, and Spooner, WI, attending school but always looking for a way or ways to earn money, whether it was selling home essentials to housewives in the early 1940s as a young boy by pushing a wheel barrell through the streets of Spooner, working as a movie theater usher or manufacturing tires at a rubber factory in Lafayette while attending high school.

Rohrman was a cook at a country club, a successful poker player and then an instructor in the military before returning to his Lafayette roots in 1954 to be married to the first of his three wives, Shirley, who is the mother of his five children.

In 1955, just a few days before the birth of his first child, son JR, Bob Rohrman accepted an offer to sell automobiles for a Lafayette-based Ford dealer. An instant success, Rohrman became the dealership's top salesman by literally using the Lafayette phone directory, starting with A and working his way to Z.

The first Saturday as a car salesman, twelve of those who Rohrman randomly had called on the phone showed up to see him and look at automobiles on the dealership's lot.

Eight years later, Rohrman opened his own used car dealership on Lafayette's Sagamore Parkway, beginning a journey that he never dreamed would be as successful as it has become, blossoming thanks to a move into the Chicago market bolstered by aligning himself with Toyota and Honda.

When Rohrman opened Schaumburg Honda in 1985 in the growing Chicago suburb, it was the springboard into sales and riches few - if any - ever believed was possible for him.

With more than 1,500 employees and more than 30 dealerships in Indiana, Illinois and Wisconsin, Rohrman has coupled highly successful TV and radio commercials and an insatiable work ethic and a love of sales into notoriety, fame and riches that few ever achieve.

In addition to Rohrman's entertaining story-telling description of his life, you will read chapters from 34 of those who know Rohrman best, including family members, friends and loyal employees who have gotten to know the complicated yet fun-loving man whose background is heaped in a drive to be successful and a keen ability to listen to those with whom he does business.

"Love the customer, and the customer will love you," is the simple yet logical mantra by which Rohrman conducts business.

Even at 82 in 2015, Rohrman proudly claims that he intends to work for at least another 30 years. He says, "This isn't work, it is my hobby, and why would I want to give up my hobby?"

It was an honor and a pleasure to spend a year with Rohrman, listening to his compelling and often funny stories of a life that most only can dream of experiencing.

--- writer Jeff Washburn

A Fantastic Ride

Part One

A Fantastic Ride

1. *In the Beginning*

On April 18, 1933, my mother gave birth to me, her ninth child among eleven, Robert V. Rohrman, on South River Road in West Lafayette, IN - believe it or not - a log cabin. Now, isn't that something.

My parents and my eight older brothers and sisters moved to Tippecanoe County from Madison, IN, where my older brothers and sisters were born, along with my parents, Velma Ringwald Rohrman and John Rohrman.

For a period in the late 1920s and then into the early 1930s, my father had moved the family to a farm in Billings, Montana, where he was a sheep herder. In Montana at that time, you either raised sheep, or you raised cattle. He decided on the sheep. At that time, it was a good business.

In 1931, the family moved back to Madison, and then in 1933, the next move was to West Lafayette, where I was born in the log cabin. They had loaded a big truck with their furniture and all of the kids, and my oldest brother, who was 18 years older than me, drove the car.

When they pulled into Lafayette, the family drove to a 150-acre farm that my father had rented near the Granville Bridge Road.

The man from whom my father had rented the farm said that the family living there could not move, but that my father could move the Rohrman family into a log cabin nearby.

On April 18, I was born right there in that log cabin. At that time, very few births took place in a hospital. Children were born in the home.

Soon after my birth, we were able to move into the farm house. Of course, I don't remember moving into the farm house because I was only two months old, but I have lots of memories of the times in the farm house.

I especially have fond memories of an older gentleman whose name escapes me that lived under the Granville Bridge when I was 5 or 6 years old. I spent many hours listening to his stories

Bob's parents, John and Velma Rohrman, on their wedding day.

and lessons about life. It taught me a great lesson about being a good listener.

During our time in that farm house, the Wabash River flooded frequently in the spring, and the water would cover the ground all the way up to our house. When I went to first grade at Montmorenci School, three or four times I had to take a motor boat to where we could board the school bus on the side of a hill.

My friend - that older gentleman - would pitch a tent during floods at the top of the hill on the other side of the bridge from where I lived. When it flooded, I didn't get to see him, because no one wanted to risk taking me over there.

But I cherished my times listening and visiting with him. He was such a good talker that I didn't have to talk very much. Imagine that. I didn't have to ask him any questions, because he answered any I might have had when he would share his wonderful stories.

There were many lessons learned when I lived on South River Road, especially the fact that my father was a disciplinarian. Man, he was tough. He was a big guy. And when I misbehaved, he grabbed a razor strap, which was used primarily to sharpen a razor.

It was tougher than a regular belt. When he spanked, he hardly ever gave up. I was probably 6 when I decided to take that razor strap off the hook and stuff it down the stool in the outhouse. No one ever knew who took that razor strap, except me.

I never told anyone what happened to that strap until my mother, who was 96 and near death in our home in Lafayette, and I talked about it. She smiled and got a big kick out of it. She probably always knew I had something to do with the missing razor strap, because she thought I was kind of ornery. But neither she nor anyone else was sure I had destroyed it.

When it finally was time for me to start first grade at Montmorenci, the bus came for the first time, and just when I thought I was ready, I suddenly got very nervous. Three of my older siblings got on the bus, but when it was my turn, I turned and ran away.

I decided that I was not getting on that bus. But my brother, Joe, who was 8 years older than me, took off after me. Of course, I had no chance of escaping him, and he caught me and then carried me onto the bus.

My first day of formal education, I went to Montmorenci screaming and crying. I did not want to go to school. I wanted to stay right there on the farm. But, yes, I did pass first grade.

Soon thereafter, my father moved the family from the farm on South River Road to Lafayette.

Left to right, Bernie, Rita and Bob Rohrman
in the late 1930s

2. *Across the River*

We moved from the farm house on South River Road into a large house on Wilson Street in Lafayette, which was a good thing except for the fact I now had to walk a mile and a half each way to school at St. Boniface.

At that time, all of the teachers at a Catholic school were nuns, and they were strict. When the weather turned cold, I lacked proper warm clothing to walk that distance, but I did so anyway. One day at about 2 p.m., my teacher told me to stay after school. I thought, "Oh, what I have I done wrong? What in the world could I have done?"

I really thought I was a pretty good kid - at least at that time - in school. I agreed to stay after the other children were gone. As I sat there, another nun entered the classroom carrying a large box, which she instructed me to open.

When I looked inside, there was a brand new bright red snowsuit just for me. The nuns knew we didn't have a lot of money, and they wanted to be sure I had warm clothing to wear to school. I was so appreciative. Wasn't that something?

I wore it every day. It was the best thing I ever had. Until then, I never had anything that was brand new, especially a snowsuit to keep me warm. That was an experience that I will never forget.

The next year - third grade - they transferred me to Saint Lawrence. It was a good school, and I was having no problem until in the middle of the school year, I was walking down the railroad tracks, and several kids jumped me and beat me up. My face was swollen to a point where I had to miss almost two months of school.

But the injuries to my face were a coincidence with a condition that really was causing me to be sick. I had to miss school because I actually had strep nose. This was a condition that no one really understood until years later — 1973 during a visit with my doctor, Jim Pickrill, who suggested that I travel to Los Angeles to visit a specialist, who operated on me when I was 40, long after I began having problems with my nose in third grade.

I woke from that surgery, and my face was completely bandaged except for slits cut for my eyes. My second wife, Linda, was with me the whole time and helped me walk up and down the hall several times, because although I was weak, the doctor who performed the operation encouraged me to walk and be active.

At the time of that surgery - as a frame of reference - I was still in the used car business in Lafayette, but in 1969, I had acquired a Toyota franchise.

For those who may be curious, I met Linda at Lafayette National Bank, where she worked in the loan department. Linda is just a great woman, and she saw me through that surgery that really helped me with a condition I had suffered with since third grade at Saint Lawrence.

Because of the swelling in my face that forced me to miss two months of school in third grade, the nuns at Saint Lawrence recommended that I repeat third grade, which I did.

While we were living on Wilson Street and I was attending Saint Lawrence, I met a friend - Dick Leill - who remains a great man and one of my dear friends. I could not write this book without mention of Dick, with whom I shared some memorable childhood antics.

During one of those hot Indiana summers, Dick, whose family lived right next door to our family, and I were playing in our backyard with one of my brothers, and after we dug a hole, Dick stuck a potato fork right through my brother Bernie's foot.

To this day, when Dick and I get together, we talk about that day in the backyard with the potato fork.

3. On (to) Wisconsin

From my early years on Wilson Street and attending Catholic schools in Lafayette, my father decided to move the family to Spooner, WI, to a property which actually was about ten miles north of Spooner. Again, I would walk to school, this time about one mile. There are beautiful woods near Spooner, and I had a great time there. The school I attended included all eight grades in one room.

We raised pigs on a farm and had a couple of horses, too.

We also chopped trees and produced pulp wood to make paper. When we cut that wood for pulp, we had to create roads through the woods, and we would stack that pulp wood in stacks of about two cords.

Bob (top left wearing a tie) at the one-room school house in Spooner, WI, 1944.

My dad's dear friend, Buck Cummings, and dad decided that dad also would build a tavern. When it was completed, they decided that Buck would run the tavern, and they would split the profits 50-50. To this day, that tavern is still there.

After the tavern was completed, we moved from the farm to another place by Dunn Lake on Little Casey Lake.

At one point, we had 644 acres, and it was all timber, except for the lakes. When we moved from the farm over there, we got out of farming, and dad got into building lake cottages. He put two buildings together for us. He dug a nice basement, built one house on one side and one on the other side. It was kind of a T shape, and that was the house.

When I was a fourth grader, my brothers Joe and Don each joined the Navy during World War II. Joe came home for a visit, and I had a very cute teacher, Lorraine, so I asked my mother if I could invite her for dinner to meet my brother.

When Joe got out of the Navy when the war ended in 1945 and came home to Spooner, they got married. Yes, I must admit that I always have taken pride in being a match maker. My fourth-grade teacher became my sister-in-law.

Family has always been such a big part of my life, and it makes me proud that Joe and Lorraine got together because of my efforts.

They always reminded me that I was responsible for their marriage. Joe moved their family to Denver, because he took a position with a construction company there.

After about ten years in Denver, Joe wanted to go into the construction business on his own. At that time, I was the used car manager and general sales manager at Glen R. Pitman Ford in Lafayette, and Joe moved his family to Lafayette.

I put up the money, and he and I ran a construction company called Rohrman and Rohrman. He built a couple of houses and sold both of them. After that, they decided to move back to near Spooner, where my mother and father were still living, along with my younger brother, Bernie, who is two years younger than me.

Brother Joe continued to do construction work in Spooner, where older brother Don also settled after he got out of the service. Don, who got married before the war, wed Maisey who was from Mulberry, IN, near Lafayette. Maisey was a nurse.

I also had an older sister, Marie, who married George Terrell, who like me was a car salesman. George sold cars in Lafayette for Ed Becker at Becker Auto Sales. Ed and George were very good friends.When Marie and George were married in 1938 at St. Boniface in Lafayette, I rode to the church in the car with mom and dad. When we were in the car, my older brother Joe told me - remember, I was 5 in 1938 - that if I walked into the church, the church would fall down. So, I was scared the church was going to fall on me, so I sat in the car during the entire wedding.

But I made it up to George, because when I left Pitman's in 1963 to start my used car lot, I hired George to sell cars. He was a great salesman. Everybody just loved George. He loved everybody, and everybody loved him. People couldn't refuse to buy a car from George.

4. *At the Core of My Success*

I have learned many valuable lessons in my life, but few are as important as the method of selling cars that brother-in-law George exhibited.

People don't buy cars. They buy people. Four of my grandsons are in the business with me, and one of them runs the biggest store I have - Schaumburg Honda - and one runs the Toyota store here in Lafayette. Another runs the Ford store in Schaumburg.

Another one, Luke, sold cars for us the last two summers and graduated from Hope College in Holland, MI, in 2015

When he graduates in the summer of 2015, he will attend the National Automobile Dealers Association school, which really is the automobile bible. He averaged selling sixteen cars a month. Luke has a great personality.

I have told them all - and I tell all of my salesmen - that if you want to be a success in selling cars, and you can sell cars well, then you can sell anything.

Also, if you can sell anything, then you can sell cars.

The thing you have to do is fall in love with the customer. If you fall in love with the customer, the customer will fall in love with you. If that customer falls in love with you, he won't buy a car from anyone else.

He will even pay you $50 more because he likes you. Of course, we don't charge them $50 more, but those who love you would pay it.

That is my philosophy, and it always has been since I started selling cars.

5. Sad but True

In every family, there are many happy stories, but there also often are sad ones. Our sad story centers on my brothers, Joe and Don.

Joe went to work for Minneapolis Power and Light, which was a big electric company in Minneapolis. Many electric companies have buildings that are fifty feet tall, but there are no individual floors. It is just a big, wide space in which they produce electricity.

Joe was working in this building about thirty feet off the floor, and he didn't have his safety belt on. He was on the plank that they walk on, and he slipped and fell. He fell all the way to the ground and hit his head on cement.

In most cases, he probably would have died, but he survived the fall. Joe spent the next six or seven years in a nursing home, the first year in Minneapolis. After that, his wife, Lorraine, talked the electric company into moving Joe to a nursing home in Louisville, KY, because their daughter, Theresa, was living in Louisville and teaching school there.

They also had an adopted son who was living in Louisville. Surrounded by family, Joe spent five or six years during the late 1960s and early 1970s in a nursing home in Louisville. I visited Joe as often as I could, but he never remembered me. He really could not remember anyone.

Finally, he was able to remember Lorraine, but I think that was because she visited him every day, and they always interacted. Essentially, Joe got reacquainted with Lorraine. Fortunately, Minneapolis Power and Light paid all the bills for Joe's care.

When I visited Joe, I would take him for a walk, but he would walk faster than me. I had to hold onto him to slow him down. Everyone in the family would travel to Louisville to visit Joe, but as far as I know, he never recognized anyone.

During those years, Lorraine was diagnosed with a brain tumor, and the doctor told her that the tumor needed to be removed in an operation. The tumor was located on the side of her brain. The surgery was performed, the tumor was removed, but Lorraine never woke up. Six months after Lorraine's death, Joe died.

Joe and Lorraine are buried next to each other in Spooner, WI, where I had arranged for them to meet at our dinner table when I was just a little guy. My parents are buried in Spooner, as are my brother Don and his wife, Maisey.

The Don and Maisey story also had a sad ending. When Dom retired after being in the construction business for many years building bridges, he and Maisey would vacation during the winter in Bonita Springs, FL, where they had a nice little place.

After retiring when he was 65, Don learned about five years later that Maisey had Alzheimer's. Don took great care of her even when some in the nursing home would not. The nurses could not get Maisey to eat. The last two times I saw her, she never opened her eyes.

But for almost 15 years, Don did a wonderful job taking care of her at a nursing home in Shell Lake, WI, not far from Spooner.

When Maisey passed away, I really think the same thing happened to Don that happened to Joe when Lorraine died. Don lived maybe a year after Maisey passed away, and then when he was 90, Don died. Don's efforts kept Maisey alive for years. Everyone in the family said she never would have lived the number of years she did had it not been for Don's wonderful care. That was Don's way.

Nine of the eleven Rohrman children.

6. *An Accidental Loss, Yet an Important Gain*

When I was young and living in Wisconsin, we were cutting pulp wood from 150 acres, so we made roads for the trucks to go through and load up. We had to stack the pulp wood in cords on the road.

Buck Cummings' son was who I worked for. He would cut the tree down, and I would trim the tree once Buck's son got done. I was 8, and I was trimming it with an axe. After I trimmed the tree, he would be cutting another one. It was easy to trim, because most of the limbs were at the top on a big Jack Pine.

I would lay 100 inches down and mark it where Buck's son had to cut it. After I would mark it, he would saw in 100-inch lengths. My major job was to stand those things up and put them over my shoulder, walk back to the road they had made and then stack them.

I am still strong from that job as an 8 and 9-year-old. With that strength, I have arm-wrestled a lot of people and never lost. I haven't arm-wrestled for 10 years, but I still don't think anyone can whip me.

But one time, we had some of the trees close to our house, and they had little limbs on them. I was trimming them with a hatchet, and I cut the end of my left ring finger off. I was bleeding terribly, and they rushed me to the hospital.

That injury always bothered me when I was in high school, trying to learn how to type. Through all of those experiences at such an early age, I learned a valuable work ethic that serves me well to this day. Work to me is not work.

Being in the car business, it's something you either like, or you don't like. If you really like the car business - or you find a job that you really like - then they say that you no longer work.

I've always loved every job, even when I was working 3-11 and 11-7 at Brown Rubber when I was in high school. I have always tried to be the best at what I do, no matter if it was trimming trees, working in a factory or selling cars.

7. Back Home Again in Indiana

After some great times in Wisconsin, it was time for me to return to the Lafayette area, Romney to be specific. John Kennedy, who lived near Romney, married my sister, Mildred, and John's father had a farm near Romney on South Raub Road.

By this time, I was about to enter seventh grade right after World War II, and my father was working for a large construction company based in Washington, D.C. and was working on the island of Attue. Dad was one of the better contractors and built military barracks in several places, mostly in Alaska.

The island was close to Japan and had an airstrip. The United States took the island from Japan and built an airstrip there. Japan bombed Attue a lot, and dad was injured in one of those bombings.

He was putting a roof on one of the barracks when there was a bombing raid, and dad was injured coming off that roof and landed on the ground. Dad was hospitalized for quite a while.

When dad was hospitalized, John Kennedy and my sister, Mildred, came to Spooner from Romney on vacation. Dad was in a hospital in Madison, WI, so I talked my mother into letting me go back to Indiana with John and Mildred.

At that time, they didn't have any children. So as a seventh-grader to be, I began living on a farm near Romney. It was fun working with John, who was crazy in a good way. He was a wild man.

He was working at Brown Rubber where I would get a job, and we went home one night at 11, and we hit the gravel just as he was driving about 90 miles an hour on South Ninth Street.

There was a cloud of dust, and the guy following us was a friend of John's, and the friend couldn't see anything. The friend ended up in a field after going through a ditch. But John was a fun guy to be around, especially when a kid like me was in seventh grade.

When school started, I rode the bus from the farm to Romney. I made a lot of friends there, including Bill German, who grew to be a 7-foot basketball player and later was the Superintendent of the Lafayette Parks Dept.

John also was working on the farm, and one time I was riding on the back of a tractor while he was disking. John had some Red Man chewing tobacco and told me that it was good stuff. He encouraged me to take some, and I put a bunch in my mouth. I chewed it, but I didn't remember that I had to spit it out. So, I swallowed it. I got so sick that I had to fall off the tractor and go over and sit underneath a tree. I sat under that tree the entire afternoon, four or five hours before I began to feel better. I learned a lesson.

Another time, one of John's buddies who had been in the Air Force was able to secure one of the trainer planes. It had an open cockpit, and he would take John up and then land in the field in Romney. They turned to me and said, "Bobby, you have to take a ride." I said OK.

That was the first time I was in an airplane. It was fun and didn't seem dangerous to me at that time, but it sure would now.

The eleven Rohrman children at their father's funeral, Aug. 25, 1962.

8. *In the Cards*

Although I was living with the Kennedys on that farm near Romney, I always enjoyed going into Lafayette and spending time with other family members.

Nick Switzer, another brother-in-law, and my older sister, Maxine, lived in Lafayette, where Nick worked at Alcoa and operated a crane. At night, Nick worked downtown running a poker game.

Poker was illegal, but you could be sitting there playing with a policeman. Many people played at the old Central Cigar Store.

On Saturday night, the poker game was held at Nick and Maxine's house on Rochester Street. I was just out of seventh grade when they would have the poker games at Nick's house, and after the other guys all left, he taught me how to play poker.

Nick and I would play head to head all night long until it was time to go to church on Sunday morning at St. Boniface.

Nick taught me when to hold them and when to fold them, and that made me a lot of money when I was in the Army some years later.

Nick and Maxine had sons Larry, Steve, Bob and Tom, and Tom just retired after working for me for 35 years in the parts department. That was a wonderful family.

Before I began eighth grade, I decided that I wanted to go back to Wisconsin with the intent of graduating from grade school there. And so I did.

The Kennedys drove me to Wisconsin during the summer, and I moved back into the house my father had built. My younger brother, Bernie, and I slept in the basement of that house in one big bed. The furnace was in the basement, so it was the warmest place in the house. We made sure that big wood-burning furnace was well stocked with wood.

I attended Dunn Lake School in eighth grade. Again, all eight grades were housed in one room. I remember that I had a very attractive teacher, and I tried to take her out on a date, but she wouldn't have any of it.

I graduated from eighth grade at 14. I played baseball that year and was a pitcher, but that really was the only sport I played because when I attended high school in Lafayette, I had to work all the time. During the summer after my eighth grade year, Nick and Maxine Switzer traveled to Wisconsin for vacation driving a 1935 Ford roadster with a rumble seat. I have tried to buy one of those ever since, but now, they go for $50,000.

I decided to come back to Lafayette with Nick and Maxine, and the funny part of that story is that at 14, I had gotten a driver's license in Wisconsin and helped them drive back to Lafayette from Wisconsin. My brother Don had taught me to drive, and while dad was out of the hospital in Madison and back home, I talked my mother into letting me go back to Lafayette again.

It's interesting how at 14 I was able to get that Wisconsin driver's license, which I still have. I hitchhiked 15 miles to the county seat to try and get my license. I went to the sheriff, because back then, that is where you got your driver's license.

He asked my name and asked if I could drive. He asked my age, and I said 16. He asked my date of birth, and I said Jan. 1 of the year that would have made me 16 at the time. The old guy gave me my copy after we had taken a drive in his car around the block and I had parked.

It worked for me in Lafayette during the two years before I turned 16 and got a regular Indiana driver's license.

At 15 and 16, I lived with Nick and Maxine in Lafayette. They already had four sons to feed, so I had to work. Their four sons slept in bunk beds, and I slept in the middle of the floor in that same room.

When I would walk home from school, I would stop at a little grocery store and buy cans of Campbell's Tomato Soup. I still like to eat it to this day. Some years ago at one of my birthday celebrations, my friend, Alan Riggs, brought me a big Campbell's Soup sign and several cans of Campbell's Tomato Soup. It was a great gift from a great guy.

9. *A Working Man*

Upon my return to Lafayette to live with the Switzers, I knew I needed to earn some money. I saw an advertisement in the paper for an usher at the Lafayette Theater. Don Dimmitt was the manager, and he and I got to be good friends. Years later, he bought quite a few cars from me. I applied for a job with Don, and he put me to work at 40 cents an hour.

A normal schedule at the theater was 25 or 30 hours, but a lot of the other guys would want someone to work for them, so I averaged about 60 hours a week. I almost had to work that many hours to help Nick and Maxine make ends meet with four children of their own. I worked at the Lafayette Theater my entire freshman year at Lafayette Jefferson High School. In the fall of my sophomore year, I decided to apply for a job at Brown Rubber where brother-in-law John Kennedy worked.

I met with the personnel manager, who told me the plant was in operation for three eight-hour shifts a day, making all that rubber for cars. At that time - just a few years after World War II - automobile dealers were selling cars as fast as the auto factories could build them.

The personnel manager took down all of my information, and I explained to him that I needed to work the 3-11 shift because I was attending high school. To work there, you had to be at least 18 years old, so I told him I was 18 but I really was 16, about to be 17 the following spring. I looked old enough to be 18. John Kennedy put in a good word for me. My starting wage was $1.10 an hour, 70 cents more than I was being paid at the Lafayette Theater.

I worked 40 hours a week, and sometimes I worked 48 if they needed us to work on Saturday.Remember, I was going to school at this time, and working at Brown Rubber meant I was covered in dust and the rubber smell, which was terrible.

But it was worth it, because I was making enough money to buy a car, a 1948 Ford convertible. I financed it through Lafayette

National Bank, and Nick Switzer co-signed for me. My payments were approximately $35 a month. I never missed a car payment and actually paid it off early.

Each night after work, I would go home and take a shower and then cruise Main Street. Whenever I saw a couple of good-looking girls, I would pull up to the curb, open the door and say, "Taxi." Sometimes, it worked.

It usually was 1:30 or 2 a.m. each night before I went to bed, and then I had to get up at 7 a.m. in the morning so I could be at school at 8. Problem was, I ended up missing about half the total number of school days because I was exhausted.

The dean of boys at Lafayette Jeff finally called me into his office. He said, "Bob, I know you need to work, but if you don't start making it to school, you are never going to graduate."

He told me I would have to find a solution. So, I went back to the personnel manager at Brown Rubber and asked if I could transfer to the 11 p.m. to 7 a.m. shift. He told me that if I made that move, I would earn an extra 10 cents an hour, which came with working the Graveyard Shift. I then was making an extra $4 a week, which in the late 1940s was a lot of money.

The following Monday, I began working the Graveyard Shift. When you are 16, 17 and 18, you can work from 11 until 7, go home and take a shower and go right onto school. You already are awake at 7 a.m. When you haven't gone to bed until 1:30 or 2 a.m., it is difficult to get up and go to school.

After I made the switch to working the Graveyard Shift, I went to school every day. Then, I started doing OK in the classroom, even though I rarely opened a book. I listened in class and really never needed to open the books. I made straight As in math and in business class. The course I had the most trouble with was English, because you had to open a textbook to do well in that subject.

I always enjoyed my business and typing teacher - Mr. Kenneth Andrews - who fought in World War II and shared military stories with us, which I really liked. Kenneth Andrews' brother, Paul, married my sister, Leotta. My final two years at Lafayette Jeff, I lived with Paul and Leotta. Paul's brother - my teacher - always was proud of me because of all I went through to graduate while earning a living.

In fact, one time Kenneth Andrews asked me to drive his car to the grocery and purchase milk and bread for his wife before attending class. He gave me money and the car keys, so I went to the store, came back and went to class. I thought that was pretty special that he would ask me to do that.

10. Double-fisted Employment

With my strong work ethic established, I took on another job in high school in Lafayette, this time between my junior and senior year at Jeff, working with my good friend Tommy Robinson at National Homes.

He and I worked 3-11 at National Homes, then drove the short distance to Brown Rubber, clocked in and worked 11 p.m. until 7 a.m. That was a lot of work, but it was fun work. That summer, I made a ton of money for a young man. Actually, it was a lot of money for anyone.

Working at National Homes was tougher. They had me loading box cars and unloading them. The box cars were insulated, and if that stuff got on you, you would itch for a week.

The previous summer also provided an interesting work experience, thanks to my dear friend Charlie Bartley. Charlie had secured jobs for us at the Midlothian Country Club in Chicago. We loaded my suitcase onto the back of Charlie's motorcycle and headed up Highways 52 and 41 towards Chicago. We got into Northwest Indiana and stopped to rest, and when I looked back at the motorcycle, my bag was gone. Somewhere along the way, it had fallen off. Every piece of clothes - except what I had on - was in that bag.

We went back 20 or 25 miles in an effort to find it, but we didn't locate it. Charlie told me not to worry about it. He said his mother would take care of what I needed. Finally, we arrived at Midlothian, which was at 147th and Cicero in Chicago. You talk about a big country club. They staged major golf tournaments there. You could take the rail from Chicago out to it. The second floor of the country club had rooms for the guests, and the third floor is where the help lived.

When we arrived, Charlie's mother said that they had uniforms for us to wear and that she also would buy me some clothes, which she did. Charlie and I had a room on the second floor, because his stepfather - E.J. Ellison - was the manager.

The Ellisons lived in a house on the property. The country club included big ballrooms and four bars. Charlie even learned to play golf, and we had a great time that summer.

I started as a pots and pans washer, and then they elevated me to dishwasher. Then, one of the cooks quit, and they elevated me to second cook, which meant I got to grill lots of steaks and pork chops. Each Sunday they had a buffet, and Charlie didn't like to work that because he didn't like to wear that big white hat a chef wears. So, I would go out there and carve the roast beef.

And did we have fun.

We still had that motorcycle, and E.J. bought Charlie a 1947 Buick convertible that had air horns on either side. It was a beautiful blue car. We would leave the country club at 11 p.m. and drive over to Calumet City, where we would go to clubs where the girls would dance on the table or the stage. I was still a kid, really, but we would go in there and drink beer, and it was no problem.

One of the second cooks told Charlie and I that we needed to meet a young lady who was a friend of the second cook. She was a bartender in Chicago Heights. To say the least, Chicago Heights was a little edgy. Charlie and I went out there, and we were playing shuffleboard and visiting this young lady.

Charlie talked her into getting in the car with us and going home with us. The young lady was in the front seat and Charlie was driving. We stopped at a traffic light in Chicago Heights, and a car pulled up alongside us. The driver of that car had the window down and pointed a 45 gun right at Charlie. The man with the gun told the young lady to get out of Charlie's car and get into the car with him. She told Charlie, "I have to go." I was on the floor in the backseat. I thought I was going to get shot.

At the end of that summer, Charlie and I returned to Lafayette for the school year. Before we came back to Lafayette, we decided to drive from Chicago to Spooner, WI, to see my sister Cathie, who was dating Charlie. We stopped for a cup of coffee in Joliet on a highway, and when we got back on the motorcycle to head out, we somehow got onto an alternate highway and were on it for 20 minutes before we realized we had made a circle and were back in Joliet.

So, we stopped at the same restaurant and had coffee again. Finally, we got to Spooner.

11. *In the Army Now*

When I was ready to start my senior year of high school, I had a little money saved from working at the Midlothian Country Club in Chicago - probably $200 - and I also was returning to work at Brown Rubber in Lafayette, working 3 p.m. until 11 p.m.

But I talked to the employment manager and asked if I could work 11 p.m. until 7 a.m. He granted my request in part because they needed help on the 11-7 shift. The car business was flying at that time right after World War II, and what we were making at Brown Rubber was all car related material, the rubber moldings around the doors and the rubber arm rests and rubber around the windshields.

Bob Rohrman's senior picture at
Lafayette Jefferson High School, in 1952

All three of the major manufacturers at that time - Chrysler, Ford and General Motors - used our materials, and we were just covered in work.

I had a lot of fun during my senior year, during which I hung out quite a bit with my friend Tommy Robinson, who worked at National Homes and was a good high school wrestler. He and I often would go across the river to Purdue and work out.

After I graduated from Lafayette Jefferson High School in the spring of 1952, I knew I wasn't going to attend college because I really couldn't afford to, although my sister, Maxine Switzer, had spoken with some people at Notre Dame who were prepared to offer me some scholarship money.

I really wanted to be an attorney, but I turned down the Notre Dame opportunity because I thought maybe that was something I could do later. In the summer of 1952, I decided I was going to eventually join the military, so I sold my 1948 Ford Convertible to Tommy Robinson. Before I joined the military, I bought yet another car - a 1949 Plymouth Convertible. I bought that car from a Chrysler plant employee in Michigan.

I continued working at Brown Rubber into 1953. In February of 1953, I sold the 1949 Plymouth Convertible to a gentleman who later would be my oldest daughter's father-in-law, Tom Isbell.

Because I had not gone to college and the Korean War was on, I received my draft papers.

Before I left for the military, I hitched a ride to Attica and bought yet another car, this one from Gale Tipton, who used to have a used car lot in Lafayette. I bought a four-door sedan that ran well and looked good. It was a 1938 model, and he sold it to me for what he had in it - $200.

Three or four days before I was to report to the Lafayette Post Office for military processing and to go to Indianapolis for a military physical, I sold the 1938 sedan to another friend for $200.

Every car I ever bought, I never lost money on it.

When I reported to the post office on April 15, 1953, there were fifteen of us, and the first sergeant, who handed out the papers, came to me and said, "Bob, you are in charge. Here are the papers for all fifteen of you."

I do not know why he picked me as the leader, but maybe he thought I looked like a leader. Because I was drafted, the commitment was only two years. Had I enlisted, it would have been a three-year stint. Going into the Army turned out to be a great choice. We took the bus to Fort Benjamin Harrison, and I handed all of the orders to the officer in charge. We took a physical, and it was a quick one. I passed. We got back on the bus and headed to Chicago and Fort Sheridan. As soon as we arrived, we received our military clothing, helmet and mess kit. We formed a line, and the supply sergeant handed everything to us.

We went to a wooden barracks and were told we would be there three days. After three days, we were told we would be given orders to ship out. We had no idea where we were going. On the third day, they took us to an airport, and we boarded a DC-3.

At that point, we learned that we would be flying to Fort Lewis, Washington, about 50 miles from Seattle between Tacoma and Olympia. On this flight, it had to be a pre-World War II plane, because we couldn't fly too high. Had we gotten too high, we would have run out of oxygen. The plane shook, but it got us there, non-stop from Chicago to near Seattle.

We unloaded the plane, boarded buses and traveled to Fort Lewis, which was a beautiful fort at that time. Like Fort Sheridan, there were wooden barracks, but they were not too old. We would take our basic training there, assigned to the Second Infantry Division, which was comprised of the Illinois National Guard. Basic training lasted thirteen weeks.

12. A Military Leader

I don't know why, but I was picked to be an instructor in a lot of cases.

I was the instructor in CBR - Chemical, Biological, Radiological Warfare. I read the books for the subject matter and then taught the classes. Fortunately, I never pulled a day of KP because I always was instructing. I also was pretty good at calling cadence.

Right away, I was made a squad leader in charge of the first squad. Soon thereafter, they sent a lot of us to the RepoDepot, a receiving depot for shipping overseas in Fort Lewis. There were about 2,000 of us there.

We were there for three days and didn't know where we were going. On the third day, they lined us up on the marching grounds and told us that we were the luckiest guys in the world. They said we were to have been shipped to Korea but that the day before, the peace was signed.

Bob (right) and a fellow soldier stand next to a wrecked jeep near Fort Lewis, WA in 1954.

They said a third of us still were going to Korea, a third were going to Germany and a third of us were to remain at Fort Lewis, and I was to stay and teach basic training. I was assigned to the recon company, the only one in the entire division. We answered only to the division commander. We had light, fast tanks that moved 50 miles an hour and personnel carriers, which would carry a platoon.

They were short of officers, and at that time, I was a Private First Class. So, they made me a second lieutenant. I was in charge of a whole platoon, which was forty people. I was the commander of the lead tank. My driver's name was Wild, and he was from Chicago. Today, he is living in Westmont, IL, which is where my Toyota Dealership is located.

Because the war actually was over, they retired the 44th Infantry Division, which was the Illinois National Guard. Then, they brought the Second Infantry Division back from Korea, because Fort Lewis was the home of the Second Infantry Division. The company commander thought I was going to re-enlist. They even gave me my own room in the new brick barracks.

The company commander came to me and told me he was sending me to officers' training school in California. I went there for a month, and at the end of our training, another guy and I hitch hiked to Los Angeles. We wore our uniforms and never had a problem getting a ride. We hitch hiked back and had a graduation ceremony.

The company commander pulled me aside and told me that I graduated No. 1 in the class, tied with a colonel. I graduated March 22, 1954. I went back to Fort Lewis, and our whole company was in Yakima, WA. That is where the summer training took place. We had a big barn that served as the motor pool. My driver told me we had to change the oil in my tank, and as he was backing it up, the left-hand side rode right up on to one of the company commander's jeep.

We smashed all of his radios. If you destroyed something, you had to pay for it. So, three months later, we each got a bill for $200 for damages.

13. Wedding Bells

With a year to go in the Army, I came home on leave and got married to Shirley Relander.

We had met in high school and had dated two years. We talked about getting married before I went into the Army, but she had a year of high school to finish. When I was in the Army, we wrote letters every day.

Bob and Shirley Rohrman's wedding day in 1954.

I had to have a car, so I went to an auto sale in Illinois and bought a 1950 Pontiac, a three speed. I came back to Lafayette from the auto sale, loaded the car and drove all the way to Fort Lewis. That was our honeymoon. We drove through mountains and almost got stuck in a snow slide.

We rented an apartment in Olympia, which only was about 10 miles from Fort Lewis. I was at the apartment about three nights a week, because that's all the time I could get off the base. Shirley got pregnant with our oldest, JR, a month after we arrived at Fort Lewis. She had a lot of morning sickness, so much so that I was afraid to leave her by herself at the apartment in Olympia. So, we decided she probably would be better off to return home to Lafayette and stay with her mother and father. Her mother was worried about her. That way, we could save a little money, too.

I kept the car with me in Washington, and she flew back to Lafayette. When I got out of the military, I left the car at a used car lot in Seattle. That lot sold cars for military personnel who were leaving. I sold it for $200 more than what I paid for it. Before I left the military, a regimental combat team had been formed at Fort Lewis, and that team included my platoon. It ended up including 1,000 troops.

We loaded on the ships in the Puget Sound, and traveled well out into the Pacific Ocean. We could not see land at all. We got overseas pay because we were outside the United States waters. I got seasick and half of the ship was sick. All I could eat was soda crackers. We slept in bunk beds, stacked three high. We sailed down the Pacific and then stormed a beach to practice combat like they did at Normandy Beach in World War II.

We stormed the beach at the Hearst Castle in California. Right next to that castle is an army training base. From our ship, some were storming the beach in life rafts. We hit the beach with our jeeps and our tanks. The first jeep goes off, hits the water, and pretty soon, the only thing showing is the pipe. Then, he started coming back up. It was so funny.

It was at night, and then we headed up as if it was into mountains with no lights. Finally, we got through the mountains. We stayed four or five days and probably flipped over a couple of jeeps.

We reloaded the ships and went back to the Puget Sound and Fort Lewis. That was the only time I was in foreign waters. Within a month, I got my discharge from the military. It was early in 1955.

When I got back to Lafayette on April 15, 1955, three days before my birthday, it was eight days before JR was born on April 23. I never will forget the month of April in 1955. That was some month.

I had a lot of fun in the military, especially playing poker, which brother-in-law Nick Switzer had taught me to play years before. Every month, we had a poker game at Fort Lewis. In three days after we got paid - in cash - only three or four of us had any money left. I would loan the guys money who had lost theirs, and they would pay me back with a little interest. That last year I was there, we did that every month. They paid me $50 a month, but when I was discharged from the Army, I had $3,000 in a savings account, all in poker winnings.

I used that money to buy appliances and furniture for our apartment in Lafayette. I also had enough money to buy a car.

14. *The Beginning of a Dynasty*

When I returned to Lafayette in April, 1955, we moved into my first wife's parents' home on Union Street in Lafayette. It was a nice, comfortable little place with a bedroom, living room and kitchen.

Three days after I was discharged from the Army, I went downtown to visit George Terrell at Becker's Used Car Lot at the corner of Ninth and Columbia Streets. We hugged. George always was one of my favorite people, in large part because he was married to one of my favorite sisters, Marie. George asked me if I had gotten a job yet. I had applied with Associates Finance as a debt collector, and they said they would call me.

I told George that I needed a car but that I didn't want to pay a lot for it. George showed me a 1952 Frazier Manhattan with push-button doors. We took the car for a drive, and we talked about what I might do for work. George was dressed to the hilt, and people loved him because he was such a good guy and a great car salesman.

I looked at him and said that I might want to sell cars. George said that if I was serious about it, I might be able to get a job with Glenn R. Pitman Ford, who had been trying to hire him away from Becker.

George said that Pitman had some employees, but that they really weren't great salespeople. George did not want to leave Becker. George said he would take me to visit Pitman, and I said, "Let's go."

Right then, we headed to Pitman's. We walked in, and George introduced me to Pitman.

Glenn's office was right there in the showroom on Fifth and South Streets. We went into Glenn's office and sat down. Glenn was smoking a cigar, which he said he never inhaled; he always had it lit and wore silk shirts. the cigar sparks would fall onto those silk shirts. Glenn had hundreds of little tiny holes in those silk shirts.

We talked a little bit, and Glenn asked me when I had gotten out of the Army. Finally, Glenn asked me if I thought I could sell cars. I said, "Oh, yeah." He then asked me when I wanted to go to work. I told him, "Right now." He said, "You're on."

Glenn told George to leave me at Pitman's and that Glenn would give me a demo car to drive. George said he first wanted to take me back to Becker's and show me how to fill out a sales order and a purchase order. At that time, you called your own deals into the bank. We spent two hours back at George's office. It would be the first time I sold a car, but back in Wisconsin, I had sold Blair products to make extra money. The ladies bought all kinds of stuff from me when I was 10, 11 and 12. I had a sample case and sold everything from pie mix to ointments.

I told George that I could sell but that I didn't know the people in Lafayette like he knew them. I knew a lot of school classmates, but many of them had joined the military and were not living in Lafayette in 1955. George pointed at a telephone book and told me that would be my best friend. George said to start anywhere in the phone book and just start dialing numbers.

Bob Rohrman working at Pitman's in the 1950s.

I would say, "Mrs. Smith, I am an automobile salesman with Glenn R. Pitman Ford, and I understand you folks are interested in buying a car." I would talk to them, and most people were friendly. I called everybody in that phone book until Glenn made me the used car manager eight months later. The second Saturday I worked there, I had about 10 people come in to see me all at one time. Some of the other guys had to help me out.

Afterwards, Glenn asked me how I got so many people to come in. I told him I used the phone book. Glenn told me I should teach the other salesmen how to do the same thing.

I always kept good records of who I had called. About ten years ago, I went to a Toyota meeting, and one of the celebrity guests was former Purdue and Kansas City Chiefs quarterback Len Dawson, who was in college when I started at Pitman's.

I reminded Len that I had sold him a 1946 Ford when he was in college. He traded in a 1938 Studebaker. At the Toyota meeting, I told Len that I had saved the card file on him when I sold him that car. Len asked me to send him a copy of that card file, and I did.

The first month I was there, I sold fifteen cars. Throughout my sales career, I never sold less than fifteen cars in any single month. When I was the used car manager, I was a salesman as well. Glenn paid me $25 a week to be the used car manager. When he made me general sales manager, I didn't have to sell, but I did.

Glenn was always really good to me. He really liked me, so much so that he sent me to dealer's sons school in Dearborn, MI for a month. It taught me a lot about the car business. Another good mentor for me was Paul Bouwkamp, who was the vice president at Pitman's. I relied on his knowledge more than anyone's.

Bob Rohrman in his early days of selling cars at Pitman's.

15. *Time to Spread Wings*

When I was 28, I sat down with Paul Bouwkamp and told him that I was thinking about leaving Pitman's to start my own used car dealership.

Paul advised me to wait until I was 30. He said I would know a lot more, and that if I waited, I absolutely would be a success. I agreed, actually waiting until I was 30, leaving Pitman's in 1963. The reason I did that was because in 1961, Ford came to Glenn, who was older and not in great health, and tried to get him to sell the dealership to me. They wanted me to buy him out on contract.

Glenn first agreed to sell but wanted to wait a couple of years. After two more years, I knew that Glenn never was going to sell. Glenn died in his early 90s, still going to the Lincoln-Mercury dealership every day.

Glenn always was a great guy with me until the end. At the end, Glenn's dealership wasn't doing so well, and some of his employees weren't the best to him. When Glenn died, his daughter and only child called me and asked if I wanted anything from his office. I took his desk and kept it in my office at my home in Lafayette.

16. *Out on My Own*

After deciding to leave Pitman, I opened my first dealership - a used-car lot - on the Sagamore Parkway, which at the time was known as the 52 Bypass before Interstate 65.

The Chrysler Dealership was on the corner of Kossuth Street and the Bypass. Plymouth was with Chrysler and also with Dodge. Right across the street was a used-car lot that was closed. I looked at it in February, and the lot was about halfway covered with snow. The lot was gravel, and the lighting system for the lot consisted of light bulbs. There were four rows of lightbulbs, and about half the bulbs were burned out. The guy who owned the lot owned all the property in that area.

I tried to call the owner, but I was told that he was vacationing in Florida for a couple of months. I was given his number in Florida, so I called and explained that I wanted to start a used-car dealership. He told me immediately that he would be willing to rent the property. The owner was willing to rent it to me for $200 a month. I told him that was a fair price and that I was willing to pay it. He told me to send him a check, and I did. It was as easy as that.

I moved in there by myself. Soon, we had a group of four of us, including my good friend Jack Shaw, who was a fireman at that time. it did not take long before we were selling 20 to 25 used cars a month from that lot. I knew a lot of people in Lafayette and had sold a lot of cars in Lafayette seven years with Glenn R. Pitman. A lot of my friends would come to our lot and sit on the couch and visit.

The building was one big office with two small offices at one end. In the middle of the waiting room, we had a kerosene stove. It was cold, so we wanted to light the stove. we checked for kerosene, and there was some in the stove's tube. We pushed the knob on the back of the stove, and threw a match into it after opening the door.

Harold Craft, who had joined our staff from Pitman, said we needed to get more kerosene into the tube. Then, I took a newspaper and set it on fire. I opened the stove, threw the flaming paper in there. Before I could shut the stove door, it went BOOM, and scattered soot all over the office. We had soot on the walls and the ceiling, just everywhere. We did not get hurt, but our first task was to clean up. I will say the stove finally worked and provided the heat we needed. We never had a problem after that.

As Bob's original dealership looked in 1963.

Finally, we really were up and running, so I bought a few cars from Lafayette dealer Bill DeFouw, who had just moved to Lafayette to be the Chevrolet dealer. I also was buying cars from dealerships in Brookston, Rensselaer and Monticello. We also bought cars at sales in Indianapolis. I had saved some money while working for Pitman, but that winter of 1963 was difficult in terms of weather, which created some problems.

One day I came to work after it had snowed all night, and we had to dig our way into the dealership doorway. You could hardly see the building, because it was covered in snow.

I had that used car lot for approximately six years.

17. A Strategy that Worked

When we began selling at the used car lot, I had about $25,000 in the bank, which in 1963 was good money. You could buy a new car for $1,500 at that time and some pretty good used cars for $1,000 or even $700 or $800.

I did a lot of business with Lafayette National Bank, and the bank president was Lloyd Newman. Lloyd and I became good friends. When I told him I was leaving Pitman's to start my dealership, he told me that if I needed some money, I should give him a call.

I called and told him that in addition to the $25,000 I had, I would like to have an additional $25,000 for the purpose of purchasing enough used cars. Lloyd arranged for me to borrow as much as $100,000.

He knew my credit was good because we had had a relationship for seven or eight years at that time.

At that point, I actually had $125,000 with which to buy cars. With $125,000, I could buy from 50 to 60 cars and fill our car lot. I started with probably ten cars.

I had Jack Shaw as a salesman, and he knew everybody in town. When we started selling 20 to 25 cars a month, I would keep my own books. Finally, I realized that I needed a part time office manager. Jack told me I should hire his wife, Liz. She went to work for me and did a great job, staying in that position for 23 years.

Then, when we took on Toyota, we had to use the factory mandated accounting system. We also had to use the Toyota monthly statement. We had to submit that monthly statement before the 10th of the next month.

Neither Liz nor I knew how to use those forms. I called Bill DeFouw, and Bill was nice enough to send his office manager to us every night for almost a month. He taught Liz what was to go in the financial statement and how to submit it.

We added Toyota in the fall of 1969. I was not that familiar with Toyota, but I learned that on the West Coast, Toyota was selling well. They had a reputation as a car with very few problems.

One morning, I was sitting at my dealership reading an automobile magazine, and on the back cover, there was a picture of a Toyota Corona. It looked good. Next to the photo was a toll-free number in California.

At that time, our used cars were selling so well that I built a four-bay service department and hired a service manager. He was my service manager, head mechanic and parts manager. That guy was Skip Raisor.

That was important when I called Toyota. They listened to what we had and put me in touch with their Midwest distributor. I told the distributor that I wanted a Toyota store in Lafayette, IN. I was told that a Toyota representative would contact me.

Two days later, I got a call from a gentleman with whom I had some history. He came in to see me later that day, driving in from Cincinnati. We sat at my desk, and I told him I wanted a Toyota dealership. He told me it was a great move.

I signed some papers, and 30 days later, I was a Toyota dealer.

18. The Toyota Springboard

So, here I am with a gravel lot, no Toyota sign and no Toyota parts, yet I am Lafayette's Toyota dealer. At that time, no one in Lafayette knew what a Toyota was.

Within a short time, they sent me 15 or 20 Toyotas. Now, Toyota has 30 or 40 different lines of cars and tracks compared to two in 1969. I showed the cars to Liz and our staff, and they each agreed that those cars would sell.

Liz thought we would sell fifteen the first month, and that is exactly how many we sold in that first month. And the great thing was, there were no mechanical issues with these cars, while during that time there were many issues with the domestic made cars.

It made me feel good when Toyota customers would come in and say there is nothing wrong with this car. I was off and running.

Since 1969, the domestic has gotten quite a bit better, especially after Chrysler and General Motors each went bankrupt. Ford almost did, too. But Toyota has gotten a lot better, too. It is a great car. When I took on Toyota, there was one other Toyota dealer in Indiana - Bob Butler in Indianapolis.

Toyota now is the No. 1 manufacture of automobiles and trucks in the world. The Toyota Camry has been the No. 1 selling car in the United States for twelve consecutive years. Before that, it was the Honda Accord.

While we were selling Toyotas, we still were selling used cars and some new cars, too, especially Fords. The best used cars I could find at that time were Oldsmobiles. At that time, Oldsmobile was the No. 1 car sold in Indiana.

In 1969, I would drive to the Oldsmobile plant in Lansing, MI. twice a month and buy 15 or 20 cars. We would put them on our lot - all cars that had been owned by employees of Oldsmobile - and they all had low mileage. I sold a lot of them to people who would have bought a new one. I sold some new ones too, ones I had purchased from Kokomo.

I sold a lot of those Oldsmobiles from 1963 through 1979. I also purchased a few Buicks and Chevrolets in Flint, MI, when I would make my trips to Lansing. I also slid down to Pontiac, MI, and purchased some Pontiacs, Chevrolets or Oldsmobiles there from General Motors employees.

During that era, I also added Honda to our dealership in 1977, which has been a wonderful complement to everything else we were doing.

Bob Rohrman Toyota on IN 26 in Lafayette, IN.

19. *In Off the Street*

One of the best hires I ever made literally walked in off the street and asked me for a job. That man is John Barrett.

John joined me in 1973 and is still with me 41 years later. He had lost a job in Lafayette and walked into my office, telling me he could sell cars. John's dad was a real estate agent, and his mother worked at Lafayette National Bank. He left me two times, but each time, not for long. Eventually, John was my new car manager in Lafayette.

Right now, John is second in command under me of my fifteen stores in the Chicago suburbs, all the way from Westmont on the south side to Kenosha, WI, on the north side. We have none in Chicago, but they all are in the suburbs, including four in Schaumburg. We started with Schaumburg Honda in 1985, and John was my first general manager there.

Along with John, the Raisor brothers were great early hires. They had operated the Sunoco station until the company closed it. Skip became my service department manager, and Mike became a car salesman.

I wanted Mike to manage a used car lot I was going to open on Main Street. I ran the Sagamore Parkway lot, and Mike ran the Main Street lot. Mike eventually went with Pontiac as their Lafayette sales manager when it was Foxworthy Pontiac.

John Shaver eventually bought that Pontiac dealership for which Mike Raisor was the sales manager. It got interesting a few years later when Shaver called me and asked if I wanted to buy that store. I said yes, so we met for lunch the next day and made the deal. I asked him for the property survey, and he said he would give it to me the next morning.

He never showed up, so two days later, I called his store, and they told me that he was on vacation in Florida. Shaver had told his office manager that he had sold it to me, but she said, "Would you sell it to me?" He said he would for the same price. She called

Mike Raisor, and the two of them bought it out from under me. Shaver ended up in Fort Wayne.

Mike ended up with Ford and Pontiac and always was a great car guy. I am always proud to say that he started with me. I have had a good knack for hiring people. I have a lot of people who have been working for me a long time. My parts manager at Toyota in Lafayette was with me 32 years before retiring. My secretary, who retired in October of 2014, was with me for 30 years.

I opened Schaumburg Honda in 1985, and I have fifteen people who are still with me. In all, we have approximately 1,500 people who work for the company.

20. Pleasantly Surprised? You Bet

My oldest brother, Don, is 18 years older than me and was in construction in Spooner, WI, and each December he loaded his car and his trailer and would head for Florida. On his way, he would stop at my used car lot in Lafayette and stay there a couple of days. We would spend a lot of time together. We went to lunch on one of those visits, and Don asked me how long did I plan to continue to work. He wanted to know if I ever planned to retire.

I was young at that time, and I told Don that when I had $250,000 in the bank, I would retire. I had $250,000 in the bank by the time I was 40. That didn't stop me. I don't know where I came up with that figure, but at that time, $250,000 was enough to retire. That was a lot of money. Don told me that was a good idea. I thought I might move back to Spooner and build a small cottage on Little Casey Lake.

Instead of stopping, I decided to move forward. It seemed like every time I got an opportunity to get another dealership from the factory, I would take it. When I got the Schaumburg Honda in 1985, I had a Honda dealership in Lafayette, which I had gotten in 1977. We were selling Toyotas and used cars, and we were doing well in Lafayette.

In 1977, a Honda rep walked into my building and said Honda wanted to put a point - or dealership - in Lafayette. I told him I would take it. He was reluctant to put Honda with Toyota, but when I told him I would have separate stores, he said he would give me Honda. In 1973, Rambler had come to me, and I took it. We sold Ramblers and Toyotas together, and then when Honda came in, I had the separate showroom for Honda.

Who would have believed that Toyota and Honda would be so red hot? We had people climb up onto the car carrier to make sure that it was their car. Every car on those carriers was sold when they got to our lots. I would shake my head and realize how amazing it all was.

But I really didn't shake my head too much, because it is the car business.

In 1972, American Motors came out with a Gremlin, and it got great gas mileage. I had good gas mileage cars with Toyota and with Gremlin, and the next fall was the first oil embargo. Toyota had told me that if I would buy at least fifty Coronas from 1972, they would take off $700 or $800 a car. Now it would be like taking off $3,000 or $4,000 a car.

I bought fifty, the oil embargo came and I sold all fifty in three weeks. Man, did I come out smelling like a rose on that transaction. I have been fortunate to do that several times.

Part of it is that I was always up late. I would do things in the middle of the night that some people would wait until the next day to do. By doing things in the middle of the night, I finished in first place.

That is what I tell my guys now. I tell them that you can't wait until tomorrow. You have to do it now to be the winner. It is just like running a race. You have to do it now. You can't wait until others are way ahead and then try to catch up.

I seem to be at the right place at the right time, just like the Honda store I got in Schaumburg.

21. A Home Run in Schaumburg

I was a member of the Toyota Dealership advertising committee for the Chicago region, and we would have a meeting once a month in Chicago.

Jerry Resnick had the Toyota dealership in Calumet City, IL. Jerry sold it to a friend of mine and contacted Toyota about opening a Toyota store in Schaumburg. Soon, the owner was selling 200 Toyotas a month in Schaumburg. In Calumet City, they were selling 25 or 35 a month.

At the next advertising committee meeting of the Chicago dealers, I asked Jerry how they were able to sell 200 a month in Schaumburg. When our meeting was over, Jerry said to follow him and he would show me why. I followed him to his Toyota store in Schaumburg. Then, I got into Jerry's car, and he drove me to the largest shopping mall in the United States at that time. We were in Schaumburg.

Jerry said that shopping mall put Schaumburg on the map. Now, the Mall of America in Minneapolis is the largest. You could barely drive all the way around the mall in Schaumburg because it was so big.

The home of Motorola also was right there. The population of Schaumburg was 50,000, but approximately one million worked in the area. I asked Jerry where the Honda dealership was in the Schaumburg area. Jerry said he did not know.

I returned to Lafayette, called Honda in California and asked if I could have the Honda dealership in Schaumburg, IL. They checked to see if Schaumburg was an open point for Honda. Two days later, they called and said Schaumburg was an open point for Honda. They told me it was mine. They said that I should buy some property.

I found some ground on a great corner, but the Honda chairman said to hold off a bit because suddenly there were others who wanted the Honda point in Schaumburg. Legally, he had to talk to each one who was interested. But he said it would be mine, but that it would take another month or so. Finally, I got the official letter from Honda that Schaumburg was mine.

I bought the ground and built the store. Later, I learned that the strongest competition I had for the Schaumburg point was my old friend Jerry Resnick. Jerry never told me until I found out about it.

It turned out to be a gold mine. Our best month at Schaumburg Honda, we sold 561 new Hondas. We average 350 or 400 a month, plus 150 to 200 used cars. Most of them are certified used Hondas. Toyota and Honda have the best reputation of any car manufactured in the world. They do make some dandy cars.

The Schaumburg Honda dealership was the first point I had outside Lafayette. It was the springboard. Soon after that, we got the fourth Honda dealership in Indianapolis, which was a good one on the south side. We also got the Hyundai store in Indianapolis, and then John Barrett and I opened the Acura store in Fort Wayne. Soon after, I got the Lexus store in Fort Wayne and bought the Nissan dealership out of bankruptcy in Fort Wayne.

We certainly had grown from our gravel used car lot on the Sagamore Parkway in Lafayette.

Bob Rohrman Schaumburg Honda.

22. *Sweet Home Chicago*

I secured a contractor for Schaumburg Honda in late summer or fall of 1984, and it took approximately a year to construct the building. The store actually is the same today as it was then, except for a few minor changes. We have built a used car building on the property since then, but the main building is the same. We also added a service drive through. That helped us control the service department.

In the fall of 1984, I decided that it was going to be quite a drive from Lafayette each time I wanted to go up there. At that time, I didn't have stores in Indianapolis or Fort Wayne. A friend suggested that I buy a plane. We could fly and land at the Schaumburg Airport in 45 minutes. We rented a plane at the Purdue Airport and flew to Pittsburgh to a manufacturer who was about to relocate in Florida. They had one Saratoga aircraft left for sale in Pittsburgh.

The plane had only 60 or 70 hours on it. We looked at it and made the deal to purchase it. We bought it for $85,000. It was a six-passenger plane with a rear door. That same plane today - new - sells for $650,000. I have been offered $150,000 for mine, and I still have it. We have it in a rented hanger at Purdue. It still is in good shape, even with about 4,000 hours on it. Bud Davis of Davis Construction is the friend who went with me to Pittsburgh to purchase that Saratoga. After we bought that plane, Bud, who has a pilot's license, flew it back to Lafayette.

I hired Dan Keene, a Lafayette policeman, to pilot my plane, and he still is my pilot today. Dan also works for the FAA, flying all over the country to investigate accidents. There is no better pilot than Dan. He can fly almost any plane.

So, it became easier for me to travel to the Schaumburg Honda, which my son, Randy, was going to oversee. I told Randy that if he was going to run the Honda store, he would have to sell some cars. I arranged for him to sell cars at the Ford dealership across the street from where we were building Schaumburg Honda.

Today, I own that Ford store, which I bought from auto nation. Randy sold cars there. When Schaumburg Honda was finished, I put Randy in as general manager, but Randy told me he wasn't sure if he wanted to remain in the car business. He wanted to return to college and become a grade school teacher. He was great with kids, and went to school at DePaul University in downtown Chicago.

I brought John Barrett in to run Schaumburg Honda. At that time, John had worked for me for about 10 years. As of the fall of 2014, John had worked for me for almost 41 years. We had the grand opening for Schaumburg Honda in May of 1985. Before the opening, they shipped us 75 or 80 new Hondas. We had them sitting on the lot while they still were working on the building. So, we started selling the new Hondas. About three weeks later, a gentleman representing the Illinois State Police - Mark Battista - stopped in and asked if we were selling cars. He said we did not have an occupancy permit yet and that we could not sell cars until we had the permit.

So, we quit selling the cars until we had the permit. But, we had sold all eighty that Honda had placed on the Schaumburg lot. Every one we had was gone.

23. *A New Friend in Chicago*

Mark Battista came to me and said he wanted to come to work for me. I hired him, and he has been working for me ever since.

Mark does many things for me in a supervisory role. Recently, Mark took over the building of our new Nissan store in Kenosha, WI, and it is done in less than a year. It is a beautiful store right on I-94. It has 15 acres and about four different levels. It is right between the Honda and Toyota stores. Mark's brother is an attorney and knows as much about the law in Illinois as anyone. Plus we are remodeling the Lincoln store in Schaumburg and the Toyota store in Westmont. We are remodeling the Toyota store in Fort Wayne and are building an almost new Lexus store in Fort Wayne.

We also are remodeling our four Kia stores to Kia's specifications. We bought 28 acres in Gurnee, right next to our Hyundai store. We are moving those wetlands back, and Mark is in charge of all that. We are building the Subaru store in Lafayette to twice the size it is now. Mark just finished the Subaru store in Fort Wayne. He just loves construction and knows how to get everything done quickly. He works seven days a week and works more than I do.

Mark loves what he is doing. He starts in at 6 a.m. Mark is like me, if you have something you really enjoy, you really aren't working. Mark and I still laugh about me selling those Hondas in 1985 without an occupancy permit. Now, 29 years later, that store is No. 1 for total Hondas sold in the entire Midwest.

From the start, we knew that would be a great store. People from other dealerships came to me and wanted to sell cars at that store. I started doing all the crazy commercials with the lion - Bob ROHRMAN - and it continued to take off. In 1988, I bought some property in Palatine, IL, right next to Arlington Heights. I got the Honda Acura store right on Dundee Road.

In 1989, I took a leap of faith with a Lexus dealership. In 2014, we had the 25th anniversary of that store. Lexus has some great cars coming out, and I have dealerships in Arlington Heights and Fort Wayne.

I also acquired the Toyota store in Westmont, IL, and it has been very successful for me. The next one was Nissan in Buffalo Grove, IL. I got it when it went bankrupt. The judge awarded it to me from among four offers. We turned the store around in one month.

We have made money in the car business, so we put money right back into the car business. Guys ask me what I am doing with my money. I tell them that I am building automobile stores. That is the truth.

While we were building in Chicago, we got the Honda franchise in Indianapolis in 1992. I was looking to get into the Indianapolis market. I had lots of competition, but we were doing so well with Honda that the guys in California normally gave us what we wanted.

I also bought the Hyundai store in Indianapolis from Tom Wood. That was right next to our Honda store. Now, we were a fixture in Lafayette, Chicago, Indianapolis and Fort Wayne.

24. The Indy Market: Autos and Real Estate

In 1991, we were doing so well with Honda in Lafayette -10 percent of the market compared to 3 or 4 percent of the market nationally - and Honda decided to place a fourth dealership in Indianapolis.

I worked with a real estate agent on U.S. Route 31 South, and I told him I needed 5, 6 or 7 acres. He told me there were 16 acres on US 31, about half a mile north of Beck Toyota. I was told there was a 22 acre plot that was owned by six people. The realtor said all were willing to sell even though all had lived there for a long time.

The realtor talked to the six owners and told me it could be the land I was seeking for $1.4 million. In all that was 22 acres right on US 31 with a lot of frontage land. I agreed but I asked if he could get the price to $1.2 million. They agreed.

The realtor went back to the six land owners, and one guy who had an acre and a half right on US 31 could not sell because the government took it from him for back taxes. The man who runs the automobile auction in Indianapolis bought that parcel of land from the government.

I called the auto auction owner who had purchased that one piece of land from the government for $35,000. That man told me he bought the land to make money. He told me he would have to have $150,000 from me in order to sell it. Since we knew each other, he said he would sell it to me for $100,000, and I said OK. At that point, I had $1.3 million invested, which is what the owners originally wanted.

Right after I bought the 22 acres, a man came to me and asked how much of that 22 acres I actually needed. I told him I needed enough to build two dealerships there - one Honda. I told the man I had to get the land zoned. He told me that if I would sell him half of the 22 acres for $1 million, he would pay for getting it zoned for automobiles.

In Indiana, automobile zoning is difficult. Some in Indiana

think of an automobile dealer as a salvage yard. Neighbors do not like that. In Illinois, it is different. The villages in Illinois like automobile dealers. For example, the village of Schaumburg gets 7 or 8 percent of sales taxes. That goes to the state, but one percent of that goes back to the village where it was collected.

Schaumburg has one of the largest malls in the United States, and every car manufacturer is represented in Schaumburg. It is the hottest area in all of Chicagoland. The village of Schaumburg gets more sales tax back from the state for automobile sales than from that entire mall. I sell a car with an average price of $30,000 or $35,000 in Schaumburg and the village gets one percent of that. That is a ton of money.

Schaumburg Honda contributes at least $500,000 a year to the village of Schaumburg in tax revenue. That's why in Illinois you can get things done when you go in to get a piece of land zoned for an automobile dealer. In Illinois, they jump up and down and want to sing Christmas Carols when an auto dealership comes to town. In Indiana, it is difficult. I have told officials in Indiana they should do the same thing.

Getting back to our land on US 31, the man who purchased half of my 22 acres brought in architects and attorneys. He had great stuff to show the officials what he planned to do. But the attorney for Indianapolis and the president of the board asked if there were any opposed. An audience of 400 opposed it. The board told me in order to build an automobile dealership on US 31; I would have to go further south - south of Beck Toyota. The land I had was north of Beck Toyota.

In the end, Tom O'Brien came to my rescue. The O'Brien family had purchased land south of Beck Toyota and across the street from Ray Skillman. O'Brien had this land and had gotten it zoned for automobiles.

A Chevrolet dealer bought one piece of O'Brien's land, Tom Wood bought the middle piece and put Hyundai there and Beck bought the third and last piece because he thought he was going to get the fourth Honda dealership, but I got it, so Beck wanted to sell me the ground. He sold it to me for just more than $1 million.

Soon thereafter, I bought out Tom Wood in 1993. But remember now, I still had that original 22 acres north of Beck Toyota that Indianapolis would not zone for an automobile dealership. I had $1.3 million in it. The land had been given the OK for commercial.

I got a call from Duke Construction and Realty from Indianapolis. They sent two representatives from Indianapolis to Lafayette to meet with me. They thought they were going to steal that land from me.

I told them that while I may be an old country boy, I know property is worth a little money. They told me I had to sell it to them. I said, no I don't. I told them to go back to Indianapolis.

They offered me $2 million. A month later, the Duke owner called me and asked why I did not get along well with his reps. I told him it was because they acted like they already owned the property.

He apologized, but I told him I would not sell it to Duke for any price. Two weeks later, another man from Indianapolis called and asked if I wanted to sell. I asked that man for $5 million. Two days later, they came to Lafayette and offered me $5 million. I took it.

25. *Staying Ahead of the Game*

While I made about $3.7 million in seven months on the land deal on US 31 in Indianapolis, it took a lot of night work to get that done.

You have to do what it takes, because if you don't, people will run over you and get there first. That is how I won. I was there. I almost lost it with that one little piece there that the government had taken for back taxes, but it worked out pretty well. A couple of years later after Tom Wood had built a building on the center piece of the three pieces south of Beck Toyota, I ended up with it.

Our Indy Honda store on US 31 was a winner right from the word go. But the Hyundai, Suzuki and Isuzu store was a different story. All but Hyundai stopped building cars in the United States. Hyundai wanted to put another store on the east side of Indianapolis, and they wanted to give it to Ray Skillman.

Ray came to me and asked if I wanted the point on the south side or on the east side. I told Ray I thought the south side was better. Ray said he would give me $1 million for the Hyundai dealership on the south side, and I took it. Ray outsmarted me on that one.

The south side sold so much better than the east side. At the time, I did not realize how much better the south side was. We are doing OK on the east side but nothing like we were doing on the south side. Ray has that south side Hyundai store No. 1 in Indianapolis. Ray got me there. I got $1 million from him, but it did not last too long. But that is business.

I have hit more home runs than I have struck out. I have had some singles, doubles, triples and home runs, and I have struck out two or three times.

That is our story in Indianapolis. In Indianapolis, Honda is outselling Toyota. That is very unusual. Nationally, Toyota outsells Honda in cars and trucks by about 400,000 and 500,000. But in Indiana, Honda outsells Toyota.

I do not have to worry about our Honda store in Indianapolis. I only go down there about once a month. Indy has been a good market for us, but I have not spread out there. I have another building there, but we use that for our Honda used cars.

In most cases, it is fair to say that I stay ahead of the game. Sometimes, I literally run out of people. I am fortunate I have not run out of money. It is such satisfaction I have gained from my success in the automobile dealership.

26. *Quiet on the Set, Take One*

Of all the things for which I am known, people always want to know about and talk about my commercials.

I began doing commercials at WASK radio in Lafayette during the 1950s when I was selling cars for Glenn R. Pitman. I started selling cars there in 1955 and began doing the commercials when I was used car manager.

An advertising salesman from WASK came to see me and told me that he thought I should be on the radio in an attempt to sell these cars. I agreed that it was a good idea, but I said I wanted to discuss it with Glenn. Glenn was supportive and encouraged me to start doing radio commercials.

I drove to WASK and started doing radio spots. They were 60-second spots. Our spots in Lafayette are all 60 seconds, but the ones in Chicago are 30 seconds. In the beginning, I advertised used cars more than I advertised new cars.

We advertised that our prices were low and that we did our own financing. I would tell the listeners that a big down payment was not required. At that time, the normal down payment on a car was one third.

Today, if you have a real good credit score, you do not need a down payment. At that time, the longest we could finance a car was 24 months. It was tougher to finance them then, but the prices were lower.

I did radio spots then every month. If we needed a change, I would change them in the middle of the month. The commercials were very successful. Those commercials were pretty straight and lacked the theatrics that we have now. I would just say that I was Bob Rohrman from Glenn R. Pitman Ford.

At first, I really was not comfortable doing the radio commercials. But that was almost 60 years ago, and I became more and more comfortable as time passed. For most of the time I did commercials for Pitman, probably less than 50 percent of the population had a TV in their home. If they did, it was an 8-inch black and white.

When I opened the used car lot in 1963, Soon thereafter, I started doing TV commercials with WLFI-TV 18 in Lafayette. The sales rep convinced me to do some, and they turned out pretty well. He told me TV was the coming thing and that TV advertising was my best move. I was all for it, but I did not drop radio. I have been on WASK forever.

I went to the TV station, and they set up a scene for me to do. I was to look at a written spot that was affixed to the camera on a cheat sheet. Now, if I don't like what it really says, I will change it right in the middle. Then something happened at WLFI that got me started doing all the crazy commercials. The station would broadcast live until midnight, but then it would air all-night movies. WLFI did not know how many people were watching movies at 2, 3 or 4 in the morning, and the station wanted me to do some late-night TV ads.

They told me to do a TV spot that I wanted, even if it lasted for five minutes. This was right after I took over Toyota, and the program director at the TV station was quite a ham. One movie was about

Bob Rohrman on the set at WGN-TV in Chicago, where he films most of his commercials, in June of 2015.

horses, so they put a big bed in the studio where we shot the commercial. I had my pajamas on with a stocking cap, and they trained two horses to run by me and grab my stocking cap and take off with it.

When they took the horses down the hall before they got outside, one of them made quite a mess that had to be cleaned up. The theme of that commercial was me saying that you are better off buying a car than a horse. I said that the expense of buying a car is less than buying, keeping and caring for a horse. At that point, I was more willing to be crazy and creative in my commercials.

Another all night movie commercial we did was for a war film. We had bunk beds as if we were in the army, and we were sleeping when we had about a dozen soldiers in uniform jump over the beds.

At the same time, Ken Double, who was working at TV 18 at that time, wanted to do my normal hours spots and he would write them. Ken and I had a blast doing those commercials. We got pretty creative with them. We came up with one saying that people just loved, and that was me saying, "That's a reallllyyyy nice" while driving a car with Ken as the passenger.

I did that commercial saying for almost a year. I was just supposed to say, "That's nice," but when I added the "reallllyyy" it worked.

Sometimes, there are just some crazy things that just work.

We started doing some commercials at the Columbian Park Zoo involving the monkeys. People thought we were crazy, but they came out very good. People remembered them because they were so crazy.

In 2013, the business editor of the Chicago Tribune wrote a column in which he said "Bob Rohrman does the craziest commercials I have ever seen." But those commercials work.

27. My Favorite: The Mummy

The commercial I like best centered on the theme of "The Mummy."

The other character was Egor. The kids today always ask me what has been my best TV spot that we have done, and this is the one. I am lying on what looks like a hospital operating table. In the commercial, the operation did not go well, so my character - The Mummy - dies. They wrapped me up in gauze like a mummy. The scene was that I was being prepared to be shipped out and buried. But Egor says no. I am lying there, and lights are flashing, and there is lightning. Egor is talking gibberish, trying to get me to come alive. Buy I am still dead.

Egor does this four or five times, and finally, I throw my feet over the edge of that operating table and stand up. I put my hands out and walk towards the camera. I say in a scary voice, "Get your hands on a Toyota, and you never will let go." That actually was the Toyota slogan at that time. It was great that we were able to incorporate that into a commercial.

Normally, I will talk to classes of school children from K-8, and then college students. Everybody always asks me in these classes to talk about my commercials. They all say that the commercials probably made me famous.

When I am walking down Michigan Avenue in Chicago, people from across the street will yell, "Bob Roooooohrman," I will go to a Chicago Bulls game in the United Center, and as I walk up an aisle, people will say the same thing. I was flying to Vegas, and a couple of young businessmen got on the plane and noticed me, and after we talked, one ended up buying a car from me several weeks later.

In October, we ran a commercial promoting a charity in which we hoped to raise $100,000 by donating $50 from each car we sold. Just a month later, we presented a $100,000 check. Again, the commercials helped out.

Another interesting thing people ask about is where the "Bob

Roooorhman!" slogan came from. The sign on our pre-owned car lot in Lafayette has the original sign from our first used car lot. It is a lit sign that we had in 1963. I company from Indianapolis made that sign, and they created a design that included a lion on the bottom.

They created it, saying that a lion roars, and I am Bob Rohrman. When I asked the creator about it, he said Bob Rohrman reminded him of a roaring lion. Quickly, we started using the saying in our commercials.

It has been with us for more than 50 years. Our radio spots always begin or end with the saying.

We also featured Count Bobula - Dracula - at Halloween. We started doing him at the Haunted House at the Tippecanoe County Fairgrounds. We also have had great success with our bloopers commercials, which are out takes. We have some good ones.

The Tax Man is another of my favorites. Until about 10 years ago in Indiana, whatever inventory you had on the lot at the first of March, you had to pay taxes on them. It amounted to about $300 a car.

We used to try to sell out down to zero by the first of March so that we did not have much tax to pay. When I got the Honda store in Schaumburg, I would have 10 or 15 semi-trucks take the extra cars to Schaumburg. We dealer-traded them to that store and paid for them. We took the inventory out of the state and placed it in Illinois.

Indiana was the only state that had that inventory tax. That is where the Tax Man spot came from. Even after Indiana removed the inventory tax, we continued to do Tax Man commercials for a couple more years because people like them.

Back then, February was our best month of the year. I always played the Tax Man in the commercials. I just kind of made up the script as we went along, but it was easy, because it was something I had to deal with - taxes.

Then there is Santa Bob, which we do in December with me

coming down the chimney with my Santa uniform on. I hand out presents, and I tell people what I will give them if they come in for a test drive. We would give away those big cans of popcorn, or maybe a dinner for two. It was so good that we started doing Christmas in July with Santa Bob, who wears a swimming suit with his beard. We would give great deals. We try to feature the previous year's cars and feature the new ones coming in. The commercials really help with that.

28. *The Pied Piper*

With my commercials, especially with young children, I am like the Pied Piper. I wish they would do that when they are 16 and old enough to purchase an automobile!

Our commercials really are as good as ever. We come up with some pretty good ones. Sometimes, I will be driving, and an idea for a commercial comes to mind. That happened with the football commercial we filmed in the fall of 2014.

I also came up with one for Thanksgiving in which I am in the kitchen cooking the turkey. We filmed it in the kitchen of a large restaurant in Chicago. The cook and the owner were there in that kitchen with me.

I like football commercials in November because everyone is watching or listening to football that month.

People mix the two at Thanksgiving with the meal and then watching football later in the day. Years ago when I was home with the kids and had Thanksgiving dinner, I would go in and watch a football game. Now, there are at least two or three football games that day.

Most of our commercials are tied to holidays, but in Lafayette, our sales increase every month. For example, in October of 2014, we sold 375 new cars and 361 used cars for a total of 736 in Lafayette. That was a record for October. In 2013, we sold 503 cars in October in Lafayette.

I credit a lot of the increase to the commercials, but I also think a lot of it is the familiarity with us in Lafayette. Lafayette is my home, and when the people of Lafayette think of automobiles, Bob Rohrman is the first one they think about. I have been here the longest of anybody, and I do more advertising than anybody.

Another part of it is the contributions I make to the city, Tippecanoe County and to Indiana. We don't advertise what we do for the city, but everybody knows it. One thing you have to remember is that

I graduated from Lafayette Jefferson High School, and I did not graduate from a college.

When I gave the money to build the Rohrman Center for Performing Arts, it was because of my association with Jefferson High School.

Groundbreaking of the Rohrman Performing Arts Center
at Lafayette Jefferson High School, Bob's alma mater.

Today when I am downtown or in a grocery store in Lafayette, so many people walk up to me and thank me for the performing arts center because their son or daughter or nephew attended Jefferson High School and got so much use of that facility. People I don't even know walk up to me and say thanks.

It helps when they know me, and of course, the advertising helps, especially the TV. The success of our commercials has surpassed all of my expectations. At first, I really did not know what the heck commercials would do for us. I thought people might say, "That guy is crazy. I am not going to buy a car from him."

But it worked exactly the other way. You worry about it a little when you are acting kind of crazy. But people get it right away. They tell me I look like I am having so much fun in those commercials. And

I am. I start laughing naturally in so many of them.

I am so comfortable doing commercials that it seems like that is what I do for a living. Some people ask me what I do for a living, and I tell them I sell cars. Some think I am an actor who works for the dealer.

I tell them, "I really am Bob Rohrman."

The recognition is amazing. This past Purdue football season, I was at the concession stand at one of the home games in Ross-Ade Stadium and when I was buying a hot dog, four fans came up to me and asked if they could have a picture taken with me. I said, "Sure, let's do it." I get a kick out of that. We visited, and that always is fun for me, especially when the good-looking ladies come up and want to have a picture taken with me!

In my way of thinking, I would like to continue doing these commercials for another 50 or 60 years.

Now, I have my grandchildren doing the commercials, too.

From my perspective, I think my personality has helped me become comfortable taking chances and being crazy in these commercials. I just laugh and have fun. I love people. Some people tell me I should have been a comedian. I tell them, "I could have been, but I couldn't afford it."

One of the unusual things that happens when I am on TV is that small children who barely are old enough to walk will run to the TV when they hear my voice. When the commercial is over, mothers tell me that the small children leave the TV. I think they love the way I say, "Bob Roooorhman."

29. Young Love, and My First Marriage

I met my first wife, Shirley Relander, when I was a junior in high school at Lafayette Jeff. Shirley was a sophomore at St. Francis High School, which was a Catholic high school for girls located behind St. Elizabeth Hospital in Lafayette.

Both of us were Catholic and went to church at St. Boniface. On a Saturday night, the church sponsored a dance at the St. Boniface gymnasium and invited all Catholic teens in Lafayette. Shirley and I each attended that dance.

There were lots of refreshments, and Shirley's mother baked lots of the cookies and cakes. At that time, Shirley didn't have a driver's license, and at that time, I owned a 1948 Ford convertible, which was my first car.

I asked Shirley to dance, and she accepted. We danced a few dances, drank a Coke and enjoyed some of the refreshments. We then sat and talked for a while, and I asked her if I could drive her home. She said that she would ask her mother, who was still there serving refreshments.

She told Shirley that I had to be introduced to her mother before her mother would trust me to drive Shirley home. It worked out well, so I drove Shirley home that night. Her father was home, so I went in so she could introduce me to her father, who operated a printing press for Warren Paper at the corner of South Street and Earl Avenue. Her dad was a great guy.

We started dating off and on - not always on - for three years, including a year I was working at Brown Rubber after I graduated from high school before I joined the military. When I joined the military, Shirley was graduating from high school. We were considering getting married before I went to the Army, but neither her mother nor her father thought that was a good idea. Shirley was 17 at the time.

We decided that it would be best to wait for about a year before we got married, which we did. Shirley graduated and continued to live with her parents while I was based at Fort Lewis in Washington. In July, three months after I had been at Fort Lewis, I got a call on a Sunday morning at the barracks from my commanding officer of the division. He said I had person at the front gate who had come to see me. They could not allow her in the gate, so she was there waiting for me.

I went to the gate, which was six to eight blocks from our barracks, and it was Shirley. She had ridden a bus all the way from Lafayette to Fort Lewis, Washington to see me.

Was I surprised. She was so tired from riding a bus for hours and hours. I took her to a hotel in Olympia, WA so that she could get some sleep. I think she slept for 24 consecutive hours. I had to go back to the post after I got her checked in, but I came back to see her later.

Shirley stayed three days and really liked it in the Seattle area, which is beautiful. I showed her Seattle, including the waterfront. When she was ready to come home to Lafayette, I had enough money to purchase an airline ticket for her so she wouldn't have to endure another long bus ride.

At that point, Shirley and I had determined that we would get married the following spring - 1954. We would write letters back and forth almost every day. She got several babysitting jobs in 1953 while she was still living at home.

In the spring of 1954, I received my first 30-day leave. At that point, I was an acting officer, so I had it pretty well made. Before I began my 30-day leave, I called Shirley and said that maybe we should wait to be married before I got out of the Army.

She did not like that idea and said no. She said, "We're getting married now, or we are not getting married." She laid it right on the line to me. So I said OK.

I flew from Washington to Chicago and hitch hiked to Lafayette for our wedding. At that time, the only Chicago airport was Midway. Dressed in my military uniform, I had no problem getting a ride. Before the wedding, Shirley's parents had moved into a home on Union Street with a smaller house in the back of the property, a dwelling in which we lived after I got out of the Army.

Shirley and I were married on a Saturday in May of 1954, and the next day, she and I were scheduled to leave for Fort Lewis. I had talked with my brother-in-law, Nick Switzer, and at that time, Nick was selling used cars.

Nick and I made a quick trip to the auto auction in Dyer, IN, where I bought a sharp looking Pontiac, a 1952 Pontiac Chieftain with a three-speed on the column. I drove that car back to Lafayette two days before the wedding.

After the wedding, we packed the car with our belongings, most of which were clothes. We took off for Fort Lewis. We got into Utah and then crossed the Columbia River into Washington and were near Spokane.

When we got to Yakima and into the mountains - about 10,000 feet - there was a bunch of snow. The police had yellow flashers out to stop us because lots of snow had fallen from the mountains onto the road. It was bearing right down on us. We had to turn around and were directed to a path down below so that we could get through to Olympia.

Before I had left for Lafayette, I rented an apartment for us so we would have a place to live near Fort Lewis after we got married. About every other night, I could leave the base and spend the night with Shirley in our apartment.

It was fun. We had a nice apartment, and Olympia is a nice town. At that time, my military assignments included teaching classes on chemical and biological warfare, along with instruction about how to use a bayonet. I would practice in our apartment with a broom, and Shirley wondered what in the heck I was doing.

Shirley got pregnant in July of 1954, and because I couldn't be with her every night, we decided it would be best for her to return to Lafayette and stay with her parents during the pregnancy. In April of 1955, I was discharged from the Army, and five days later, our son, JR, was born. I just made it to St. Elizabeth Hospital in time for the birth, because I was selling a car when I got the call.

Today, you are discharged from the hospital the next day after giving birth. In 1955, you stayed in the hospital four or five days. Five days later, she was released, and we took JR to our little house on Union Street just behind her parents' house.

It was just one big room, but we put up partitions to create the look of several rooms. After a time, we rented an apartment on

Bob (top left) and first wife Shirley (holding baby JR) with Shirley's parents (front) and Shirley's sister and brother-in-law, in 1955.

Alabama Street, about a block from the Pitman Dealership where I sold cars. I had a demo car, but I walked to and from work each day.

That apartment was on the second floor, and the only problem was that the steps to get to it were on the outside of the building, which wasn't too great in the winter. The nice thing about that apartment being so close to Pitman's was that we had a sales meeting six mornings a week. I led the meetings because I was the sales manager at that time.

Nationally, Chevrolet was leading Ford in sales in 1955, but in Lafayette, we were No. 1. We were selling lots of cars, and Shirley and I were having fun. She was a very pretty girl. Her dad and mom were very nice people. She and I just kind of clicked.

We always had a lot of fun together. I knew we would have kids, and I always told her, "Our kids are going to be good looking kids. And they were." About 10 years ago, she reminded me of that conversation.

Our second child was Rhonda, who was born in 1957. She has four girls of her own. Shirley was a good mother, and not long after that, Randy was born. All five kids were born in a window from 1955 through 1964. Our fourth child was Richelle, and Rick was the fifth.

30. The Struggles within My First Marriage

We had five children pretty quickly, and while that didn't bother me, it did bother Shirley. For her, it was too many kids too quickly. It seemed as if she was fine through the third one, but the fourth one kind of tied her down. Then the fifth one really tied her down.

That was kind of a problem with our marriage. In a way, she was kind of tied down with five children from the ages of 8 through an infant. Of course, I was working long hours six days a week. I was a go-getter. I was the general sales manager at Pitman's from the time our second child was born through the birth of our fifth and final child. It affected our marriage, because she felt like she was just tied down, and she was.

Bob (right) plays with son JR in the backyard of their home in 1956.

I was working at least 10 hours every day except for Sunday. And then sometimes on Sunday, I would play golf, and Shirley did not play golf. It put a strain on our marriage. So, we decided to take a nice trip.

Shirley and I had gone to Jamaica a couple of times and kind of liked Jamaica, so we decided that Shirley and Rhonda would vacation in Jamaica and that JR and I would join them four or five days later.

Then, we would spend another four or five days there as a family and then come back. They met JR and I at the airport, and we went to the hotel. We got along pretty well, but when we decided it was time to come back to Lafayette, Shirley decided she wasn't ready to come back.

She wanted to stay a while by herself. She did. So, JR, Rhonda and I came back together. That was a sad time, especially for the children. For Rhonda, her mother was the love of her life. I think Rhonda continues to think about that trip and what happened during it today.

There was quite a bit of stress there. I thought Shirley would be coming home in a couple of days, but she didn't. I tried to call her, but she never answered the phone. She never contacted us. That event really put a strain on the marriage. It really hurt JR and Rhonda, because they were the oldest at that time at 16 and 15, respectively. They could sense there was some friction in the marriage.

Shirley stayed in Jamaica for an additional two weeks after the rest of us had come home to Lafayette. I, with the help of her mother, Olivia, was taking care of the kids. Olivia didn't know what was going on.

Shirley's mother thought there was something crazy going on, which there was. Finally, Shirley came home. She just walked in the door. After that, it really wasn't the same between Shirley and I. I was hurt more than I was bitter.

We didn't get along too well after that. It wasn't too much longer before Shirley left again by herself, this time to Mexico City. She was there for a couple of weeks, maybe three. Again, her mother took care of our kids when I was working.

Shirley's mother couldn't figure her out, either. After that, we continued to grow apart. The kids all were in school. We tried to talk things out for a couple of years, and it would be OK for a month, and then it wasn't OK for a month.

We didn't argue very much, but we didn't communicate well. Shirley was not a good communicator. After the third or fourth time that she just took off to go to Mexico, I began to think that maybe she had met someone there.

I couldn't go on like that, so I filed for divorce in 1973. The divorce was finalized in June of 1973, and I bought Shirley a house. The kids were going to live with Shirley, but they could come to me at any time.

JR was going to attend the University of New Mexico in the fall, so he moved in with me, and Rhonda, who was going to be a senior at Jeff, also moved in with me.

Shirley got a house as well as alimony for a number of years, about $20,000 a year. We talked from time to time because of the children, but we went our separate ways. She had the three youngest ones with her, but from time to time, they would move in with me, mostly in the summer when they weren't in school.

31. Finding the Love of My Life, Linda

After my divorce in 1973, I was single and pretty happy, because the relationship of Shirley and I during the final three or four years of marriage was pretty rocky.

My bank was Lafayette National, and soon after my divorce, I met Linda Louise Lindsey, who was employed at my bank in the consumer loan department. That is where we financed the cars. When I was at Pitman's, I set up the deal with Lafayette National Bank to finance the cars Pitman's sold.

We had a real good relationship with Lafayette National, especially with Lloyd Newman, who was a really good friend. He was the chief executive officer at the bank. Linda was working for Harry Von Segren at Lafayette National, and Harry and I became good friends. I went into the consumer loan department and met Linda. We hit it off right away. I asked her out, and she accepted.

We went to dinner at Hour Time after I picked her up at her apartment on Ninth Street Hill. When we met, I was 40, and she was 26. I always told her I was 39. What was interesting about our early courtship was that she was dating another guy. After a few dates, she told me that she had a date with him that night. That very day, my friend Jack Shaw said he wanted to fix me up with a lady that he knew. I called her and asked her to dinner, and she said OK.

Linda had a date, and I had a date that same night. We ended up at the same restaurant as Linda and her date. Linda smiled at me. I was having a nice time with my date. I got up to go to the restroom, and when I came out of the door, Linda was standing there.

She said, "Can you take her home?" I said, "I think I can." Linda said, "And then come over and see me."

When Linda saw me with another girl, she forgot about going with somebody else. We laughed about that night many, many times.

That night was the last time she went out with somebody else, and I went out with somebody else. Quickly, Linda and I got to be pretty close.

Early on when we were dating, I had an appointment with a doctor in California to repair a problem with my nose, and Linda ended up being there with me. She had a girlfriend who lived in Arizona. The two had gone to college together at Ball State. Linda grew up on a farm near Muncie.

Bob and his second wife, Linda, soon after being married in 1973.

When I was going to go to Los Angeles about my nose, Linda took vacation and visited her girlfriend in Arizona. I went to Arizona with her, and instead of going back to Lafayette, she went to LA, where the doctor performed surgery on my nose. When I woke up five or six hours after the operation, Linda was standing right there. She stayed with me for two or three days, and then she had to get back to work.

I was really in love with Linda, and I still am. It was great of her to come to LA to be with me.

The sad thing is that we eventually broke up, and to this day, I wish that had not happened. I think she still loves me, too. When I got home from having surgery in Los Angeles, I felt like I was beat up badly. It was then that I asked Linda to marry me. She said yes.

We got married at her boss' home on Christmas Eve, 1973. He and his wife stood up for us. After the wedding, we were hungry, because we hadn't had anything to eat all day. We got a room at the Howard Johnson's, which now is the Best Western. But we wanted to get something to eat, and nothing was open. It was 10:30 at night, so we had nothing but snacks from the vending machine.

Linda and I were married from 1973 until 1999. I made a terrible mistake when it ended. She is such a wonderful person and a beautiful lady. Linda and I always had fun. And she is a very intelligent lady. She did an awful lot of things for our company.

When we built new buildings, Linda kept track of all that. She wrote the checks and paid the contractors. Linda would go through all of the bills and make sure they were correct. I never had to check her. She never made mistakes. She had a lot of experience at the bank, and she has a great head for business.

We never, ever should have gotten a divorce. It was my fault, 100 percent my fault. I still love her, but I got caught up with a girl that worked for me in Chicago. That was a big mistake. If Linda would marry me, I would marry her again today.

Another thing with Linda, while she had no children - she got pregnant once but lost the baby after about three months - she always treated my children like her own. When my kids come to Lafayette, they don't stay at my house, they stay at Linda's.

My grandson Trey got married at Linda's house. She had a beautiful setting or the wedding. When one of our grandchildren graduates from high school, she takes them on a trip of their choice. They all just think the world of Linda.

She was my soul mate, and to be honest, she still is, as far as I am concerned. To this day, we still talk whenever the family gets together, or if I need something that she may have. As I have mentioned, I would marry her again in a minute. I still love her. Maybe we will get back together one day. I sure hope so.

32. My Third Trip into Marriage

This was a bad mistake on my part. I have not made many mistakes in business, but in other facets of my life, I have. This probably was my biggest mistake, because Linda and I were married for 25 years.

The story begins after I opened Schaumburg Honda in 1985. That dealership was given to me because we had done such a good job with Honda in Lafayette. It was an open point, and Honda decided to give it to me.

It was very successful. In 1992, I bought the Toyota store in Downers Grove, IL. That building was kind of run down, but the store started making money right away because our concentration was with used cars.

In 1995, my lease ran out, and I decided to build a new Toyota store about two miles away. We moved into that store about 18 months later, and it looks like new today. At that time, we hired some new people, and my general manager hired a real nice-looking lady. He hired her to do customer relations work. Her job was to make sure we had good customer relations before and after a sale. Her name was Ronda. She had two daughters, who at that time were 6 and 8. The younger one was Molly, and the older one was Amy.

I stopped in there on a Monday and talked with the general manager. I walked out and got into my car, Ronda came out and introduced herself to me as I sat there with my window rolled down. She had a very nice personality and was very good in the role as a customer relations specialist. We talked, and I asked her if she would like to have dinner that night. She said she would love to.

There was a Mexican restaurant just down the street in Downers Grove, and we decided that she would meet me there at 7:30. We had dinner and a nice conversation. That was the start of the relationship.

I viewed it as just being friendly, but after that dinner, I guess I changed my mind from friendly to extremely friendly. I was still married to Linda and not unhappy at all. Everybody thought that Linda and I would be married for the rest of our lives. So did I.

The mistake I made was that I would go to Chicago and would spend a night or two each week in Chicago. I bought a condominium while we were building a new Honda store. For a time, my son, Randy, and I lived there.

I took Ronda to that condo, and that really was the beginning of the relationship. The relationship went on for three or four months before Linda found out about it. I think she hired a private detective to follow me. Linda found out where Ronda lived in Downers Grove.

Unbeknownst to me, Linda and one of my daughter's-in-law drove to where Ronda lived. Linda knocked on the door, and Ronda answered. Linda asked to come in, and Ronda said no. Then, she let Linda in, and Linda said, "I am Bob Rohrman's wife. I am here to tell you that you are involved in a bad thing."

Ronda told Linda that she knew I was married but that she didn't think I was getting along with my wife. Ronda said she would give me up. Two days later, Ronda told me about the encounter with Linda.

At that point - it was 1998 - Linda and I decided that we loved each other. Linda did not want a divorce. I decided that this thing with Ronda was over. And for about two months, it was over.

Ronda and I tried to stay away from each other, and for a couple of months, we did. But, then we got back together again, which was a mistake. Linda found out about it again. I think she knew where I was all the time because of the detective. It was not a good thing.

Linda and I tried to get back together again, and we did for another month. Then, I got together with Ronda again. It was not something Linda wanted to do, but she knew I had made a lot of money during the 25 years we were married, so she secured the services of a very good attorney.

I had to get an attorney at the point she filed for divorce. The process went on for six months, and then we settled. It cost me a plenty.

Another terrible thing was that near the end of the proceedings, Linda's mother died. She, like Linda, was a great lady. I really felt badly. I went to her mother's visitation in Muncie and still had a lot of feelings for Linda. We had had so much fun traveling to Italy, Spain, Japan and Hawaii.

After my divorce from Linda, I did not marry Ronda for two years. That marriage lasted ten years, but we almost didn't get married. When we finally decided to marry, we selected Hawaii. We took Ronda's two daughters and Ronda's mother with us to Hawaii. Ronda grew up in Cicero, IN, and lived for a time in Noblesville, IN before she moved to Chicago.

She had married her high school sweetheart, divorced him and married another man with whom she had the two girls. So, before we left for Hawaii to get married, I had my attorney draft a prenuptial agreement. I waited until a week before we were scheduled to travel to Hawaii before I had my attorney draft it. I didn't tell Ronda anything about it until the day before we were scheduled to be married in Hawaii.

I said, "You have to sign this." I think she thought she really was going to get wealthy in this marriage. She read it and said she wasn't going to sign it. I replied by telling her that there would not be a marriage unless she signed.

She took the paperwork and went to a place to review it. She came back and said she didn't want to disappoint her mother or her daughters, so she signed it. We got married, and her two girls stood up with us. It was beautiful getting married with the ocean in the background.

Problem was, it turned out that Ronda was not a faithful wife.

33. *The End of Marriage No. 3*

I knew Ronda was unfaithful to me once, but the second time was the end for me. The first time, in 2006 or 2007, she said she was very sorry and that it wouldn't happen again. I took her word for, it. We got back together. Until that point, we had gotten along pretty well.

I even bought the home in Downers Grove that she always wanted, a home that cost $1.5 million.

I still have that home. The relationship began to come apart when Ronda came to me and said that her daughter, Amy, wanted to see a plastic surgeon. I really cared for Amy and wanted to make her happy. In fact, I still have her in my grandkids trust.

I told Ronda and Amy that Amy should discuss this with her biological father, who was against the surgery. But he told Ronda and Amy, who was about 20 at the time, that he wouldn't stand in the way if she really wanted it done.

I agreed to pay for the procedure, which was $8,000 or $10,000. There was a problem with the initial procedure, and she went in and had the work done again. The doctor said he would fix it for $3,000 or $4,000 more.

Ronda then went back to the doctor - she had large breasts - and wanted to get them downsized. The doctor told Ronda that he could do it, but that it would require extensive work. He talked her out of it, and then the two of them got together.

After Amy had her surgery, Molly wanted the same operation, so I agreed to pay for it, too. Molly went to a different doctor. The doctor who was involved with Ronda had a history of trying to date his patients. When we went through the divorce, my attorney had testimony from four or five other husbands whose wives had been involved with this doctor.

The divorce took place in 2012, and it did not come out quite as well as I thought it would. She had signed the prenuptial agreement, but it called for only about half of what she got. The problem I had was that while she signed the prenuptial agreement, she had not had her attorney look at it.

She said the only reason she signed it was because of the daughters. I still had to pay her a pretty good chunk - seven figures - and I have to pay her $7,500 a year for 15 years. We do not see each other at all any more.

She texts me once in a while to remind me that a payment is due soon.

I was attracted to her originally because she had a really good personality, and it seems like I go for very good looking women, which she is. But I should have stayed with Linda. Linda never lied to me. Plus, there was 30 years difference in age between Ronda and I. I was 69, and she was 39 when we married.

To this day, I love Ronda's daughters. I think they love me more than they love their mother. They blame their mother for what happened in our marriage.

I sure learned that I made a bad decision. I've tried to get back with Linda several times, but while she says she forgives me, she doesn't want to get back together.

34. *The Secrets - Some of Them - To My Success*

Success in business is the result of success with people. That results in trust, which you have to have, otherwise they are not coming back.

In all of my dealerships, a couple of signs are posted. One reads, "If you are not satisfied for any particular reason, call me personally." They have my cell phone number. Some call me, and they will call about good things as well as bad. I have had a lot of calls - I answer "Bob Rohrman, here." - and they will ask, "Is this really Bob Rohrman?" Then they will tell me they called just to see if I would answer the phone. Some will call just to tell me they love my commercials and can't wait for the next one. They remember that they have heard my ads all of their lives, at least they think they have.

I realized the significance of the people element when I was in high school. You have to get people to like you. The only way you will get people to like you is if you like them. If you don't like somebody, everybody can see it. There is no comfort level.

Frequently when a customer comes into a dealership, there is a wall they have built because they do not trust an automobile dealer. So, we have to take that wall down. In a conversation as we are selling them a car, they will tell us they just left a dealer down the street and that they don't know how they ever sell a car.

If you have a customer who is angry with another dealer, all you have to do is be nice to him. Pretty quickly, he will buy a car from you because of trust you have instilled. Tell them the truth, and you will instill that trust.

In our dealerships, there is no lying, no cheating, no stealing and always be nice to the ladies. Those four elements are part of our company policy. Treating ladies with respect is a significant part of our policy. When a gentleman comes into a dealership with his wife, some salesmen talk directly to the man. But the best thing to do is to talk to the lady, because the lady controls the eventual purchase of a car.

Eighty percent or more of women control what kind of car the gentleman purchases. I share that information with all of our sales staff. The female decides the kind of car, the color, the interior and everything.

Women are stronger than men, especially a man's wife.

When I was married to Linda, I tried to sell her on a Lexus, but she would not drive anything but an Acura. Along with my four primary rules, there are a lot of little things that add to success. A lot of people, unfortunately, don't do the little things. To me, talking with people is a must. When I walk into a dealership, people recognize me and want to meet me. I always go over and talk with them. I always talk to the lady. They usually also want to have a picture taken with me.

It's also important to do nice things for the people who work for you. I have had a lot of people tell me that I am a nice guy to work for, which makes me feel good. If they don't enjoy working for me, they aren't going to work very hard for me, or for themselves.

I tell my employees that in actuality, they are working for themselves. The better they work for themselves, the more money they are going to make and they better jobs they will have. If they do a poor job, they probably aren't going to be around for very long.

Really, they are working for the people. For example, I got a call from a lady who had brought her car in for service and had a special Rosary around the gearshift knob. She had gotten the Rosary in the Philippines, and it had been blessed by a Cardinal.

When she called, she told me the Rosary was missing after they washed the car. We looked all over for it. I went into the dealership to try to find it for her. I knew it was priceless to her. I left her a long message telling her we were still looking.

I told her about a cross I had gotten in Italy, a cross that the Pope had blessed. We talked for a long time, and she and I developed a bond. People feel comfortable calling me, and after I help them, they say they never will buy another car anyplace else. That makes me feel good. I want all of my people to do the same and to take care of our customers. That doesn't cost anything.

The advertising you spend to get one person into a dealership costs $500. I may give someone something that may be worth $100 or $150, but that is much less expensive than $500. The best thing about that is that they will tell their friends and neighbors. It is all about trust in people, and their trust in you. It sure has paid off for me during the years.

It is an amazing story. I understand why people will ask how in the world I went from living with my sister and brother-in-law and working nights at Brown Rubber and then going to the Army for two years to having all of this.

The Army helped me develop into a leader. When I was a PFC, they made me a second lieutenant.

I often wonder if something like my story could happen again. It would be very difficult. You would have to start with a lot of money. They don't give you the stores today like they gave me mine. You have to purchase them.

I had to do it myself, because nobody gave me anything when I was young, but I am glad I did it my way.

35. The Tax Man Doesn't Get it All

When you are paying a Federal Income Tax of $15 million a year, you know you are making money. But you still have a lot left, even at that tax rate. But it's really not the money. It's the fact you are doing a good job to make that kind of money. I have plenty of money. It is, to a degree, the money in that I am building a new Lexus store in Arlington Heights, IL that is going to cost me $45 million. But it is paid for.

And that is because of my customers, who I love. They like me too, or I wouldn't be making that kind of money. They like buying cars from me, and their children like buying cars from me. Their neighbors buy cars from me.

I think it's great that Lafayette is my home, and everybody in Lafayette knows me. And now, I have been in Chicago for 30 years, and everybody there knows me. We do a lot for the people in Chicago because the people have been generous to me.

We're going to give away four cars in 2015 in Chicago. The first one was to a group that has children, third grade and younger, read to dogs. It builds the child's confidence. The group has 65 dogs who work with 2,000 kids at ten lower-income schools in Chicago.

To me, it was great just being there seeing the kids and their teachers and the dogs. For me, you have to give back to the people. It's not that I do it to sell more cars, but it works that way, though. And another thing I always do is answer calls. My general managers know that if they call me, I will answer. The same for my customers. But I get very few calls, which means I am taking care of the customers.

I wish I didn't have any bad calls, but I have more good calls than bad ones. By far. It is a great feeling for me. People say, "Bob, when are you going to retire?" I tell them that I think I have another 35 or 40 years. My work keeps me young. Besides, what are people really going to do if they retire? Are they just going to sit in a chair and play a guitar? I don't know how to play a guitar. And I can only go to Las Vegas so many times. You can get tired of going to Vegas.

As I look at this wonderful life and career, I always come back to the fact that it is because of the people. You have to surround yourself with good people. In my case, it carries into the family. JR's four boys are tremendous. They were raised perfectly, and they love the car business. Those young men know how to answer my questions, but better yet, they know how to answer customers' questions.

Before my mother died at 96, she just couldn't believe how successful I had become. It's interesting, because she thought I was the ornery one among all of her children. She kept telling people, "I don't know what Bob is going to do when he grows up. I don't know if he ever will make it or not." But I know this, when she died, she sure was proud of me.

I had a great upbringing with great parents, especially my mother, Velma, who went to church at least five times a week. Among her eleven children, four were still living as of 2015.

I have had a good, long run, and I hope it lasts another 35 or 40 years before I retire.

36. My First Born, JR Rohrman

JR, who attended St. Mary's School in Lafayette and then Lafayette Jefferson High School, was a very good athlete, especially in track. He ran the half mile and participated in the high school state finals twice and almost won the half mile. I attended the state finals each time he competed. The first time, he stayed near the back of the pack too long to catch up to the front and ended up about third place.

The next time, he started so quickly that when he got near the end of the race, he was in second or third place but didn't have enough gas left in his tank to win it. Because of his track skills, he received a full athletic scholarship to the University of New Mexico in Albuquerque. He attended New Mexico for a year, but he had a girlfriend at Purdue, and she convinced him to come back to Lafayette.

JR attended Purdue for a period of time, but he decided to go into the automobile business and transferred to a business school in Michigan, where he met his wife, Kathy. When JR graduated from college, he and Kathy married. Kathy is a native of Michigan, and her father was in the clothing store business.

When they got married, they moved to Lafayette, and JR went into business with me for quite a while. He was a manager for me. When we picked up Lincoln-Mercury and Subaru, I made JR the general manager for that store. We did so well with Subaru that we ended up buying some Subarus from dealers in Chicago.

After a few years, he came to me and said, "Pops, we should get into the Buy Here, Pay Here used car business." I really didn't want to do that. You are selling cars to people who don't have good credit to be financed through a bank or a finance company.

I told JR that it can be profitable if you can get it to work. Actually, it kind of scares me. I prefer the franchises and the used car business but not a Buy Here, Pay Here setting. Two weeks later, JR told me he wanted to go into the Buy Here, Pay Here used car business.

I asked him if he was sure. He said yes. I was disappointed with his decision, but I said OK. I was disappointed because I had to replace him. He was doing a fantastic job. I never have been able to replace him.

He would have been good as my general manager for Toyota,

Bob's five children.

Honda or whatever. But he opened three Buy Here, Pay Here stores - two in Lafayette and one in Monticello - and did very well with them.

JR and Kathy have four fantastic boys, and when the children were young, they lived in Lafayette. When they were living here, I would take the kids to Spooner, WI because I had spent six years living there when I was young. They liked it there.

It is a great place for fishing and relaxing. Soon, JR and Kathy were taking the four boys to Spooner for vacations. They built a nice cottage there and decided to move there. They moved to Eau Claire, WI and raised the kids there.

JR sold the Buy Here, Pay Here stores in Lafayette and opened one in Eau Claire. Again, he did very well. The three oldest graduated from high school there, and the two oldest graduated from Bethel University in St. Paul, MN.

Kathy and JR are very religious, and their four children graduated from religious high schools and colleges. As soon as their oldest, Ryan, graduated, JR sold his location to Walgreen's in Eau Claire and got out of the Buy Here, Pay Here. They moved to Niles, IN, near where Kathy grew up in Michigan, right across the Indiana state line and only a few minutes from South Bend.

A month or so later, I called JR and asked what he was doing. He said, "Pops, are you sitting down? I am preaching. I am traveling around to churches, mostly in the south, and preaching in different churches."

He had the strong religious beliefs that Kathy had. She is such a sweet girl and a beautiful woman to be in her 50s. She looks like she is 30, maybe 25. Her boys have never uttered a curse word.

JR continued preaching for some time. But finally when I hired JR's son Ryan to be a manager at the Honda store in Schaumburg and Chase to be the manager of the Ford store in Schaumburg and Trey was in college at Indiana Wesleyan, JR called me and said, "Pops, you've got all my boys. Kathy and I are kind of here in South Bend by ourselves. I wonder if you have a spot for me for me in Chicago, because it looks like you are going to have all of them in Chicago."

I told him that of course I did. I was talking to Ryan, and we agreed that we were having a difficult time hiring good salespeople, both in the car business and in the service departments. We had trouble hiring enough good ones for all the stores we have, fifteen in Chicago. Ryan and I talked about possibly opening a Rohrman University in Chicago, just to teach people how to act when they talk to a customer. That is the whole key. You don't really have to learn how to sell. If you act nicely and you are friendly, it takes care of itself.

You have to be friendly and listen. You can sell more cars listening than you can talking. So, I told Ryan about my conversation with his father about the possibility of working in Chicago. Ryan said that his father would be the perfect person to be the professor at Rohrman University.

Ryan knew that his father could teach. I told Ryan that it was a great idea. I called JR to ask if he would be interested, and he said yes. That is how JR and Kathy moved to the Chicago area, buying a home in Arlington Heights, IL.

The only difference between JR and I is that at 60, he is losing some of his hair, and at 82, I still have all of mine. I give him a hard time about that from time to time. But I am so proud of him. He is a fantastic father, husband and worker. He always has put in a lot of extra hours in any job he has had. He also is very intelligent. He is a wonderful son.

37. Rhonda Rohrman, My Oldest Daughter

Rhonda is a sweetheart. A wonderful mother and wife. She attended Lafayette Jeff, and during her senior year in high school, she began dating Vic Isbell. Quickly, they developed a serious relationship. I always liked Vic, but I told Rhonda that she really should date around a bit. So, she had a friendship with Ron Alting, now an Indiana State Senator, but she went back to dating Vic, which was great.

Vic and Rhonda graduated from Jeff, and Vic went on to college at Purdue, majoring in and graduating in engineering. He was an excellent student. To this day, I feel badly that I tried to tell Rhonda she shouldn't marry the first guy she ever dated, but it ended happily for everyone.

Rhonda and Vic married, and we had the reception at our Lafayette home. What a wedding. The cake was approximately 5 feet tall. We had tents in the backyard. To do that, we took our fences down and our neighbor's fence down. We had two big tents. We had one tent for the cake and one tent for the band and dancing. Rhonda and Vic arrived from their wedding at St. Mary's, and it started to rain. What a storm.

That night, a tornado ripped through Lafayette and struck the old Holiday Inn. We didn't get the tornado at our home, but we got lots of high wind. Everyone had to go into the house because sirens were sounding. Our basement wouldn't hold everyone, so some of our guests had to go to the second floor.

I stayed outside and guarded that huge wedding cake. I guarded the cake, but I got soaking wet. The rain finally stopped at 11 p.m., and everyone came back outside, and the band began to play.

The reception party lasted until about 3 a.m., and the backyard was nothing but mud. I was the last person up. My second wife, Linda, who was such a good mother to those kids and still is, had such a good time that night, too.

Linda went to bed at about 3 a.m., and I stayed up to make sure everything was OK. I cleaned as best I could, but inside in every waste basket, there were women's hose. Their hose had gotten soaking wet and muddy. They all danced in bare feet.

Vic went to work for Caterpillar in Peoria, IL. He was there for five years, and my first grand daughter was born in Peoria. Vic called Linda to tell us that he had taken Rhonda to the hospital to have the baby.

That night, Linda and I drove to Peoria and arrived at 11 p.m., just after Rhonda had the baby, Christina, who I call Tina. The funny thing about that night was that after Linda and I had been in Peoria for three or four hours, we decided to drive back to Lafayette. We both had to work the next day.

Linda said she would drive, and I said OK. Coming across Illinois, Linda, who always drove fast, was speeding. She was cruising along at about 90 miles an hour when an Illinois State Policeman pulled her over. He told Linda that the fine would be $200 and that she would have to pay the fine, or surrender her driver's license until the fine was paid. The officer also mentioned that he might take her to jail unless the fine was paid.

She turned to me and asked what we should do. I said, "I don't know. Do you want to spend the night in jail?" I was kidding her and told her I might just go on home to Lafayette. So I pulled out a credit card and paid the fine.

Of course, I drove us home. I still tease Linda about that today. Not long ago, I shared that story with Christina. Christina now has two little girls of her own. Rhonda and Vic had four daughters and no sons. Rhonda and Vic are very happy and live in Indianapolis. After Vic left Caterpillar, he went to work for General Motors' transmission factory in Indianapolis, which is Allison's.

Vic helped develop the six-speed transmission. About ten years ago, Vic left Allison's to enter the real estate business, which was pretty good timing on his part. They now own quite about of real estate in Indianapolis. A couple of their daughters have an interest in that business. They do very well.

Rhonda spends an awful lot of time in Chicago, because she has two granddaughters there. Christina is a partner in our Orange Media Group advertising business in Chicago, as is Rhonda's second daughter, Laura.

Christina and her husband bought a home in a Chicago suburb. Christina's husband also works for Orange Media Group. Laura, who was married in 2012, found a home in the same suburb, right next door to her sister, Christina. Each home is on five acres. I told them they have enough land to raise thoroughbred race horses.

Laura now has a son, the first in that family. Vic is so happy, he is jumping up and down singing Christmas Carols because it's a boy. I am sure that if Vic and Rhonda didn't own all of those properties in Indianapolis that they would be moving to Chicago. The third daughter, Kaitlyn, moved to Chicago and also is working for Orange Media Group. The fourth daughter, Alexa, was entering her junior year at Purdue in the fall of 2015.

Those four girls are beautiful young women. Rhonda just has such a gorgeous family.

Bob's daughter, Rhonda and her family in November, 2014.

38. Third Child Randy Rohrman Does it His Way

Like all of my children, Randy attended school in Lafayette, first at St. Mary's grade school and then began high school at Central Catholic before finishing at Lafayette Jeff.

Randy was a great athlete, especially as a left-handed baseball pitcher. When he was young, he finished third in a Punt, Pass and Kick contest. His good friend, Dave Thomas, finished second. Until then, I didn't know Randy was such a good football player.

Unlike his older brother and older sister, Randy was a little ornery. For example, each of our sons had his own bedroom. The two girls shared a bedroom, although it was a lot larger than the other three. Randy's bedroom had one window and opened up onto the top of the garage. I didn't know it until years later, but when everyone else was sleeping, he would climb onto the garage and then jump onto the ground and be gone for a couple of hours. He got back in through the back door. I don't think the other kids even knew, but if they did, they did not tell me.

Randy always was his own guy and still is. And he always has been a good car man.

After starting at Central Catholic, he transferred to Lafayette Jeff to play baseball. He was great. He had a tremendous fastball. He was so good that he had scholarship offers to play baseball, one at Indiana State and one at Georgia Southern. He also had offers from Purdue, Indiana and Notre Dame. I took him to visit Georgia Southern, because that is where I really wanted him to play. They play a lot of warm weather games each year. We drove to Savannah, GA and had a meeting with the head coach in his office.

When we arrived, the coach said the Cincinnati Reds were staging a tryout camp there that day. Including Randy, there were 27 pitchers and about 250 position players. Each pitcher got to face three batters. The temperature was about 100.

We went to the baseball field, and the stands were full of parents. Randy was the third to pitch. He struck out all three batters he faced. I was sitting in the stands clapping. A little later, they asked Randy to go back out there and face three more batters. Again, he struck out each of the three batters he faced.

After that, we returned to the Georgia Southern coach's office, and he offered Randy a full ride scholarship. I told Randy that we

Randy Rohrman (No. 9) waits to bat in a high school baseball game at Lafayette's Loeb Stadium in 1974 as Bob (standing in the bleachers) looks on.

had to accept that offer. We got in the car and headed back to the hotel, and I asked Randy how he struck out all six. He said, "Pops, I didn't want to disappoint you."

We talked about the two scholarship offers, and Randy said he liked Georgia Southern. But after we got home, he decided to accept the offer from Indiana State. Why would you go to Indiana State when you could go to Georgia Southern?

It turned out that the reason he picked Indiana State was because he had a girlfriend at Jeff that ended up attending Purdue. Funny thing was, he broke up with her, and a friend of Randy's began dating that girl. The friend married Randy's ex-girlfriend.

Randy never has been one to want to be tied down. He pitched well at Indiana State as a freshman, but that summer, he started working for me cleaning cars. But when it was time to return to school at Indiana State, Randy said he was going to transfer to Purdue.

The Indiana State baseball coach called me about a dozen times and actually drove to Lafayette from Terre Haute twice to try to talk Randy into going back to Indiana State. But when Randy gets something in his mind, you don't change his mind, even though he has done several things that were against my wishes.

He does well at what he wants to do, but it always is his way. I don't think he really even had a desire to play professional baseball. He has a son, Cal, who is 6-foot-5 and is a right-handed pitcher for the University of Dayton.

In 1984, right after I was awarded the Honda franchise in Schaumburg, Randy stopped attending Purdue and asked if he could move to Chicago and oversee construction of the Honda dealership in Schaumburg.

He did, and he also got a job selling Fords at a dealership right across the street from where we were building Schaumburg Honda. At the time, the Ford store was selling 300 or 400 new cars a month and 200 or 300 used. Randy sold Fords for quite a while until Schaumburg Honda was almost completed.

At that point, I made Randy my first general manager at Schaumburg Honda. I brought on Johnny Barrett later to be my general manager at the Honda store when we opened the Acura store a couple of years later in Palatine, IL. When we opened the Acura store, Randy owned half of it.

I loaned him the money to buy half. Randy and I each put in $300,000. He didn't do a bad job with Acura, which was a new car. Soon after, he came to me and told me he wanted to finish college and become an elementary school teacher. So, he began studying at DePaul in downtown Chicago. I bought Randy out.

Randy moved downtown in Chicago and bought a condo in a building that had been a warehouse. They changed it into six stories of flats. He bought the third floor for $220,000. Two years later, he sold the place and made some money on the deal. I didn't think it was worth $220,000. But, young kids seem to like those kinds of places. At that time, they didn't want a fancy downtown apartment. I have a fancy downtown apartment that I bought for $350,000 after the guy selling it wanted $450,000. Now, it probably is worth $600,000.

Randy graduated from DePaul with a degree in elementary education. Soon after graduating, Randy accepted an offer to do his student teaching at an elementary school on Chicago's south side.

After teaching sixth grade for several months, his students came into the classroom and one had gotten into a fight with a teacher. One day after the student had gotten into the fight with the teacher, Randy disciplined them pretty harshly. He was trying to teach them to be good kids.

The kids then went to lunch, but they did not return to Randy's class. At 1 p.m., the principal asked Randy if the kids were back in class. He said no. They did not return until it was time for class the next morning. The next morning, Randy walked into the classroom, and the kids were there on time. Randy took his coat off, walked to the front of the classroom and welcomed the kids back to school. He told them that they had left him but that they were back now.

Randy walked to the back of the room, put his coat on and told them he was going to do the same thing to them that they had done to him. He walked out and never came back.

He called me and said he wanted to come back to work in the car business. We opened a Saturn store on Green Bay Road in Waukegan, IL, and I made him general manager of that store. We started making money hand over fists. We were selling 205 a month.

I had a regular monthly meeting at Saturn of Waukegan, and as I was ready to leave, Randy said he wanted to talk to me. We went into his office, and he said his five-year plan at that store was ending. I didn't know we had a five-year plan. That's Randy.

He said he was going to go into business for himself. He said he was going to open an office in Lake Geneva, WI, and buy and sell cars and write commercials among other things. That lasted a year until he ran out of money. He has worked for me three or four times since, but as Randy is Randy, he doesn't last five years with me now.

As of the summer of 2015, he was living in Illinois but right on the Wisconsin border. He likes to buy and sell cars on the internet. He buys and sells expensive cars, those that sell from $75,000 to $150,000 each. When he sells one, he will make $10,000 to $20,000. He also is doing some day trading on the stock exchange.

He is his own guy and always has been. Everybody loves him.

39. *Daughter Richelle - Shelly - Has a Mind of Her Own*

Richelle - we call her Shelly - is my fourth child and second and final daughter.

It's kind of funny, but all five children have a different personality. Shelly certainly is different than Rhonda. Rhonda is more of a mother type, and actually, was a mother to each of the other four kids, even though JR actually is older than Rhonda.

On the other hand, Shelly was her own girl. Rhonda had a sweet personality. Shelly was a little different in that if she disagreed with you, you were in for an argument. Not that it is bad or good, it is just the way she is. She is probably more like her mother than she is like me. But Shelly and I get along well. One thing that hurt Shelly more than Rhonda is that Shelly was like 12 or 13 when her mother and I got the divorce. It bothered Shelly more than it did Rhonda because Rhonda was older.

After my second wife, Linda, and I were married, we tried to get Shelly to move in with us, like Rhonda did, but Shelly did not want to move in with us. Shelly wanted to stay with her mother. I am not sure why, but she did.

Shelly's mother probably was a little easier on her than I would have been. That might be some of the reason why Shelly chose to live with her mother. Shelly grew up to be a good person. I tried to get her to attend college, but she did not want to go to college.

At that time, it would have been very reasonable for her to attend Purdue, but instead, she really wanted to go to work for me in the automobile business. And so, she did. She started in Lafayette as the receptionist and phone operator. She greeted people and took the money for service department tickets. She was very well liked and did an excellent job.

Then, when we opened Schaumburg Honda, she wanted to move to Chicago and work for us there. A bit later, she went to work for us at the Lexus store, which at that time was a beautiful store. In

2015, it was 30 years old.

We had a lot of nice customers, but at the start, business was a little slow. It was a new line for us. It took two or three years before it finally got pretty good. Shelly worked for Lexus as the cashier and receptionist and did a fantastic job.

Her life changed during a vacation she took while she was working at Lexus. She went to Cancun, Mexico with a female friend. In Cancun, Shelly met Joe Posh, with whom she fell in love. Joe was from Pennsylvania and graduated from Villanova University near Philadelphia but was living and working in Florida at the time he and Shelly met. He was an executive for the Nestle group in Florida. He traveled throughout Florida for his job, making sure each product was being managed and operated correctly.

They fell in love, and Shelly left her job with us and moved to Florida. With it being Shelly, I was not shocked. Had it been Rhonda, I would have been shocked, but not Shelly. To put her in perspective, Shelly is more like my third child, Randy. At Christmas time of the year she moved to Florida, Shelly and Joe were married in The Keys.

To this day, even though they now are divorced, I still talk with Joe. Shelly and Joe have two children, a boy and a girl. In 2015, their son turned 19 and their daughter was 17. Shelly and Joe had a beautiful home in St. Petersburg Beach, FL. The house was on a canal that flowed into the Gulf of Mexico. They had a boat, which they would take down the canal and into the Gulf of Mexico. In 2011 or 2012, Shelly and Joe divorced. I don't really know why. I traveled to Florida to try and help when they were disagreeing about alimony and child custody.

Shelly did have a source of income from me because each of my five children own a piece of the Schaumburg Honda property. Not the dealership, but the property. So, my children get the rent every month from the Schaumburg Honda property. Schaumburg Honda is the biggest property that I have, not in terms of land, but in terms of sales.

Joe brought that up to his attorney, and of course, I probably would have done the same thing. Shelly did get the house in St. Petersburg Beach. At that time, the home was worth about $1 million. We tried to sell it recently and were offered $850,000. The property values in that part of Florida have not bounced back quite as much as other parts of the country.

Shelly got the children, but Joe has visiting rights any time he wants. Another important factor was that they knew that their entire educations for each of the two children was paid for through my trust that I have for each of my grandchildren.

After the divorce, Shelly moved back to Chicago, where many members of her family live and work. She bought a house in a suburb of Chicago. I loaned her the money to purchase the home in Chicago and she will pay me back when she sells the home in Florida. That home in Florida is paid for.

Her son, Jake, who I thought would decide to live with his father in Florida, is living in Chicago with Shelly. Their daughter, who I thought would end up with her mother in Chicago, is living in Florida with her father. Their daughter wanted to remain in Florida because she is attending a Christian high school and is an excellent athlete, especially in basketball and softball. She is almost 6 feet tall and is a strong girl. In 2014, she was an all-star in basketball.

Joe is taking really good care of her, and she stays busy attending basketball camps. Jake also was a good basketball player. Shelly tells me she is not going to remarry, but of course, I said that a couple of times, too. With her income, she does not have to work, but I told her she should work. I have offered her a job in one of my stores selling cars. I think she would be a good saleswoman.

We have several women selling cars for us, and our best sales person at our Arlington Lexus store during the past three months is a female. She has a great personality. Shelly has a great personality and can talk your leg off. I would like for her to sell cars for me.

It is too bad things did not work out with Shelly and Joe, because he is a good guy. I was a little disturbed when Joe's attorney tried to acquire more of what would be Shelly's inheritance.

Shelly, like Randy, is a great person, but she likes to do her own thing. Shelly and Randy get along very well.

40. Child No. 5 - Son Rick

Rick was my little baby, and my divorce from Shirley probably hurt him more than any of the kids with the exception of Shelly. Rick was young and impressionable. My second wife, Linda, tried to get Rick to move in with us. Linda was a great mother to my children and would have been a great mother had she had children of her own.

She is not their biological mother, but they are her kids and her grand kids and her great grand kids. I think they like Linda more than they like me. Rick was in elementary school when Shirley and I were divorced. I think the reason he didn't move in with Linda and I was because Shirley let him do just about anything he wanted. That actually hurt Rick more than it helped him. Today, I think he probably would agree with me about that.

Shirley moved to Arizona, and Rick moved with her. He actually graduated from high school in Arizona in the Phoenix area. I attended his high school graduation and tried to get him to come back to Lafayette with me. About six months after his high school graduation, he did come back to Lafayette. Shirley stayed in Arizona for about another year, and then she came back to Lafayette.

When Rick came back to Lafayette, I bought him a mobile home. He lived there for a couple of years. During that time, he met a girl from Indianapolis, Vicki. What a nice young lady she was then, and what a nice lady she turned out to be.

Rick and Vicki got married and are still married today. They have three sons. They dated for a year before they were married. They were both young when they were married, probably in their early 20s.

They live on the south side of Indianapolis, and the three boys attended Indianapolis Roncalli High School, a Catholic school on Indy's south side. All of them played football at Roncalli.

All of Rick and Vicki's sons are very good boys.

Rick runs my Hyundai store on the east side of Indianapolis, and in May of 2015, Rick had one of the best months he ever has had. Rick has been the general manager of Indy Hyundai for several years.

Before that, Rick was the sales manager at our Honda store in Indianapolis after starting there as a salesman working for my old friend Johnny Barrett. Rick and Vicki have lived in Indianapolis ever since they got married.

The only time Rick hasn't worked for me was a brief period at Hyundai when he got mad at me and quit. I told him he wasn't selling enough cars, and that made him mad. He actually went to work briefly for one of the auto auctions in Indianapolis.

He knew the auto auction guys, so they gave him a job. That didn't last long. He came back to work for me pretty quickly and has been there ever since. I think he was at the auto auction for two months.

It took Rick a long time to grow up. When I say grow up, I mean knowing what he actually wanted to do. I have to take the blame for a lot of that because of my divorce from Rick's mother. I think that caused a lot of hurt for the two young ones - Richelle and Rick.

I'm not sure he really ever would have grown up if not for his wife, Vicki. I give Vicki a lot of credit. Vicki kept Rick out of trouble. I saw that several times. I think a lot of Vicki.

Meeting Vicki was the turning point in Rick's life. When they met, Rick was living in the mobile home and was working for me in Lafayette, cleaning cars at the original Toyota store. Rick met Vicki when he was going to Indianapolis a lot as a single guy from Lafayette.

I would say Rick has been successful since he got married. Before he got married, Rick was on the edge all the time. He didn't just walk on the edge, he had one foot over it. It is a wonder he did not get into a whole bunch of trouble. He was very lucky. He was a free spirit. Everybody liked Rick, who is very personable, but he lived on the edge.

He is, however, a good car salesman who now has done well in that business. You also have to give Rick credit for taking on Hyundai when that line of cars wasn't accepted as well as it is today. Hyundai and KIA are good sellers today. When I took them on, they were selling a combined 50,000 or 60,000 cars a year. Now, they are selling 600,000 to 700,000 a year.

I am proud of Rick, especially during the last 10 to 15 years. There was a time with Rick when that edge was close. But he has done a great job in business and with his sons. They all love him. Whenever Rick's sons have a football or basketball game, he is there. That is a regret I have with my children, because it seems like I always was working. That didn't help.

My relationship with Rick always has been good, but it is even better now. At one point, I was a little worried about him, and the same with Shelly. But they always tell me they love me, and I tell them that I love them.

Rick Rohrman (front right), wife Vicki and two of their three sons in the late 1990s.

41. *A Traveling Man*

As a kid from Lafayette, IN, I rarely had an opportunity to take vacations, but when I did, it always was back to Spooner, WI, to see my mother and father, younger brother Bernie and other family members.

Spooner is a vacation area, and I took my kids there when they were young. In fact, I took them every year when they were young. To this day, they love going there, and some have built cottages on the lake.

My grandsons Ryan, Chase and Trey go up there all the time. It takes six or seven hours to drive there. It used to take me 12 hours to make the drive from Lafayette, because there wasn't an interstate. Now, I have had an opportunity to take many, many trips because of all of the franchises and the automobile companies that I represent. Every year, it seemed like we won a trip. I don't take all of them, because I can't. I let my general managers take about half of them.

Johnny Barrett, my director of operations for our Illinois Bob Rohrman auto group, took one to Eastern Europe in 2015. That was a fantastic trip from Acura.

Among the trips, the ones that Linda and I took together were the most memorable for me. She loved the trips, too, and that was really good because we both liked to travel. It worked out real well with she and I.

One that I remember quite well was a trip to Italy. We went to Rome on a Toyota trip. All of us on the trip were Toyota dealers. One day, we went up into a mountain area from Rome. We took a bus in the morning and stayed all day.

In Italy, whether you are having breakfast, lunch or dinner, you have at least two big wine bottles on the table, regardless of what you are eating. It gets kind of funny, because you are drinking a little bit of wine here, and then a little bit more for lunch.

Once you get on the bus, they bring the cases of wine along. You start passing those bottles around in the bus. It was very good wine. Sitting in front of me on the bus was a good friend of mine, a Toyota dealer from northern Indiana.

He was wearing a light tan suit, which was very nice. We had drank quite a bit of the wine when somebody handed me a glass of red wine. Somebody dared me to pour the glass of red wine on my friend in the light tan suit. When they dare me, I generally take the dare. So, I reached over and poured the glass of wine onto the beautiful tan suit.

Linda was sitting next to me, and she told me not to do it. She really didn't convince me not to do it. We spent the night, which was Saturday, and the next morning, we went to church, and that was the Pope's summer place. We went to church, which was staged outside, and the Pope was standing two stories up in the balcony saying mass. Isn't that something?

It was fantastic to go to church with the Pope. After mass, I went to the store there, which had items the Pope had blessed and bought a beautiful cross, which I still wear today. I have had to change a broken chain a couple of times, but I still wear that same cross.

The next day, when we were on the bus going back down the mountain, we were drinking more wine. Halfway down, Linda asked the bus driver to stop the bus. She needed to use the restroom, and some others had to go as well.

On that same trip, they had extra bottles of wine, and they told us we could take those bottles to our rooms. I picked up two bottles to take to our room, which had a beautiful marble floor. One of the bottles slipped from my hand and shattered on the marble floor.

The hotel staff rushed to clean it up and told us not to worry. That was a great trip, and I loved Rome. We toured the Roman Coliseum, and they told us how they would release the lions, who would eat people. We were in Italy on that trip for about a week and visited the island of Sicily. They took us across the water on a boat. We saw where they shot scenes from the movie The Godfather.

On another trip to Rome, we went on a ship in the Mediterranean. We boarded the ship in northern Italy in Venice and went completely around Italy before we docked. We stayed on the ship at night but were on land during the daylight hours.

Another great trip, we boarded a ship in Italy or France and sailed to Athens, Greece. We toured Athens and then visited the Greek Islands. That was great. We also visited Turkey after spending time in Greece.

I remember Turkey quite well, because we boarded a bus and traveled to a city known for its rugs.

On a lot of our trips to Europe, we would land either in London or Berlin and go from there. One of those trips to Europe, we took my granddaughters Laura and Christina with us. We toured London, and one day, we got on the train under the channel and went to Paris.

The girls just loved that trip. We stayed in Paris for a day and went back to London. We visited Stonehedge and a lot of castles. Visiting all those castles wears you out. We went to Buckingham Palace and the home of Winston Churchill. I loved Churchill.

Earlier, we had taken another trip to Paris with the Mitsubishi dealers. All were first-class trips. In Paris, we stayed at a famous hotel two blocks from the Eifel Tower. We were going to go to the top, but I said I didn't want to go up that high in an elevator. So, we did not go to the top of the Eifel Tower. We also went to the Louvre and saw the beautiful paintings.

I needed a haircut, so we found a side street with a barber. A girl began to cut my hair, and while I was telling her not to make it too short, Linda kept telling her to take some more off. Linda said it was too long and to cut some more off. The barber didn't speak English, but she understood what Linda and I were trying to tell her. She listened to Linda.

I came out of there with the shortest haircut I think I ever have had. When we got back to the United States, I think I wore a hat for a while. We went all over Paris, which is huge. They have some very beautiful streets there. Paris and London both were very interesting.

42. On to Japan and Other Ports of Call

I counted, and Linda and I have been to Japan thirteen times.

We would win this Holiday in Japan that Honda had every year. And we won it every year, and at that time, I just had the Honda store in Lafayette. I asked why I continued to win the Japan trips, but they never came out with the rules how you win. They told me that they just like certain people to go on the trips with them. And then, Toyota trips went to Japan, too.

On one trip to Tokyo with Toyota, we were on the top floor of a 40-story building, where they served dinner. They were getting ready to serve dinner to us, which was a group of Toyota dealers from the Chicago region. We were with my friend Doug Smith and his wife.

As we were sitting there, all of a sudden, our waitress dove under the table. Just then, the room started shaking. I thought, "Why is she diving under the table?" They said they were going to turn off the gas, because there was an earthquake. It shook, and I thought the windows were going to break. But they didn't.

They got us up and told us that we needed to get down to the ground without using the elevator. We had to walk down 40 flights of stairs. The building was shaking the whole way down until we got to the 10th floor. At that point, they told us we could ride the elevator. So we rode the elevator the final 10 floors, but we did not go back up to the top floor to eat. We went someplace else to eat.

Toyota and Honda would put us up in the nicest hotels. The Japanese hotels are really, really nice. They give you everything you want. In fact, they give you extra service. It seems like the Japanese people try to give you the best service there is.

On a lot of our trips to Japan, we would take the fast train, which is called a Shinkansen or bullet. It travels at a speed of well over 100 miles an hour. One trip, we took the train to Hiroshima, where the United States dropped an atomic bomb in World War II.

Hiroshima was a city of almost 1,000,000, and it wiped out many of them. It destroyed the city, which still had not been rebuilt when we were there. The only buildings that were standing were the museums that were built to show and explain the story.

We went through the museums, and they gave us headphones for the walking tour, where we saw all the pictures. It was really dramatic, very emotional and kind of sickening. Some of those who survived and lived in the city could hardly walk. We were there in the late 1970s, more than 30 years after the bombing. We did not visit the other city that was bombed - Nagasaki - but it was smaller and not as many were killed.

We stayed in Tokyo all the time, but we were taken on side trips, including Mount Fuji. It sits off by itself, and you can see the snow all year long. We also took some boat trips. During those trips to Japan, I had an opportunity to acquire a taste for Japanese art. I think we also visited every Toyota and Honda factory in Japan. It was interesting, because the Honda and Toyota factories at that time all were automated. There weren't very many people working in those factories. They had the robots.

The robots are coming to the factories in the United States now, but not as much as there is in Japan. I got to know a lot of the Japanese people on those trips, and some of them got to be real good friends of mine. I hated to see some of them retire.

When the Honda guys in the US get to be 65, they send them back to Japan. They either retire them, or they have them work in Japan. A couple of them got to be real good friends of mine, and even after they went back to Japan to work, some of their families stayed and lived in California. They got used to living in the United States. They were here for so long that they got to be citizens.

One of the Japanese executives really got into automobile racing, and any time there was a race, he would invite me to sit with him at the race. I always did. He spoke perfect English and is a very intelligent man. Their cars are the best in the world.

They enjoyed being around me, and they still do. I always was very friendly with the Japanese, because they are such good people. I am friendly with everybody.

The other thing about it is that my hobby is selling cars. It's not a job to me, and you have to be friendly. As I tell all my grandkids, if you want to sell cars, you have to fall in love with the customer. Because I enjoy sitting down and talking to people, they enjoy sitting down and talking to me. And I love to travel and meet people along the way.

Another favorite trip for Linda and I was one we took to Australia. We enjoyed Sydney, and then visited Melbourne. We also toured the rain forest. We took a submarine ride to the Great Barrier Reef. That was very interesting.

I liked going to Australia, although some people said a flight of 20 hours to get there is too long. I did not mind, because we were in first class, plus we were sleeping half the time. I kind of enjoyed it.

I love listening to the Australians speak. You can tell the difference between someone from England and someone from Australia.

Another trip we took was to Fiji. It was a great trip. When you go there, you stay in huts out in the water. When my daughter, Rhonda, and her husband, Vic, got married, I sent them on their honeymoon there. They were there for a week and then spent a week in Hawaii.

We also have visited almost all of the Caribbean Islands. A lot of the manufacturers take their trips to the islands because it is a shorter trip. In Aruba, I took my grandson, Ryan, and we stayed in a hut in which you just closed the drapes when you were going to sleep. Ryan and I also went white water rafting in Peru. That was something I never imagined doing. But I enjoyed it. I thought I would fall out of the raft and hit my head on a rock.

I also have been to Russia. We began in Sweden and boarded a cruise ship to St. Petersburg. We stayed in a real nice hotel there, which was owned by the Swedes, but the rest of it was tough, because I don't think they had repaired any of the roads since the early 1900s. We toured the entire city. They showed us where the Germans bombed during World War II. Hitler said the Germans were going to take Russia. Well, they took 200 miles in and turned around and went 200 miles back out.

On another trip, we flew into Moscow, which was taken care of much better than St. Petersburg. We saw all of the government buildings in Moscow along with a big art museum.

We also visited the French Riviera, Spain and Portugal. In 2010, I finally got to tour Germany. They got me a very fast car in Munich, and I wanted to drive on the autobahn up to Nuremburg, where the Nazi war criminals were tried.

I got the car up to 150 miles an hour, but about halfway there, I realized it was going to take too much time, so I turned around and drove back. At 150, I wasn't the fastest one on there. It is a beautiful road, but you have to stay in your lane. There is no speed limit, but if someone is coming up behind you, you have to move over.

Today, I would like to take Linda and go on that river cruise through Germany.

I think all my travels have helped me in the business world. And if I ever think about retiring, I think I might build a home on the Baja in Mexico, where I could play lots of golf, which I enjoy. I enjoy the Mexican people, who are very hard working. If you have something you need done, they will put in 20 hours a day to get it done. Because I get along so well with people everywhere, I think I could live anywhere, especially if someone could help me with the different languages. I know a little Japanese, but so many of them have learned English.

43. *A Man for All Seasons, and Songs*

Outside of my family, most people don't realize that I enjoy singing, and I am pretty good.

Ever since my kids were 7 or 8 years old, I started singing Happy Birthday to each one on the phone. I still sing Happy Birthday to the kids, the grand kids, my kids' wives or husbands and the great grand kids.

Every month, I get my daytime book out and check the birthday sheet. I also look at it, because on the grand kids' birthdays, I also make a deposit into their trusts. I write down how old each will be, and I call and sing Happy Birthday.

My granddaughter Christina knows that I am calling to sing to her or to the great grandkids Happy Birthday, so she doesn't answer the phone. I think she has saved that voicemail for each of the past 15 years. The other kids have saved some of them. Christina is my oldest grandchild.

I always have enjoyed singing. I sang in the shower. I also especially enjoy singing when I am driving alone in the car. When Linda and I were married, she would try to sleep in the car, and I would sing.

Some of my favorite singers are Bing Crosby, Elvis Presley, Dean Martin and Frank Sinatra. When Linda and I would go to Las Vegas, we had to go see Elvis. Elvis was Linda's favorite. She loved Elvis. We had to sit up close to the front, because she wanted to catch the scarf when he threw it. Elvis always performed at the Hilton in Las Vegas.

And we also had to see Sinatra when we were in Vegas. He performed there a lot. Bing Crosby also was out there a lot. I always loved the Rat Pack, and I have the movie made about the Rat Pack.

We went to Vegas a lot, because a lot of the car manufacturers meetings are held in Vegas. That is because they have enough hotel rooms to house everyone. Plus, the hotel rooms are reasonably priced. I remember when you could get a really nice hotel room in Vegas for $50. Now, it is a little bit more, but it still is reasonably priced, a lot less expensive than it is in downtown Chicago.

A have collected a lot of albums from my favorite singers. The one I have in my car - I plug it in - has about 100 songs on it. Those songs all are from Crosby, Presley, Martin and Sinatra. I really didn't start to like music until I was 15 or 16.

I think part of my interest in singing comes from the fact my father was a good singer. He would sing popular songs from the 1920s and 1930s. He was born in the 1890s. My mother told me that when they were living in Montana for a time, my father sang on the radio.

My parents were from Madison, IN, and moved to Billings, MT. for a time and had a sheep ranch. And while they were there, he sang on the radio several times. They moved back to Madison and then moved to Lafayette. I was the first of their children to be born in Lafayette. That was in a log cabin just a few days after they arrived. The other two younger than me also were born in Lafayette before my dad moved the family to Wisconsin.

I really enjoy singing when I am in the car at night, and I do drive a lot at night back and forth from Lafayette to Chicago. I will sing up a storm. Not only do I enjoy it, but it keeps me awake.

Singing makes me feel good. I enjoyed singing "I Did it My Way" at the dedication of the Rohrman Center for Performing Arts at Lafayette Jefferson High School.

I would have to say Frank Sinatra and Dean Martin are my favorites. I loved the old Dean Martin Show on TV. He always had a lot of guests on his show who were funny. He also had politicians and movie stars. His guests would knock on a door, and Dean would say, "Who is here?"

I also enjoy movies, although I don't watch as many as I used to. A lot of today's movies are wild. They are about outer space and crazy stuff like that. They are not real. A lot of people love those movies, and they draw big crowds, but I always have liked the love stories.

I always enjoyed Doris Day movies, but there were a lot of good actors and actresses that made great love story movies. I also was a big fan of Jane Russell. She was beautiful. One of my favorite movies is The Godfather. Actually, I enjoyed all of the Godfather movies with Robert De Niro and Al Pacino. But the love story movies are my favorite.

Some of those love story movies made me cry because they are so sad. In some of the love stories, the stars would be killed or die, and I would start crying.

I also liked John Wayne movies, and growing up, I also loved Roy Rogers and Dale Evans. I also was a fan of the Lone Ranger and Tonto. I still have those movies. I bet I have from 300 to 400 movies on tape. Sometimes, I will watch one of those old movies when I am home in the middle of the night.

I spend more time in Downer's Grove than I do in Lafayette, but I have a collection of movies in each home. I also have a great set of Jerry Lewis and Dean Martin movies.

I also love sports, and for some reason, I am able to remember sports statistics. I enjoy watching the Chicago Cubs and like their young talent. Being in Chicago has me watching the Cubs, the White Sox and hockey.

I enjoy watching the Blackhawks, especially after I figured out what the heck is happening. At first, I didn't know what was going on. The puck would be at one end of the rink, and I would be watching the other end. They would call a penalty or an infraction, and I would ask what the heck that was all about. Now, I figured it out. My kids and grandkids know what is going on.

To me, baseball in Chicago is the best. I am really enjoying that Clayton Richard, who is from Lafayette, now is pitching for the Cubs. I enjoyed watching him when he was with the White Sox and the San Diego Padres.

I also enjoy Purdue University football, which I have followed forever, ever since I came back from the Army in April of 1955. Lenny Dawson, the former Purdue quarterback who won a Super Bowl with the Kansas City Chiefs, bought a car from me when I working for Glenn R. Pitman downtown in Lafayette.

Over the years, I have gotten to know a lot of the Purdue players. They had some good teams with Lenny Dawson, Bob Griese, Mike Phipps, Leroy Keyes, Mark Herrmann and Drew Brees.

Now, I love to watch Brees and the New Orleans Saints. I watched the San Diego Chargers when he played for them. I was at the Super Bowl when Brees and the Saints won, beating the Indianapolis Colts.

I watch baseball games when I can, or if I am driving in the car, I will listen to the games on the radio. Football probably is my favorite sport; college football, even more than pro football, except for the Colts, the Bears and the Saints.

When New Orleans is playing either one of them, I am for Drew Brees. Drew is a great guy. The people in New Orleans say he brought the city back from the hurricane. I have twelve season tickets to Purdue football. I have had those for more than 30 years. I have ten season tickets to Purdue men's basketball, and they are the best seats. They even have a parking sign over there that says Bob Rohrman. Purdue sports really are my favorite.

44. *From Tomato Soup to Kobe Beef*

When I was in high school, for lunch, I would stop at the little corner grocery store and buy a can of Campbell's Tomato Soup. I would have that almost every day for lunch. It was fast, and it was good.

To this day, I still love Campbell's Tomato Soup. I have some of it in the pantry in every home I own. Every once in a while, I will reach in and grab a can. You can mix water with it, or, you can mix milk with it. I always liked it made with milk the best. When I was in high school, we could not afford that much milk, but water essentially was free.

Now, as I have traveled with the automobile manufacturers on different trips, I have grown to love beef, especially steak. I have grown to love the best steak, which to me, is the ribeye. Why do I love the ribeye? One reason is that a ribeye has more fat in it. As you look at a ribeye steak, it has a lot of fat lines in it.

I know that the fat adds a lot of flavor to that steak. In addition to the flavor, the ribeye is the tenderest steak there is, regardless if it is prime. You must get the prime to really get the tender ribeye that can be cut with a fork. Some restaurants don't have prime steak, which restaurant owners tell me is very expensive. You can end up spending at least $60 for a prime ribeye, and then they sell you the potato and the salad. The salad or soup, along with a ribeye, is my favorite meal.

Another interesting thing about my love for steak was acquired during my thirteen trips to Japan. I learned to appreciate Kobe beef, which comes from a special type of cattle. Those cattle are not allowed to run around in the pastures. They are kept in the barn, and they are fed grain and beer. That process makes the beef very, very tender.

The center for Kobe beef is Kobe, Japan. Every time I have a chance to order Kobe beef, I order Kobe beef. It is the best steak I ever have had. You can get Kobe beef in a strip steak or whatever you want, but I like Kobe beef in a ribeye. I love the steak from those Kobe cattle.

When I go into a restaurant today, I know that almost all of them offer a ribeye steak, but I ask if they have prime beef. There are many great steak restaurants in Chicago, which was born from the stockyards being there. Most of the waiters say that the beef is not prime but is very close to it.

Only some grocery stores will offer prime beef, and when they do offer if, there is not much of it. I will take some of the prime home with me and cook it. I am a pretty darned good cook.

When I was young, I was what was known as a second cook at the Midlothian Country Club, and most of that cooking was steak. There is a good grocery in Downer's Grove where I can get prime. You can buy Campbell's Tomato Soup at the corner grocery, but you cannot get prime beef there. I have a big grill in the backyard at my Downer's Grove home, and I enjoy grilling steaks there.

Normally, I will cook my own breakfast before I go to work, and then I cook at night, too, unless it is late at night, and if that is the case, I will stop somewhere and eat out. But to this day, if given a choice, I will go with the Kobe beef and a prime ribeye. All you really need with that is a big, loaded baked potato.

There is a restaurant in Westmont next to the Toyota store that serves a great steak and a loaded baked potato like I have never seen before. The first time I saw one of their loaded baked potatoes, I could not believe how big it was. The waitress told me that often, the first time a customer orders one of those loaded baked potatoes, they tell her they have to take a picture of it. And they do.

In Chicago, when all the kids, grandkids and great grandkids come up for Christmas, I take a group of forty-six to Mike Ditka's steak house. I tell them we are coming, and they bring out these appetizers that are four stories high and include lobster and shrimp and some kind of meat.

We have one of those for each table, and that is enough for an appetizer. Then, we order from the menu, and a lot of people order the Ditka pork chops or the steak that they call the tomahawk, because it is a ribeye with the bone in, and you can hold it like you are about to throw a tomahawk.

Bob surrounded by his great grandchildren at a family gathering in 2014.

When they know I am coming with my group, they cut more tomahawks. They tell me they normally sell about twelve tomahawks a day, and when they are out, they are out. When I make my reservation, they double the amount of tomahawks. Some in my Christmas group also order big salads, but many order one of those big tomahawk steaks or the Ditka pork chops.

Ditka's is one of the best steak houses in Chicago, but there are so many good ones that it would be difficult to say one is the best. There are six or seven in Chicago that I honestly could say are the best. It would be tough to pick one, because a steak house in Chicago is a steak house in Chicago.

I am a steak guy, but when I am in Italy, especially in Rome, I love their fettuccini Alfredo with those bottles of wine. France is another country with great food, as is Germany. In Germany, I love the sauerkraut and brats with some beer. I also am fond of a sweet German wine that is made from grapes that are over ripe. My real estate guy in Chicago buys me a case of that sweet German wine every Christmas. That case will last me an entire year, because I don't drink that much.

Wine is about the only alcohol I drink, along with a good margarita from Pepe's once in a while. My grandson Ryan lived with me for a while, and he knows how much I enjoy Pepe's and a margarita from there. I like Mexican food, especially Pepe's.

It seems like every country has a famous food that I really have come to enjoy. I like sushi when I am in Japan. At each of the new automobile shows in Japan, they serve lots of sushi. They really feed us well when we travel to Japan.

When I think of all the wonderful things I have been fortunate enough to experience, I truly am blessed. I have experienced so many countries around the world and the food for which each one is known, including Russia and China.

Oh, my, it has been a whirlwind journey. I love it. It keeps me young. It has been a fantastic ride, and I would do it all over again.

Part Two

Along for the Ride

45. *Shirley Relander*

Bob Rohrman's first wife and the mother of his five children

Until I met Bob at a dance for teens at St. Boniface, I did not know him. In fact, I had never seen him before that evening.

Actually, there was a dinner upstairs at St. Boniface, and the dance was downstairs. Before that evening, I had gotten into trouble with my mother for coming home too late at night, and she didn't want me to leave the dinner and go downstairs to the dance.

But, I talked her into letting me go down there. When I went down there, there he was. It all started when he came over to me and asked me to dance. I liked Bob right away. I think I liked him because he was fun, although he was much quieter then than he is now. He wasn't like he is today.

Now, he is kind of silly, but when I met him, he was more serious. So, we began dating while he was a student at Lafayette Jeff, and I was attending St. Francis. When we met, he also was working at Brown Rubber.

After Bob finished work at 11 p.m., he would come to visit me at my parents' home on Union Street. He always smelled like rubber. I didn't care, because I was falling in love. I am surprised that my mother and dad let him come over. But my dad liked him right away. My dad saw dollar bills in Bob's eyes. Dad thought Bob might be successful. Dad was right.

All Bob ever talked about was selling cars and making money. I guess my mom liked him, too, because she never said yay or nay.

Bob graduated from high school and joined the military. He was assigned to Fort Lewis near Seattle, WA. After a time, I missed him, so I got on a bus and went to visit him in Washington. I couldn't believe my parents let me go. I ended up staying in Washington a bit longer than I intended to stay.

It was a long trip on a bus. I had no idea it was that long. I had been to Chicago once with the Girl Scouts, but other than that, I never had been out of Lafayette when I got on that bus to Washington. But I didn't care, because I just wanted to see Bob. I missed him.

After riding on a bus for three days, I was tired, but the night I arrived, we went out with a couple of Bob's friends. I had never had an alcoholic drink, but I had my first one that night. I actually stayed for a while and got a job at the Ten-Cent Store. I went out there with nothing but the clothes on my back. I just had a small bag.

So, I had to buy a sweater, and that is when I went into the Ten-Cent Store. They said they were hiring, so I worked in that store for a few weeks and then came back to Indiana.

We had talked about getting married and had plans. We actually got engaged in the mail. He bought a diamond for me at the Army base. And he sent it to me. You could say we got engaged thanks to the United States Postal Service.

The announcement was in the newspaper, all the girls had their dresses, and I had my wedding dress. Then Bob calls from Washington and says he cannot come home for the wedding. I was mad. I said, "OK, that is it."

A couple of days later, he shows up in Lafayette. That's Bob. And we got married. That was June of 1954. I don't remember every detail of our wedding, but I know I lost 10 or 15 pounds that week because of the stress of trying to get everything together in one week. It was crazy. We had the wedding reception in the little house behind my parents' home on Union Street.

We packed everything in a car he bought while he was home, and we drove back to Washington. It was fun being there. We met some nice people. Then, Bob learned he was going to be shipped somewhere else in the United States, and he didn't want me staying in Washington by myself. So, he wanted me to come home to Lafayette. At that point, I knew I was pregnant with JR.

I came home to live with my parents while I was pregnant and got a job at Indiana Bell as a long-distance telephone operator.

Bob was discharged from the military in April of 1955, and

several days after he returned to Lafayette, JR was born. The day JR was born, Bob and his brother in law, Nick Switzer, were gone, looking for a car for Bob to buy. My mother, Olivia, drove me to the hospital. But Bob made it to the hospital just in time for JR's birth. It was about 2 a.m.

I remember the apartment in which we lived on Alabama Street. Bob was selling cars for Pitman, and Bob was working a lot of hours, which ruined the marriage. He was never home. He would come home late at night, and I would have reheated his dinner two or three times. By the third time, the food wasn't too good.

In the early years of marriage, we were pretty happy. I got pregnant with Rhonda, who was born in 1957, and then I got pregnant with Randy. Those two were born 10 months apart. That was hard for me. By then, we had moved into a house on Sioux Place.

Bob was working six days a week and playing golf on Sundays, and when I didn't see him very much, it was hard. I imagined a marriage like my parents. Then, I kept getting pregnant. With Rick, I had blood clots and had to stay in bed for three months.

It wasn't another man that caused our marital problems. The problem was Bob never being home, and me being pregnant all the time, five times in eight years. Thank God I had my mother's help. She was a Godsend. Everybody liked my mother.

However, when I was growing up, my mother was very tough on me in everything. I don't know why that was, but she raised me tough. My dad, Louis, never said boo. He was very quiet. I guess you could say my mom was demanding and expected a lot of me.

My mom liked Bob and knew Bob's mother, Velma, very well. Velma gave me my first hug, and I didn't know what to do. My family members weren't affectionate. They never gave hugs. I think it was the German upbringing. Velma gave me a hug when I was 15. She was very nice. I loved her. And I loved all of Bob's sisters. We used to do things together.

I was especially close to Bob's sisters Rita and Kathy. Rita and I were only two years apart in age. Bob has a great family, and I liked all of them very much. I knew Bob's father, John, who built a room onto our basement when we lived on Sioux Place.

Velma had plenty of her own kids to go see, but she always treated me like her own daughter. Bob's father, John, was quiet, more like my dad. Velma and my mother, Olivia, got along great.

A big part of the problems between Bob and I was that I never got to go anywhere. I never had a car. I didn't have a car until our fourth child, Shelly, was little. She was going to daycare, and that is when he finally brought a car home to me. The only time until then that I had access to a car was when he was home. But I had to wait for him to come home, because he always was late. He still is late.

I was even afraid Bob would be late to our wedding, but my brother in law, Paul Andrews, promised me that he would make sure Bob was on time for that. And he was.

I loved being a mother and I loved my children, but I was stuck. I loved the babies. The only thing I ever wanted was to get married and have kids. Bob was a good provider. But I don't know that he was a good father, because he never was there. He got home late at night, and if the kids were still awake, he would go up and talk to them and tell them stories.

He was all business, but he did get to some of the ballgames when JR, Randy and Rick were playing sports. Bob and I, however, rarely went out as a couple. During Lent, I always wanted to go out and eat fish on a Friday night and never got to. A few times, we went out with some other couples, but not many.

I got frustrated. It was hard on me. But we were married more than 19 years. During those later years, I had a pretty serious automobile accident. I was driving the three older children to school, and it was icy when a guy hit me from behind and injured my back.

I told JR to go to the front door of a neighbor's house, knock on the door and tell them I had a wreck. He didn't want to go do that, but he did. I won a lawsuit from the injuries I sustained in that accident and took the money and bought a home after we got divorced.

Eventually, I just had to get away, just to have some time for me, more than anything. I liked going to Jamaica and to Mexico and being away, but I missed the kids. I would stay a couple of weeks each time. I needed some alone time. The main reason we got a divorce was because there just was no time for me or for us, and Bob knew it.

He would tell me I was pretty. And from time to time he would tell me he loved me, but I didn't feel it was sincere. He would say he loved me but never showed a lot of affection.

At one point, I just could not handle it any more. He knew we were not happy, but I would not have left had things been different.

When we got divorced, I didn't care about money. I just wanted my kids. We both had the same lawyer to start with, but then I was told to go see someone else. I went to another lawyer, who told me I must be crazy because I wasn't suing Bob for anything. I said no, I just want my kids.

After the divorce, Bob still tried to be together, but I said no. I thought we would be married for a long time, but it did not happen.

A few years later, I realized what I had done, but today, the kids and I are very close because of that. Bob and the kids don't talk that much. It has hurt the kids over the years, especially JR and Rhonda. I would say Randy, too, but the two younger ones, not as much. That is my opinion.

Bob expected a lot from JR, and at times, didn't treat him very well. Bob would get made at JR at the car lot and yell at him. When Bob blows, he blows.

Bob always said that he would be a millionaire by the time he was 40, and he made it at 35. I never thought Bob would be as successful as he has become. If somebody would have told me back then what he would achieve, I would have said I don't know. I never really thought about it.

It is amazing what he has achieved, but look at what it has cost him in the process. It cost him some of the closeness with his kids.

I am hoping the older Bob gets that it will hit him.

With Bob, everything is business, but you must understand that he grew up poor in a big family. His goal was to become financially strong, and he made it. He went for it and got it.

I hope he can say that he loves the kids more today. JR needs to hear that more than anyone. In Randy's case, I think he put all of his frustrations into sports. Rhonda and I are very close, but I am close to all five kids. They can come to me with everything. Randy calls me the Monarch.

Bob and I had almost 20 years together, but I needed more support from him on the home front. I saw all my friends having good marriages with their husbands home at night, and that is what I wished for. I loved Bob. I really did. I can even remember crying at the railroad station when he left to go to the Army.

We have five wonderful children together, and that makes me very proud. I did something right.

The Rohrman family is saddened by the September 4, 2015 death of Shirley Relander, the loving mother of Bob's five children and a wonderful member of the Rohrman family.

46. *Linda Rohrman*

Bob's second wife and stepmother to his children

I moved to Lafayette in 1969 and began a banking career at Lafayette National Bank in 1970. I was on the dealer desk in the Consumer Loan Department in 1973, and that is when I met Bob. Not being from Lafayette, I didn't know much about him.

I knew he was an automobile dealer and had recently gone through a divorce after 19 years and was very personable. During our dating period, he was very attentive and we spent a lot of time together. Both of us share a great sense of humor.

I really enjoyed his company and fell in love with him. We were married on Christmas Eve 1973. I continued to work at the bank until the fall of 1981.

The automobile business provided several opportunities to travel, which was not very conducive for the available vacation time I had at the bank. With my background in business, I began to do more and more for the company.

The automobile business has a lot of moving parts, which makes it very interesting. When we were married in 1973, he had the Jeep and Toyota franchises in Lafayette. As he began to expand, I would be the point person for completing the franchise applications.

The one problem with this was the applications were so thoroughly completed that he was never turned down for a franchise. He was awarded the new point for a Honda franchise in Schaumburg, IL in 1985.

From there, franchises were popping up all over the place - Indianapolis, Fort Wayne, Schaumburg, Arlington Heights, Westmont and Gurnee.

As the empire grew, so did Bob's ego.

Everywhere we went, he was recognized, usually with someone saying, "There's BOB ROHRman." I am not an 'in the limelight' kind of person, so this was not something I enjoyed.

I would say that we were not on the same page when he expanded to the Illinois market. His goal was to be one of, if not the one, largest automobile dealerships in the nation.

I asked him once to take one night a week off, plus Saturdays. His response, "You're asking me to retire?" That is his way of life. I asked how much is too much, and how big is too big. Well, I think the answer to that question is pretty obvious. As I look back now, it is evident that Bob is married to the car business.

When I found out about the affair with the person in Chicago, I admit, I was devastated. As stressful and difficult as it was to be married to Bob, I did love the guy. Several steps were taken to try to save the marriage, but when it became obvious that the person in Chicago had stolen his heart, I filed for divorce.

As much as I loved the kids and all the grandkids, I couldn't stay married to their father/grandfather. My mother passed away in the same time period as we were going through the divorce, so I really went through a period of grief, one for my mother and one for my marriage.

It took some time for me to look inside myself to find out what was important to me. It came down to faith, family and friends. My faith grew during this period and has become very important in my life.

As for the family, I am eternally grateful to both Bob and Shirley for producing these five beautiful children who have become like my own. We have gone through some rough patches through the years, but I believe our bond is unbreakable. I love them all dearly.

The first grandchild graduated from high school the year after the divorce. I knew that Bob's graduation gift would be a car of their choosing.

I wanted to share memories with my grandchildren, so I began the tradition of a trip with each one. They would do the research to pick where they wanted to go, but I had veto power if it was really out of the question. We have gone to some amazing places, but the best part is the time together.

On one trip, which was a cruise, my grandson, Ryan, and I were seated at just a table for two. I told him this was quite unusual, since normally we would be at a table with six or more. He said, "This is great, grandma, we can talk to each other!" Still melts my heart today!

I now have sixteen grandchildren, eight great grandchildren and probably many more in the years ahead.

To have them all in my life is the biggest blessing. I say if I wasn't where I was before, I would not be where I am today. I am so thankful they are on this journey with me.

47. Cathie Rohrman Morehouse

Bob's older sister and the eighth of eleven Rohrman children

From the time Bob was a small boy, he always was trying to earn money, or in the early years, do something to get someone to give him candy.

When the insurance men would come to collect, Bob would roll his eyes, and they would give him candy or dimes. When they would give him candy, he wouldn't share it. And he would play all the time while I had to stay in the house and wash the dishes.

When we lived on River Road in West Lafayette, we rode the bus to school, but Bob didn't want to go. He wanted to stay home and play. Bob also enjoyed talking to an older man who lived under the Granville Bridge. The man was nice, and my mom and dad let us talk to him. All of us would go down there and slide down the banks and into the Wabash River.

Also when he was little, Bob would trim the pine trees in the front yard, and one time, he cut the end of a finger off. After it happened, Bob didn't want to come into the house, because he wanted to find the end of his finger.

Dad moved the family often, and we lived in a big house on 18th Street in Lafayette before we moved to Wilson Street. Being a big family, I didn't realize that we were poor. Dad would bring home a sack of oranges or a sack of bananas, and that was all I wanted. We also had a garden and raised vegetables.

Once we moved to Spooner, WI, we lived on a farm, and I remember that dad was a contractor, and he would do projects for neighbors for food. Dad was very handy. Bob helped dad do some work around the lake, and they would cut ice when the lake froze, and they would bring it home. Dad would store it somehow, and we would have homemade ice cream.

Bob, Bernie, Rita and I attended the same one-room school house together for one year. Bob was smart. I'm not sure Bob paid attention, but he knew all of the answers. Bob was great in math. He got all of that ability, and I didn't get any of that ability in math. You could tell later in life when Bob pulled all those numbers out of a hat and got all of those cars.

It is amazing, but Bob worked hard.

In 1944, I moved to Lafayette to live with my sister, Maxine, and her husband Nick Switzer, and I attended St. Francis School. I graduated from St. Francis in 1948, got an apartment and got a job at Lafayette General Telephone.

While I still was living with the Switzers in 1947, I was babysitting one night, and the other kids were playing with matches, and there was a fire in the house. The fire was confined to the living room.

Bob then returned to Lafayette from Spooner, and he moved in with Nick and Maxine.

But I almost never saw Bob, because he either was attending school at Lafayette Jeff or working at Brown Rubber. My husband and I got married in 1950. Shortly thereafter, Bob met Shirley, and he was bound and determined she was the one he was going to marry.

Bob always had a gift of gab. He had it then, and he has it now. I was not in their wedding, but I remember the wedding. Once he started selling cars for Pitman, he always was selling cars. He put every penny he made back into cars.

I remember when Bob told Pitman that he was leaving the dealership to go out on his own, and Pitman said he wouldn't make it. Bob told Pitman that someday, he would buy Pitman out.

I knew that Bob would make it, because he had so much bull, and that is what makes it in the car business. They have to have a gift of gab. Had he not made it, I don't know what Bob would have done.

My husband, Jim, and I did see Bob and Shirley some. We would attend convocations with them at Purdue. But we had to pay a babysitter if we went out - we had five kids - so we didn't go out too often.

Most of the time, though, Bob was working, trying to make his first million. But at times he worked so hard that he forgot to come and visit his relation. Shirley did almost all of the raising of the children. In fact, I wondered at times if they would remember him.

Bob was driven, but at times, he forgot to look around and see other things. He just wanted to make that million. He didn't have to be so distant. We would have parties, and Bob would either not show up, or he would show up late.

I remember once we had a spaghetti dinner on New Year's Day at our house, and Bob was invited. The other brothers and sisters were invited. Bob came in really late, even though Linda tried to get him here earlier. So, Bob had to eat cold spaghetti.

Bob worked so hard that he almost never was there during his marriage to Shirley, and after that, he met Linda. Linda is a very nice person, and so is Shirley.

Eventually, he moved into the Chicago market with Schaumburg Honda, and that really took off. Jim and I even bought two Hondas from him.

Now, I really can't imagine what his life is really like. I can't remember the last time I saw him. It probably was at a funeral. What he has achieved is amazing, but at times, it was like he didn't have a wife or kids. Shirley and Linda each did a wonderful job raising Bob's kids.

We told Bob he ought to retire, and he said, "I don't like doing dishes." If you enjoy what you do, it's not work. I know Bob enjoys what he does. I just wish I would have seen him more while he was making all of his millions.

To me, he is just that guy doing the commercials on TV who just happens to be my little brother. I am proud of him.

48. Rita Rohrman Crowell

Eleventh and final member of the Rohrman children

My earliest memories of my brother Bob are from the time we lived on Wilson Street in Lafayette.

We had moved there from River Road, where Bob, Bernie and I were born.

I recall one time when he was lying on a bed on the front porch at Wilson Street with a swollen face and broken nose. He told mom and dad that another boy was chasing him down the railroad track, and Bob fell and broke his nose.

He had a staph infection, and the doctor put little cotton sticks in his injured nose. I was 4 or 5 at that time, which was during a period when Bob was attending St. Boniface School.

Then in May of 1942, when I was 5, we moved from Lafayette to Spooner, WI. At that time, Cathy, Bob, Bernie and I were the only ones of school age. The others were older, and some already were married.

We moved onto a small farm in a wooden area. We had a big farm house, a barn and a chicken coup. There was no electricity, and we had an outhouse and a pump. During the winter, the pump would freeze, and one time Bob placed his lips or tongue on that pump handle, and got stuck.

Another time, Bob was told to go outside and read the thermometer to see what the temperature was. He lit a match to read it, and you know what a match does to a thermometer. Dad was very upset with Bob, because we didn't have the money to buy another thermometer.

Bob helped put up hay, counted eggs, and Bob and Bernie always picked on me. Bob was very ornery. He would milk cows, and I didn't dare go out there, because they would squirt milk on me as they were milking a cow.

We had to walk about a mile to school, and there were no other houses along the path. We had a long lane from the house, and once we turned left off the lane, you no longer could see the house. The first thing Bob and Bernie did once we were out of sight from the house was run off and leave me to find my way to school on my own.

I was in first grade and was scared to death. There was a path through the woods to school that was shorter, and we always did that, but I didn't like to go through the woods by myself.

When we got home from school, Bob and Bernie got into trouble for that, because I told dad.

Every once in a while, Bob and Bernie would get a whipping.

During World War II, dad went to work for the corps of engineers. They needed help, and there was no work to be found around Spooner at that time. At that same time, dad moved us from the farm into the town of Spooner.

After we moved into town, Bob's roots as a salesman were planted. He sold products to homemakers and delivered them in a wheel barrel that he pushed all over town. He was good at it. He had the gift.

Bob also would make money from the insurance agents who would come to the house to collect, and they would give him a dime if he would roll his big eyes for them. He still rolls his eyes.

When dad came home from helping with the war effort, we moved back to the country. About a year later, we moved to a property about a mile or two away. Shortly thereafter, dad had a nervous breakdown. That put everything on hold, and things really never were the same again.

Dad was hospitalized in Madison, WI, and I went to live with my older brother, Don, and his wife. Bernie stayed with our brother Joe, and Bob moved to Romney, IN, which is a small community just south of Lafayette. He lived with John and Judy Kennedy.

Kathy stayed in Spooner, lived with a friend and finished school. After graduation, Kathy moved back to Lafayette. Bob attended

Romney School in seventh grade and then went back to Spooner for eighth grade and graduated from a little one-room school house.

Bob left Romney after the seventh grade because John Kennedy introduced Bob to Redman Chewing Tobacco and whiskey. Bob claims that John told him, "You better go back to Spooner and sober up."

After eighth grade, Bob once again moved from Spooner to Lafayette, moved in with our sister Maxine and her husband, Nick Switzer, and enrolled at Lafayette Jeff.

While Bob was in high school, I still was in Spooner and did not see him a lot, although I knew he was working at Brown Rubber while attending Jeff. I would see him if he came to Spooner for a week visit.

In 1953, I moved to Lafayette, and in 1954, I was in Bob's wedding to Shirley. I know Shirley really wanted to get married, and Bob came home on leave from the military to get married. It was a big wedding at St. Boniface Church, and the reception was at Shirley's parents' home on Union Street.

I graduated from St. Francis High School in Lafayette in 1955. After Bob and Shirley were married, I wasn't around them much. Bob was selling cars for Glenn R. Pitman and was working six days a week.

When Bob was working for Pitman, I was working at Lafayette National Bank, right across the street from Pitman's. Bob sold me my first car, a 1955 Chevy. I really didn't think that much about Bob being Salesman of the Month or Salesman of the Year.

Then when he left Pitman in 1963 to start his own car lot, I would see Mr. Pitman at lunch at a little downtown restaurant where I ate from time to time. One day, Mr. Pitman came to my table and said something about my brother going off on his own to sell cars.

He said, "All these young salesmen get the big head because they sell all of these cars and think they can start their own business and make it. (Bob) will never make it."

It is too bad Mr. Pitman didn't live to see that Bob made it. When Bob started with the gravel lot on Sagamore Parkway in Lafayette, I guess I really didn't think a lot about it, because it was not a very big lot. I did not know for sure what he was going to sell.

He sold used cars and Winabagos until he got Honda and Toyota. At one point, he thought he was going to get the Chrysler dealership, too.

For a while, I thought selling cars was just a fun thing for him. He is such a social person, and guys like that tend to drink, but not Bob. Maybe that is because he had such a bad experience with whiskey in seventh grade.

While Bob was married to Shirley, I didn't see them that often. In fact, I don't think I ever babysat for his kids. They didn't do a lot of things, and when they did, they took the kids with them.

Bob and Shirley got a divorce, and then Bob met Linda, who worked at Lafayette National Bank. She was a loan officer and had reason to do business with Bob. When Bob and Shirley were married, he really wasn't into business that much.

I really like Linda, who is very social and a very good person. I know Bob is sorry about what happened with his marriage to Linda. Bob partly is what he is today because of Linda. She was a partner in that business. When she left the dealership, they really had to find some good help.

Then, Bob opened that Honda dealership in Schaumburg, and I thought, "Holy, cow, why would he put that kind of money in a dealership?"

It is a beautiful place, and I am sure that is what made him. From that point on, it just took off. But you know, everything Bob ever has done has been good. It is like everything he touches turns to gold. He has a knack for knowing when to get rid of something and when to hold onto it.

The funny thing is, when we were growing up, I never saw him as someone who is exceptionally smart. I don't think he ever really liked school. He wanted to get out, work and make money. He was the first in his high school class to have a car. That is what he wanted and what he worked for.

Growing up, I really couldn't see that he was intelligent, but he always has had a lot of go-get-it, and if he wanted something, he would go after it. But he always had common sense and street smarts.

Our brother Bernie always said Bob was going to be a millionaire by the time he was 35; and he was. I thought after he made his first million that he would retire, but no way.

People ask me why he doesn't stop, or at least slow down, but Bob says it is his hobby, and why would you give up a hobby? Bob says you do not retire from a hobby.

49. JR Rohrman

Bob's first child and director of Rohrman University

The most important thing to know about my dad is that he loves unconditionally, even if you are having problems, which I brought on many myself.

The last thing Joe Heath, the former basketball coach and athletic director at Lafayette Jefferson High School, said to me before he died was, "Why do you always do things the hard way?" That was at the time I left my dad and started my own car lots, the Buy Here, Pay Here lots. When I proposed that idea to my father, he said he was not interested, but in the back of my mind, I always wanted to try it. Despite that, my dad always has loved unconditionally. He loves Kathy and me, and he is a great Grandpa. As a parent, what more can you ask for? You want your kids to have all the best and to have a great relationship with their Grandpa.

As they were growing up, I never shared with my boys my relationship with my dad, because we had our moments, and I didn't want them to go into their relationship with my dad with any preconceived notions. I said to Kathy many times that I don't want the guys to know about this, or that I don't want to talk about this. I just prayed that they would have a great relationship and they do.

Business is business, and you are going to have disagreements. Going back to my early memories with my dad, I remember that he played golf quite a bit, and even was in a golf league at Edwood Glen. When I was 9 or 10, I remember that he asked me to carry his bag for him, which I thought was the greatest thing.

A side note now is that my son, Trey, is a good golfer and played in a summer league right before he played in college. Trey asked me to caddy for him, and I said sure. I was all pumped up and thought I knew everything about golf. I get there, and Trey said, "Before we get started, I have only one rule, which is don't say anything and just let me play." That reminded me of carrying dad's bag years ago at Edwood Glen, which for me was the cat's meow. Dad was a very busy guy who worked a ton of hours. That time at Edwood Glen was just me and him.

Then at 10 in 1965, my first job working for dad was filling gravel holes in the car lot. When it would rain, we would get all these mud puddles. I also changed the light bulbs in the lot. The third part of my job was to take two sticks and a string, make a straight line and pull all the weeds on one side of the string. Weeds were a big deal in a gravel lot. Then, I remember washing cars when my dad had one garage with three service bays. One of the cars I cleaned was a big Riviera that he had sold and was about to deliver it. I pulled it back to a bay, but when I pulled in, I took the whole body side molding off the car. I have had some tough conversations with my dad, but I had to walk back into his office and tell him. I said, "Dad, can I talk to you for a moment?"

He was with a customer and told me he was busy. I told him I needed to talk to him right now. He came out, and I told him I had wrecked the car. He was angry, but somehow, he saved the deal and fixed the car. Today, when I train people, I tell them that I was blessed that I actually sold cars with my dad. Back in the day, he was the best salesman. When talking about negotiations, I tell guys that when I TOd a deal - brought a manager in - my dad came in, and most of the time, we sold the car. When my dad would come in, he would not talk about cars or money. It would all be about stories and relationships. I knew that when my dad would get the customer laughing, the customer was buying the car. After 15 or 20 minutes of talking, the customer would say, "Come on, Bob, you can do something." He may or may not do something, but after he got the customer laughing, the deal was done.

He is all about relationships, and that is what the car business still is about.

Another of my favorite stories was when I was a junior or senior at Lafayette Jeff, I took this girl out on a date, and it had rained for two or three days straight. The ground was really wet. I asked my dad if I could use his demo car for my date. It probably was the nicest demo on the lot, a Toyota.

I don't know why he let me do it, because I had my own 1964 Impala. I picked the girl up, we went to a movie and then went parking in Murdock Park. I pulled down the dirt road behind the basketball courts and got stuck. I told her that I was going to put the floor mats behind the rear tires, and when I tell you to put the car in reverse, put it in reverse. She kept putting the car in drive instead.

She didn't know how to drive a car, so at 1 a.m., we were stuck real good! The differential was on the ground because it had spun all the way down. So, we go to the basketball court, and a couple of guys are playing. I asked them if they could give she and I a ride home. They gave us a ride home.

I don't remember sleeping much that night. In the morning - it was a Saturday - my dad was leaving for the weekly sales meeting. I am awake, because I know he is going to kill me. About 7:30, I hear the door shut, and then I hear him come back in and yell, "Rohrman!" He says, "Where is my car?" I told him it was stuck. He said, "What do you mean it is stuck?"

I told him it was stuck at Murdock Park. He reminded me how much the car was worth. I told him I knew but that I could not get it out. He told me to get the car out of there right now and instructed me to give him the keys to my car right now. So, he drove my 1964 Impala to the sales meeting.

I asked my mom to help me out, so she called Nelson's Towing. We met the truck at Murdock Park, and that truck gets stuck. So, they had to call a second truck. The second truck got the first truck out and then got my car out.

It took me three or four hours to clean dad's demo. I lost my driving privileges with my 1964 Impala for a week or two. My dad knew how to ground me. He would take my car away.

Keeping with that unconditional love theme, my dad instilled in me at an early age never to lie. The worst thing you could do with my dad was lie. He can handle the truth, because I gave him some pretty bad truth over the years. When I thought he was going to kill me, he would surprise me by saying, "OK." He drilled into me to never lie or cheat. In 1976, I was selling cars with John Barrett and John Davis, and John Davis and I went to the Ground Round to have a beer. One thing led to another, and he said to me that he was thinking about moving to Florida. Davis had a real good friend he went to high school with that lived down there.

That night, we decided that we were going to Florida. I had a 1955 Chevy that was worth only about $300. The next morning, we take off for Fort Lauderdale, FL, I didn't tell anyone. My dad found out because I wrote him a letter, and he remembers the letter.

John Davis moved back to Lafayette pretty quickly, but I was down there for quite a while. The first night we were there, we were in a bar, and I asked a girl to dance, and we danced. She told me to go to this apartment complex in Fort Lauderdale, because they had just fired their maintenance man and needed one.

I went in there, and an older lady told me I was the answer to her prayers. They hired me as their maintenance man for $5 an hour. It was so easy, but it wasn't enough money, so I worked several other odd jobs. I stayed six months, came home and then went to live with my mom for a while.

I came back and worked in parts and service for my dad. My dad told me I should go to Northwood, a college in Michigan, and get my automotive degree. I agreed it was a good idea, and I was tired of being broke. I went up there never intending to run track.

I kind of was disappointed in my track career, because I had these lofty goals of attending the Olympic trials and making the Olympic team in the 800. I had gone to the University of New Mexico out of high school, and the coach there was not good.

The problem with running for Phil Hurt at Lafayette Jeff is that when you went to college, you went to a lesser coach. Usually when you go to college, you assume your coach is going to be better. But nobody gets your potential out of you like Phil. If you are willing to work, he will get the maximum out of you. He used training that was way ahead of his time.

I enrolled at Northwood in the spring of 1977, not intending to run track. But one day I walked by the track and smelled the rub that we used to call root beer because it smelled just like root beer.

I got the fever to run. I had gained 20 pounds since I stopped running at New Mexico. Before, I looked sickly, so an extra 20 pounds probably was alright on weight. I approached the track coach, Jim Knapp, and told him that I was interested in running for the track team.

He asked if I had ever run before. I told him I ran in high school and at the University of New Mexico. He asked what kind of times I had run. I could tell that he thought I was lying to him, because the times I told him would have been school records at Northwood.

Coach Knapp told me to come back the next day, and he would let me know. I went back the next day, and he told me he had called New Mexico coach Hugh Hackett. Coach Knapp said he called to check me out and that coach Hackett had some nice things to say about me.

I had a great career at Northwood. I wasn't on scholarship, which in a way was nice, because at an NAIA school, there is no pressure like there is for a scholarship athlete at a Division I school.

In 1978, the athletic director asked me to coach the cross country team and told me he would pay me $500. I was 23, coaching a team of 18, 19 and 20-year-olds. The problem with that was that if I set a really hard workout, I had to run it. That always was in the back of my mind. We had fun.

During the time I was attending Northwood, my dad asked my brothers Randy and Rick and I to go with him on a fishing trip to Canada. We stopped at Spooner, WI, on our way to Canada and saw our grandmother Rohrman. Dad told us he had a really good boat and that we would take it. I wondered if the boat ever had been started, but dad said it would be fine. We packed all of our stuff in the boat, which was great. We get to Canada, and dad says we are going to take the boat out.

None of us knew much about boating, but we take the boat off the trailer, and it won't start, so then we had to figure out how to get it back in. We were kind of upset, but we were laughing. We never got it started, but the greatest thing about that trip was that we had a great time with dad, with a lot of great laughs. It was a special time.

During my senior year at Northwood, I met my wife, Kathy, who was a freshman. My friend Blake Taylor, who was on the cross country team with me, and I were getting ready to go to a race. We are getting in my car, and these two girls go by on their bikes on campus.

I looked, and Kathy was a little thing, but she had the cutest legs and was wearing shorts. I looked at Blake and said, "I am going to ask her out." Blake, who was afraid to even talk to girls, just looked at me. He asked me why I would ask her out, and I told him that she was gorgeous. He told me I was crazy. She and I had an advertising class together, so I called her and asked her out. She told me later that she thought I was cute. In class, I was handing back the tests we had taken, and she got an A. She knew who I was.

When I called, she said she wasn't interested in going out. I got my persistence from my dad, so I called her again a couple of days later. I called the third time and told her she really should go out with me. She explained that she had just gotten out of a long relationship with a guy from high school and was not interested in getting involved with another guy.

I called a fourth time, and again she said no. Finally, the fifth time I called, she was tired of saying no and agreed to go out with me. She asked what we were going to do, and I told her my roommate was a really good cook and that he would cook a meal for us.

He cooked a chicken and rice dish for us. I thought it was great, and Kathy thought it was pretty simple. We had carrot cake for dessert and had a great time. We just hit it off, although she thought I was weird. Within a couple of months, we were talking about getting married. Kathy had a twin brother going to school there, and he didn't like our relationship at all, because he thought we were getting way too serious, which we were.

My senior year, I had hair down to my shoulders and was the president of the Fellowship of Christian Athletes chapter at Northwood. The newspaper in Midland, MI, takes a picture of me and prints it with me wearing a New Mexico tee shirt with a beard. That is the first picture that Kathy's dad ever saw of me.

She sent the picture to her dad and told him it was her boyfriend. I am graduating, so I tell her we have to get her transferred to Purdue. It was seven hours from Lafayette to Midland, and I told her I would be working a lot of hours selling cars for my dad. She said she did not know if her dad would let her transfer.

I suggested that we go to her house, meet her dad and talk to him about the Purdue transfer. She and I are scared to death about this meeting, in part because I never had met her dad. We traveled to Stevensville, MI, which is four or five hours south of Midland.

Her mom was not there, but we are having this serious discussion at the kitchen table. I told her dad that Kathy and I are really serious and are talking about getting married and that we love each other and that I really would like her to transfer to Purdue because I would be working in Lafayette.

He asked me what I was going to be doing. I told him that my dad was always proud of being a car salesman but that some people don't always look at it that way and that I was going to be selling cars. Her dad said, "You just got a college degree and you are going to sell cars?" I told him that I was going to be working for my dad, but Kathy's dad - at that time - didn't know my dad from Adam.

So, her dad left the table and went upstairs. I told Kathy, "He is not going to let you transfer to Purdue." Kathy said, "Well, I am doing it anyway." She said she would pay for her education herself if he wasn't going to let her do it.

Two hours later, he comes back downstairs. His eyes were all red from crying. He looked at us and said it would be OK for her to transfer. She transferred to Purdue and graduated from Purdue.

We got married in 1980 and had our first son, Ryan, in 1984. Kathy is a great mom, and my dad sees the values that she has instilled in our sons. He tells Kathy and I all the time that we have done a great job raising those boys.

When I started selling cars for dad after graduation, I was working for Lincoln Mercury and Subaru. I was a Jeep Eagle manager. Then I was a Honda and Toyota manager for a while. I was going to go to Indianapolis and run the Honda store. It was so serious that Kathy and I put a deposit on a house in Greenwood and had put our Lafayette house in East Tipp Heights up for sale.

We had put a $3,000 deposit down on the house in Greenwood, but about a week after that, my dad told me that he wanted me to stay in Lafayette and run the Lafayette operation. I told him we had put the deposit on the house in Greenwood and that I really wanted to go down there. I said, "Well, what about the deposit on the house?" He said, "I never told you to buy a house, babe." We lost the deposit, but that is neither here nor there.

We went ahead and sold our Lafayette house and asked my friend Dave Skelton if he wanted to sell his house on South Ninth Street in Lafayette. Kathy and I looked at his house, put an offer on it and ended up buying it. For about six months, we were making payments on two houses. That is where the boys were raised from 1989 when we moved in until 1999. Then, we moved to Eau Claire, WI.

I left my dad's business in March of 1993. I had a good job and was making good money, but we butted heads. Something happened with some cars we were going to take to the auto auction, and he called me to come to his office. I went up there, and he asked what I was doing with those cars. I told him I was taking them to the auction.

He told me I wasn't taking those cars to the auction. That was a tipping point. Some other things had happened, and I was thinking about the Buy Here, Pay Here thing. There were a lot of things going on. I laid my keys on his desk and told him I was leaving. He didn't think I was quitting. He asked me what I was going to do, and I told him I was going to start my own used car lot. He told me I would fail, and I said if I fail, I will come back to work for you. He then said "I won't hire you back".

I think he was expecting me to come back to work the very next morning, but I didn't. Kathy and I really started praying. The day I quit, I came home at 2 in the afternoon. I told Kathy, and she said, "You can't quit. We have a mortgage and four children."

I started talking to some guys at the Lafayette auction, and I ended up buying a couple of lots and another lot where a Standard gas station had been. Two different banks turned me down, but finally, Joe Seaman, who was president of Bank One at that time, loaned me the money.

I bought one lot in Monticello and ended up with four car lots. God really blessed our business, and business was really, really good. When we decided to move to Wisconsin, I wanted to get the boys out from under the Rohrman bubble. Dad is really popular in Chicago, but in Lafayette, it is just at a totally different level of popularity.

When Trey was a really young guy in Lafayette, he would go into a Marsh grocery and say, "Do you know who my grandpa is?" So, I knew there was an issue. We prayed about it and decided to move to Wisconsin.

Looking back, it was hard on Ryan, because he was entering his freshman year of high school. I never will forget dropping Ryan off for his first day at Eau Claire Memorial High School, which is a big high school. We raised the boys in a pretty controlled environment, and all of a sudden, he is going to school with kids dressed gothic. He never had seen this stuff. He adapted and really did well.

I really tried to talk my four guys out of the car business, because I didn't want them to go into the car business just because it was there. It is kind of funny that all four went into the car business. I figured one or two of them would not.

Chase got an education degree, and for a time, I thought he would teach and coach before he decided he wanted to be in the car business in Chicago. At one time, Ryan, Chase and Trey all were at Schaumburg Honda. Kathy and I would stop by, and they would try and sell us a car.

In Eau Claire, I had a gas station and a car lot and loved it there. Then, Life Action Ministries came to our church, and we fell in love with ministry, which really changed our lives. We joined Life Action Ministries, sold the businesses in Eau Claire and moved to Michigan to be active in Life Action Ministries, just north of South Bend.

I never thought I would go back into the car business. I thought I would retire from the ministry but maybe have a used car lot. After being in the ministry for six years, money was getting kind of tight, so I talked to dad about maybe coming back. He said maybe I could run Lincoln Mercury. I didn't know what to do, and then Ryan called and told me they were going to start this university training sales staff and that I might be a good guy to run it. I always enjoyed teaching, so I told him I wanted to talk to Kathy about it. We decided to do it in August of 2011.

My dad called and said that Ryan told him I was the best guy for the job, and while dad didn't necessarily agree, he was going to go with Ryan's judgment on it. That's my dad. Kathy and I got a kick out of it. But it has been good, and I have helped out as well from time to time with some of the Chicago dealerships.

I have said to my dad many times that I don't know if anybody could do what he has done. I have asked him two or three times how he does it. The last time I asked him, he said it just kind of evolved. It obviously has evolved very well.

A sprinkling of various Rohrman family members vacationing at Indiana's Lemon Lake.

50. Rhonda Rohrman Isbell

Bob's second child and first daughter

My dad, Bob Rohrman, is the hardest-working person that I have ever met.

One of my earliest memories from childhood is when I was in grade school at St. Mary's in Lafayette. Dad would drive the three oldest kids to school every morning before going to work. Dad would turn off the radio and sing at the top of his lungs some of his favorite songs, like Dean Martin's "That's Amore," or Frank Sinatra's "Strangers in the Night."

My brothers would cover their ears and yell, "No, no, turn on the radio!" I would sit in the back seat and in my quiet little voice would say, "I love dad's singing." Dad would say, "See, Rhonda likes my singing."I am sure I was annoying to my brothers, as they would have preferred listening to the radio. But dad actually is a pretty good singer. Often, I didn't see dad again until late at night when he came home from work. But he always made a point of coming into our bedrooms to ask how our day had gone.

He would say goodnight with a sweet daddy kiss and hug. He worked many hours growing up, trying to build his business. I know that was hard on my mom, but luckily, she had her parents close by in Lafayette. They were wonderful grandparents to us.

I always knew that my dad loved me. I never questioned that, even when he was upset with me. He is the type of dad who tells you he loves you all of the time. I can't begin to tell you how many times I have heard, "I love you honey" over the years.

My dad is always making some sort of deal. One year, a customer traded two Shetland ponies for a car. We got to keep the horses at my grandparents' home on Union Street, where they had two acres with a barn, so it was perfect. We named them Princess and Sugar. We kids loved having those horses. We loved going over to ride them, and we were allowed to give them sugar cubes as a treat. We didn't get to keep them too long, because one day, while my brother Randy was riding Princess, Princess decided that she wanted to go back into the barn. She ran back into the barn with Randy sitting on her back.

He was pretty young, maybe 8 or 9. His head hit the top of the barn door, almost knocking Randy out. Soon after that, Princess and Sugar found a new home.

Dad always wanted the best for us, wanting us to strive to be the very best that we can be. When I was a senior in high school, I was trying to decide where I wanted to go to college. He wanted me to go to Radcliffe, an Ivy League-like college for women, but that wasn't going to happen, although he had high hopes.

I ended up going to an art and business school in Milwaukee. I wanted to study interior design and fashion design, but he talked me into business. He thought that would be the best in the long run. My dad always had good advice, so I listened to him and studied business.

While I was away at school, he would call me every Sunday to check in on me and ask, "Did you go to church today, honey?" He is a very religious, Catholic man who goes to church every Sunday, no matter where he is in the world or no matter what he is doing. He passed that along to us kids.

After I graduated from college, I went to work at Purdue University. While I was working there, my dad invited me to go on a trip to Japan with him with the Honda Motor Company. I was so excited. We went with a group of other Honda Dealers from around the country.

For the first few days, everyone on the trip with us thought I was dad's girlfriend. It took a few days for them to realize that I was indeed his daughter. Dad and I had a great time on the trip. Ever since then, I have had a love of travel.

While we were on the trip, we met another dealer who owned some National Car Rental franchises, one of which was at the Purdue University Airport. He got to know dad and I and asked me to manage his car rental business there.

After doing that for a couple of years, dad asked me to come work for him. I worked as dad's administrative assistant for several years, and I loved working for the business and for him.He expects a lot from his employees, and there were a couple of times when he made me cry when he got mad at me about something. I think he felt bad when he saw tears in my eyes. That only worked for me. It was a different story for my brothers.

For a couple of years, all five kids were working for him at the same time. During those years, my maternal grandmother would invite us to her home for lunch once a week. She would feed us tons of food, including her famous desserts. We all would go back to work with a food coma.

In 1980, I married my high school sweetheart, Vic Isbell, and as of 2015, we have been happily married for 35 years. We have been blessed with four wonderful daughters, who I am so proud of. We have two great sons in law and three adorable grandchildren, who are the joys of my life. Being a grandma overflows my heart with so much love.

Dad is a wonderful grandpa. Surprisingly, for the hours that he works, he always makes time to be at each of the special events for each of the grandkids. He always remembers everyone's birthday. He calls each of us on our birthday and sings Happy Birthday to us. It is so fun to get that call. He also sends cards to each family member for their birthday. He actually is better than I am when it comes to that.

He has a Christmas celebration each year at his home for all of us. Our girls would get so excited to see their grandpa when he would come to our house. They would run to the door when the doorbell rang and run into his open arms. He was in heaven, and so were they. They still get excited to see their grandpa.

Our three older girls have been in a couple of his commercials, and in 2014, our oldest granddaughter was in her first commercial with her great grandpa. She was only a year and a half old, but she did a fabulous job. It was so adorable. I think it was one of my dad's favorite commercials. He always talks about it.

He has taken our girls on fun trips, like Disney World, Door

County, WI, and even took the two oldest girls to London when they were about 9 and 12, respectively.

We have a lot of fun memories with my dad, and I think of him as a wonderful father who has had to give up a lot to make his business what it is today. But we all know that he loves us so much and wants the very best for each one of us thirty-nine and growing family members.

He is a very loving, generous dad, grandpa and great grandpa. I believe he has passed those qualities along to his five children and sixteen grandchildren. He should be proud of not only the business that he has built but also the awesome family that he has.

Rhonda Rohrman and family on vacation in 2015.

51. Randy Rohrman

Bob's third child and second son

Dad was always working, but one of my earliest memories is of him taking the entire family camping at Raccoon Lake near Rockville, IN. He had bartered for a camper.

I remember that dad was a Winabago dealer, and I used to work for him by washing and cleaning them. I started working for him when I was 13. I would get inside, turn on the vacuum like I was working and sleep.

He also would take us on trips to Florida and to Spooner, WI, which was great. He would take us to Little Casey Lake in Wisconsin and to grandma's house.

It was also during that time that I began to play lots of baseball. Originally, I was an outfielder. I threw left-handed and batted right-handed. Dad would go to the games, and Perry Gaines' dad was our coach. The pitcher threw me a knuckleball, and I hit my first home run at Breakfast Optimist field. Dad took that home run ball and wrote, "Randy's first home run."

He would write messages on the milestone balls. We hung onto them, and to this day, when my kids would do something special in baseball, I would write notes on the baseballs.

I know now that my dad enjoyed attending my games and enjoyed my success, but at the time, I did not realize it, because dad was not a really big communicator. He never would come up to me and say, "I am proud of you." He would tell other people, but he would never say anything to me.

As I said, I began as an outfielder, but when I played for coach Jerry Rife, we won city championships with Schnaible Drugs, and he had me pitch. My first pitching experience, I walked a guy, he stole second, and when he attempted to steal third, our catcher threw the ball over the third baseman's head, and the winning run scored. I got a loss in my first pitching appearance.

As a 13-year-old, I pitched for coach Tim Wolf in Pony League at the old field at Sunnyside Middle School. He really got me started as a pitcher. It progressed from there.

I remember that as I got older, my girlfriend, Mary Ruppert, asked me, "Why are you always mad when you pitch?" I told her that I wasn't mad. Rather, I was just focused on the game.

After playing high school baseball first at Central Catholic and then at Lafayette Jeff, I decided to attend Indiana State, and as a freshman there, I pitched quite a bit. I had a stretch in which I gave up no hits or runs in ten innings, but then I could not move my arm for about a month.

At that point, I asked myself if I really wanted to continue doing this. I loved cars, and my dad was in the business, so I began to sell cars and enjoyed it. People ask me today if I regret giving up baseball. I can't change things now, but I don't really regret it.

The Cincinnati Reds and the Detroit Tigers showed some interest in me, which was kind of cool, but down deep, as I young guy then, I didn't have a lot of guidance. I really never thought that much about it.

I started selling cars for Pops in 1978 at his first tent sale. In 1980, at age 22, I started doing finance for him and really enjoyed it. Then I told him that I wanted to be the Toyota sales manager. At that time, we had three stores in Lafayette, and then Schaumburg Honda was about to open.

I told him that I wanted to go to Chicago. I was involved in the development of Schaumburg Honda for about two years. I worked for Ford for a while and got the Schaumburg Honda store going.

From there, I went back to college at DePaul and finished at age 29. In 1989, we opened the Arlington Acura store, and he asked me if I wanted to buy in, so I bought 25 percent.

After doing this for so many years, I think my MO is moving from one project to another. I like the challenge of a new project. It has to be a challenge, and then I will move on. Money is important, but with these new challenges, it's not that the money is all important.

Financially, all of us should be fine. Dad always has been very generous when it comes to that stuff. You always want to continue to make more money with these ventures. He always has been there for us. Even though he always was working, any situation that I have had, he was right there for me.

During my early years in the Chicago car market, I met my first wife, Joelle. I sold her dad a car at Arlington Acura. I also sold her boyfriend a car. I was 30 and pretty aggressive, and I wanted to get married and have children.

I called her in 1989, asked her out, got engaged in three weeks and were married in five months. She is 10 years younger than I am. We were married for 14 years, and she is the mother of each of my three children.

My oldest son is Chaz, who was born in 1992 and is 6-foot-3. He is a graduate of Columbia in Chicago and is selling cars at Schaumburg Honda. Our second son, Cal, was born in 1994 and is 6-5. He pitched for Dayton University.

He was a better baseball player than I was. He didn't have my fastball, but his pitching motion and defensive skills were better than mine. My pitching motion was funky. Plus, my first pitch at Loeb Stadium in Lafayette usually hit the backstop.

Our third child is daughter Khol, who in 2015 was entering her senior year in high school. She is beautiful, like her mother, who was a model. Our daughter is beautiful on the inside, too.

Unfortunately, my first marriage didn't work, and I think you always blame yourself when that happens. I miss the kids coming home to me, because they are going home to her house.

Now, I have a great second wife, Robin. She is a great lady, and we are the same age. I was divorced for five years. I met Robin because of my ex-wife, Joelle. We lived in a small town in Wisconsin.

I pursued her, and Robin and I were married in 2008. Robin has two children by a previous marriage.

I have been successful in the car business, but I always tell people that Pops is the James Brown of the automotive industry - the hardest working man in the business.

I have met a lot of owners and dealers, and I never have seen anyone work as hard as he has. He is relentless, but he also has the personality to work it. When he got Toyota then added Schaumburg Honda and built his empire, he had a way with the people who work for the franchises. They loved him, he worked hard and he made money for them. He would order 300 cars, which is crazy. They loved that he was very aggressive.

To me, it never has been an issue or difficult to be Bob Rohrman's son. Maybe it was because I was an athlete, or when I was in high school, all the crazy commercials had not started yet. I would rather be in the situation I am in now than not have it.

When you have a very famous father, sometimes you live in the shadow, but that never has bothered me, because I have enough confidence in myself. But you think about it when people tell you that you have this famous father who gives you everything.

I try to live my own life and balance my life with my family and my work. I am more of a balanced person than Pop is. He is all in one basket. I have a good relationship with him, but it could be even better had we communicated better when I was younger.

I definitely I am proud to be his son. The big thing I learned from Pop is that he is very honest, and he also is a great number guy.

A favorite story is when we were about to open Schaumburg Honda, and we were in Chicago for a meeting. On our way back, we had to pass through a toll booth. The toll was 30 cents, and he had 35 cents. He went to the booth with a person and waited five minutes so he could get that nickel back.

Another favorite story is from 2008 when I was running Oakbrook Toyota, and there was a winter storm. We had a meeting, and I told a friend, "Watch this." I walked out to Pop's car and placed a penny next to his door. It was zero degrees, and the wind was blowing hard, but I told my friend that Pop would pick up that penny. Later, we walked out there, and the penny was gone.

That is Bob Rohrman.

Randy Rohrman and family.

52. Shelly Rohrman

Bob's fourth child and second daughter

Among my early childhood memories, I remember that my dad loved to cook breakfast. He would take the grease from the bacon and make our eggs. Every Sunday, he would cook a big breakfast for all of us, and the eggs always were sunny side up.

He would cook breakfast after church, because he always was gung ho on church. To this day, it doesn't matter where he is - any country - he will go to church.

Another fond memory is that I loved to go grocery shopping with him at Marsh, because he would buy all the junk. He loved to buy the circus peanuts. He also would buy potato chips and candy. I loved that, because I am a big sweets person.

My dad also likes fast food, and when my son came to Chicago for a couple of weeks, my son sat in meetings with dad and was surprised that my dad likes fast food. I am sure my son loved it.

When I was young, I also would fake like I was asleep when he got home. Everyone would say, "Just wait until your father gets home!" I wasn't asleep. He just thought I was. So, he wouldn't wake me up to scold me. That was nice of him.

I remember we had a trailer on the Tippecanoe River, and we would go there on weekends. All seven of us would go. The current was strong, and I lost a couple of rings in that current.

We had another vehicle known as the Green Wienie that we would take on vacation to Florida. Dad would hate it if we got sand in the Green Wienie. It is a little tough to go to Florida and not get sand in it. But he loved driving that Green Wienie, which was a Winabago.

He liked that thing so much that sometimes, he would drive it home instead of his car. I think he still has it.

When we were kids, we also had a go-kart and mini bikes. I was a big Tomboy. I loved to take that go-kart to parking lots and drive. Rick and I enjoyed driving it. We would ride our mini bikes around the Central Catholic High School football field.

Shelly Rohrmam and her four siblings.

When I was older, I remember a trip we took to California with dad, Linda and my ex-husband. We arrived at about 1 a.m., and dad drove around until he found the least expensive hotel. He hadn't made a reservation. We checked several, and he said it was too much money, so we drove around for about an hour and a half looking for the least expensive hotel.

During that trip, he also looked for the cheapest gas, which was good. At the same time, my dad is very generous and very giving. He doesn't have to give us what he gives us. You might think he would say, "Get a job and buy it yourself."

Our dad always tells us he loves us, but it is difficult for him to sit down and tell us we have done a good job. It is about what we did wrong. I remember wrecking a car one time, and he said it was my fault even though the other driver hit me.

Along those lines, I played basketball in junior high school and high school, and even now, people will tell me that he talks so much about me and those times, and my response is "He does?" I think sometimes he just has a hard time talking about us, and I don't know why.

It could be a generational thing, especially for men, considering the way he was raised. Yet he has a heart of gold.

When my mom and dad were divorced, I went to live with my mom, but then mom would bring me to my dad's and knock on the door and say, "I can't handle her anymore." I was probably 15 when that happened, and I lasted for about a week at my dad's. Then I would go back to my mom's.

My mom was a very loving mom, but she was trying to raise five kids with no car. I think the divorce affected me. I had a lot of anxiety, and dad took me to a psychiatrist when I was 17. I still have anxiety. That's what they diagnosed.

Growing up, I did pretty much whatever I wanted. I had a car, but if I got bad grades, dad would take it away. Then, I would get it back. But growing up, I didn't see a lot of my dad. That started when I was young, and it got worse and worse.

Linda was like our second mom, and while I may not have gotten along with her at first, we grew to get along just fine. She worked, too, at the bank, so Rick and I especially had to kind of fend for ourselves. I think I turned out pretty well. I know they were worried about me until I was about 30. I could have turned out worse.

At one point, I moved from Lafayette to Schaumburg and worked for dad at Arlington Lexus. It was during that time that I vacationed in Cancun. My friends refer to that trip as, "tan and the man."

The story of that trip is that I had a girlfriend who had a time share in Cancun. We were there all week, and there were no guys. I thought, "What the heck?" My ex-husband, Joe, lived in Florida when I met him at the end of that trip. Our final weekend in Cancun, 10 guys from Florida showed up at the pool.

It was like, "Where have you all been?" Joe was one of the guys at the pool, and we all went out together that night. The rest is history. I didn't really like him at first. In fact, I wasn't really attracted to him right away.

We met in May, and in July, I moved to Florida. I told my dad that I was quitting my job, I am moving to Florida, and this is Joe. I remember that Joe came to Lafayette for July 4th, and JR and Kathy had a party at their home on Ninth Street.

That was the day I introduced Joe to my dad and told my dad that I was quitting and moving to Florida. Linda went over and had a long talk with Joe. It was pretty quick, but Joe was a nice guy.

After meeting in May, we got married in December in Key West and then had a wedding party in March at our house in Florida, and all of my family came.

It happened quickly. I was 30 when Joe and I were married, and I was 36 and then 38 when I had our son and then our daughter. I wasn't one to want a big family. I hated babysitting, which I can only remember doing once.

I didn't like kids. When I was young, we would go to the country club for Easter, and all these kids were running around. I looked at that and thought, "Oh my God, no way." Rhonda would say, "Someday, pay back."

Joe and I were married 11 years, and those were good times. We had a good life. He was doing well, and then Nestlé let him go. He was a good guy, my dad liked him and my brothers got along with him. He was a good athlete.

We have two great kids, although I think it was hard for Jake to move to Chicago because he had lots of friends in Florida. My daughter is doing well and really wants to attend Notre Dame. She is an excellent basketball player.

To sum up me, I am a lot like my dad in that I am stubborn and hard headed. It is kind of my way or the highway. I stick to my guns, and that is him. Rhonda is a lot more like our mom. More quiet and can get her feelings hurt easily. I pretty much say what

I think.

What my dad has done is amazing. People see my last name - Rohrman - but they don't always know my dad's story, that he came from a family of 11 with nothing. You don't see that many guys today that work like that, and he still works every day.

His energy level is awesome, He has more energy than I do. I don't know how he does it. I admire him very much and am very proud of him. Nobody is going to talk badly about my dad around me.

Shelly and two kids.

53. Rick Rohrman

General Manager of Indy Hyundai

My earliest memories are from the time I was about 10, and dad and my mother got a divorce, and then he married Linda.

It was a difficult time for me, because my dad always was at work. All of a sudden, I have a new figure in my house that replaced my mom. That was the way I saw it. As a 10-year-old, I am wondering, "Who is she?"

My dad would drive me to school in the morning, and then he would be sure that he saw me at 11 at night. When I was in the 14-to-16 range, I bounced back and forth between my dad's house and my mom's house, but at 10, I was living with dad and Linda.

I remember we would leave the house at 8 a.m., and school started at 8. In the winter, we would get into the car, and the windows would be completely frosted. He would make a little hole in the frost, and we would drive all the way with him looking through a little hole.

Then he would go to work, and I wouldn't see him until 10 or 11 at night unless I had a track meet or baseball game, which he would attend and then go back to work.

On Sundays, he would go to church and cut the grass, and I would bring my friends from church back to our house, and we would play ball. Then, we would go to the car dealership, and he would give me the key to the pop machine, and I would fill the pop machine and the candy machines.

I would fill them, collect the money and give it to him. I never stole any money, but I did eat a few candy bars. He would walk around the corner, and my mouth would be full of candy.

We never did that during football season, because he always wanted to watch the Chicago Bears. In the 1970s, there weren't as many different games on TV.

At that time, he had the Toyota/Honda store, and the Lincoln Mercury and the Subaru. After church, we would drive through the Lincoln Mercury lot and go up and down each row. He would look, stop and walk up to a car and open a door. Everything was supposed to be locked on a weekend. He had the knack for being able to stop at one car among 300 and would know that car was unlocked. He would just know. Once he found that car unlocked, he was on the phone, and a lot of times, it was JR or Craig Gipson or Carlos Asay.

I would fill the pop machine, we would go down to Toyota, and he would do the same thing. I always knew that if our car came to a stop, somebody was in trouble. He would call someone and make them come out and check every car to be sure it was locked.

If one car was unlocked, someone had to come out and check every car. It was impressive that he could do that. It was like a magic trick.

At that time, I would describe our relationship as being pretty good. Maybe it was because we weren't together a lot. You know the saying, distance makes the heart grow fonder?

If I would do something wrong in the afternoon, I knew Linda would call and tell him, but instead of him coming right home to deal with the issue, I would have to sweat it out for three or four hours, which always was tough. The anxiety would build.

Another good story from those days was the time when Randy was still attending Lafayette Jeff, and we were playing nerf basketball in the hallway upstairs. I was supposed to be in bed, but Randy was allowed to stay up later.

At 10 or 11 o'clock, my dad and Linda still would be downstairs. He got so mad that he went and got a belt. He would hit me one time, and I would get the point. Then he would leave my room and head over to whip Randy.

I stopped crying, and I heard giggling. So I walked into Randy's room, and dad was hitting the bed next to Randy. The two of them were laughing. He was acting like he was hitting Randy.

As the years passed, I would bounce back and forth between my dad's house and my mom's house. If I would get mad at Linda, I would hop on my bike and take off for my mom's.

Shelly was with my mom. Randy mostly was with my dad. JR, at that time, was away at college. If I didn't get my way at one place, I would go to the other. The rules were different living with my mom and living with my dad.

At mom's, it was just be home early and do your homework. At dad's, it was come right home and do your homework. Linda was tough on the homework, which turned out helping my grades a lot. I didn't want to do the work, but it did help. Linda definitely was good for my grades, just not for my social life.

When I was at my mom's, that is when I had my social life

I attended Tecumseh Junior High School, and then as a sophomore and junior, I attended Lafayette Jeff. In high school, I participated in baseball for a time, and then in cross country and track. I had part of JR (track) in me, and part of Randy (baseball) in me.

I just couldn't throw it as hard as Randy, or run as fast as JR.

Just before my senior year at Jeff, Rhonda had gotten married, and my mom was living in Tucson, Arizona at the time. The first week of my senior year at Jeff, a couple of my buddies had tickets to a Journey concert at Poplar Creek in Chicago. So, I had Rhonda call into Jeff and tell them I was sick - that probably is the worst thing Rhonda has ever done in her life - and I went with a bunch of guys to the concert.

I wasn't really thinking much about being home that late, but by the time I got back to Lafayette, it was 3 a.m. At about 7 p.m., I knew I was in trouble. I crawled up and into a bedroom window upstairs. Right when I stepped inside the window, the light flipped on, and there he was.

He really didn't care where I was, it was just that school called him when I wasn't there. I had not shown up for work after school. I cleaned cars for him after school.

Needless to say, we had a pretty good argument. My mom was

in town at that time, and a day or two later, I told her I wanted to go to Arizona with her and attend school there. I went to Arizona and enrolled at Amphi High School.

I graduated from Amphi. Having kids now, that would have crushed me if my children left and attended school in another state. I would have been mad and upset all at the same time. It wasn't easy to leave Lafayette but maybe it was good for me to get away for a little while.

While I was still in Lafayette, a kid came up to me in Columbian Park, threatened me and chased me all the way home because he thought my dad had sold his dad a bad car.

That track and cross country experience came in handy on that bike, escaping a bad situation. So it may have been good for me to leave town for a period of time.

I didn't know anyone in Tucson, but it didn't take long to make some good friends. One of my friends from there and I met it Las Vegas for our 50th birthdays.

I didn't do badly in school my senior year, and I graduated. Dad and Linda came to Tucson for my graduation. I was glad to see him, and I think he wanted me to come back to Lafayette. I was not ready to go back.

I loved Tucson. One hour, and you are up in snow. I had a girlfriend while I was in Tucson. After graduation, I did come back to Lafayette for one summer and lived in a trailer while I delivered parts for my dad's dealership. That lasted for a few months, and then I went back to Tucson.

I enrolled at Pima Community College, and I got a job at Precision Toyota in Tucson. Two months into school at Pima, the Toyota dealership offered me a full time job delivering parts, making $300 a week, which in 1983 was good money for a 19 year old.

Then in late 1984, I moved to Chicago when Schaumburg Honda was getting ready to open. Randy was in Chicago helping get the store ready, and he called me. I showed up at Schaumburg Honda about a month before the store opened.

From late 1984 until 1989, I was in Chicago. I worked at Schaumburg Honda and then at Arlington Acura, where I was the used car manager. I got caught up in the Chicago night life, which is easy to do. It kind of helped that I worked 12-9.

I was seeing the sun come up too many times. I was living about 45 minutes from downtown Chicago. Finally, one night I realized that I was done and had to get some help.

I was afraid I was going to get into an accident and kill myself. I needed a break. The next day, I got a ride to Lebanon, IN, to check into the KOALA treatment center. That was September, 1989.

I knew that I had a problem with alcohol and was an accident looking to happen. I was never in jail or even pulled over for drinking and driving, but physically, I was a mess. I drank all night and wasn't drunk. And my drink then was Jack Daniels. I was drinking myself sober.

Two weeks into my stay at KOALA, we had a field trip to a museum in Indianapolis. Almost everyone at the treatment center, except me, was there because of the police or a court ordered situation.

A lot of the counselors looked at me to be a leader. I didn't have to be there, but I still was there. We went into the museum for a while, but one of the guys told me we should run across the street to the Red Garter, a strip joint.

We ended up going from 12 until 2. As we were walking back, the group was standing outside. The counselor who was with us was so mad. When we got back from the field trip, the guy with me at the Red Garter asked if he could move into the room with me.

He moves into my room and puts up a picture of his wife and his wife's sister, who was not married. I told the guy to call his sister in law and get her phone number. A day before I was to get out, he gave me her number.

I called her, and she said she had told Albie, my roommate, not to give me her number. Two hours later, we finally hung up, and a year later, Vicki and I got married. I would never have known Albie had we not sneaked away to the Red Garter.

How crazy is that?

I know my dad likes her a lot, and I think that is because she is a lot like him. Like with my dad, when you get on Vicki's bad side, it is not fun. If you are on her good side, it's great. She is a disciplinarian.

To be very honest, she probably is the reason I am still living. I fell off the wagon one time in 25 years, and when I didn't come to work for a few days, my dad replaced me at Indy Honda.

I was making the big money and had a slip from my sobriety. I checked into the Fairbanks treatment center in Indianapolis for 10 days in 2000 and got clean.

My dad holds his employees accountable, and Vicki is the same way. She does not miss anything. She grew up on the west side of Indianapolis and went to Washington High School.

She was working for Anthem Blue Cross and Blue Shield when I met her. The day after I had gotten out of KOALA, I drove to Indianapolis and took her to lunch.

In 2015, we celebrated our 25th wedding anniversary on Sept, 29. They told me at KOALA not to get involved in a relationship for at least a year. Leave it to me to change the percentages.

We have three sons - Connor, who was 21 in 2015. Bryce, our second son, graduated from high school in 2015. Third child Logan entered high school in 2015.

Looking back, I think it was hard for me to be Bob Rohrman's son during the time I lived in Lafayette. Now, I am just happy to be here. The decisions I made in the last 25 years turned out to be good ones after making all those bad ones for the first 25 years of my life.

Rick and Vicki Rohrman.

54. *Kathy Rohrman*

JR's wife and Bob Rohrman's daughter in law

When I met my father in law, he was just so funny. He always made me laugh.

We would go to dinner at the Lafayette Country Club with he and Linda, and he and I shared a love of baby beef liver. Bob and I would both order that, which kind of made everybody else sick.

JR and I were married four years before we had children, so on Sundays, we often would play golf. Linda and I would ride in the same cart and always talk.

Bob and JR had their own cart. Whenever Bob would tee off, if he hit a bad drive, it always was the fault of Linda and me because we were talking. That would only make us laugh harder. We couldn't stop laughing. Linda and I grew up together. I was 20, and Linda was 32.

At the birth of our sons, I have wonderful pictures of Bob at Home Hospital holding the boys. That is very special to us. It's interesting that I was only 19 when I met Bob, and I was married at 20 in 1980. JR is five years older than I am.

As we were making plans for our wedding, one night we were having dinner at Bob's house, and JR, Randy, Rick and Linda were sitting there with Bob. Linda was the person who always gave me a chance when it came to Bob, because I was raised a Baptist, and Bob was a Catholic.

He did not like that. He said, "So, where are you getting married?" I said, "In Stevensville, MI." He said, "Well, no one is going to go there. Why don't you get married in Lafayette?" Then Linda said to Bob, "Oh, no honey, almost all weddings are in the bride's hometown."

His next question was, "So, what kind of church are you getting married in?" I said, "Well, it is a Baptist church." He was not happy with that and said, "Well, nobody is going to come." He stood up, said a few things and left the table.

That was our engagement year, and for the most part, he did not have a lot to do with the plans. But over the years, our relationship changed and became great. Part of that was that he asked us to go to premarital counseling in the Catholic church with Father Duncan, and I agreed.

Plus, we had a family friend who married us, along with my pastor. So we had all kinds of clergy involved. We were good there. Of those involved, Father Duncan gave us the best advice.

Father Duncan told us that during those times we can't agree on something, compromise. He told us that it is going to happen, so land in the middle. We used that for years and years.

Now, JR and I are so much alike, but in the early years, we were like night and day. I came from a super strict environment, and JR's background was totally different.

My dad had to interview every guy before I could go out with them. My dad was pretty picky, and I didn't go out a lot. It was easier just to not go out.

But my dad is a lot like Bob in that he was a successful businessman. My dad was in retail, but he started an insurance agency, and my mother ran that. I was born in 1960 and had a babysitter, along with my twin brother, from the time I was two until I was in fifth grade.

My dad's way of keeping track of us was that we had a pool that had to be vacuumed every day, and I did that from the time I was in kindergarten. We also had a big yard and didn't have weed eaters then. We had a long fence, and I had to go every week around every post and every tree and pull weeds.

Dad also was a developer and developed a shopping center, which was beautiful. He also had three clothing stores and the insurance agency. He also had two stores in South Bend, IN. His way of keeping track of us was to make us work.

In sixth grade, my twin Mark Van Osdal was in one store, and I was in another. We would wait on customers. He taught me a lot.

I think their similar backgrounds are why my dad and Bob get along so well.

When JR and I were married, everyone in the Rohrman family showed up. I loved Bob's sisters and brothers. His brother Don, who was in Spooner, WI, and I were very close.

JR's aunts, uncles and cousins are very kind and also made me feel very welcomed into the Rohrman family. I love them very much.

Another thing that was wonderful for me is that I got to know Bob's mother, Velma, who was a tiny, wonderful lady. She would sit and tell me stories of when her husband would move the family to Spooner, and then out west. Bob's dad would go ahead and get established and then send money for the family to come out on the train.

Kathy Rohrman with husband JR and their four sons.

She would cook for all the hired hands as well as for her eleven children. She was in her 90s when she would share these stories.

In her day, to raise eleven kids, make her own bread, work the fields, have her own animals and milk her own cows, was amazing. And she told me all of this. Then, she fed fifteen cow hands every meal.

I also got to know JR's maternal grandmother, Olivia, who was the most loving and giving woman you ever could have the good fortune to know. Just like Velma, she loved her Lord. She always called him, "The Good Lord."

She used to babysit our oldest, Ryan. In her late 70s, she still was babysitting. At that time, she still was mowing her own two-acre yard. I would drive by the house, and when it was 85 degrees, I would mow the yard for her. She was an amazing, loving woman who helped take care of each of Bob and Shirley's five children.

Another thing my dad and Bob have in common is that they were born during the depression and came from super, hard-working parents that just barely made it. Neither Bob nor my dad graduated from college, yet they were able to build their businesses on their own.

When my dad and Bob are together, they laugh and joke around a lot and have fun.

As our sons were growing up in Lafayette, they were getting into YMCA basketball, so we would have a game at 8 a.m., 9, 10 and 11. Bob would come to the boys' games, and it was hilarious. He loved going to their games. And then there were the baseball games at Armstrong Park.

If I had duct tape, I would have covered Bob's mouth, because he would yell, "That's my boy!" He was so loud that I would cover my eyes.

Getting back to the basketball games, at halftime, he would yell to Ryan and Trey to come up to him. He would have these watches that he would buy from New York City, and in the middle of the basketball games, he would tell them that if they scored 20 points, they could have a watch.

The team was going crazy, and I am thinking, "I can't believe he is doing this."

Inside, I was laughing. He is just hilarious. There were lots of games and lots of fun times.

Another of my favorite Bob stories centers on the time in the late 1990s when he took Ryan and I to a Purdue-Michigan State football game in West Lafayette. JR was working. Purdue was trailing by like three touchdowns with not much time left to play, and Bob turns to me and says, "We are going to win this game."

Bob predicted what was going to happen, and it did. Purdue won. I couldn't believe that everything Bob said was going to happen happened.

By that time, Bob and I had a wonderful relationship. He loves the fact that JR and I gave him four grandsons, and he loves all four of them.

I tend to be a work before play kind of person, and that is what I taught our sons in our home. The other thing was that every day, we had something in the word of God. That was super important to me, because I never had that. But I found the Lord when I was 16. I always knew I was missing something. I saw it at church. Today, I know what it is. It is true love.

Once we were in Wisconsin, a couple of times Bob flew up to Spooner, having his pilot land at the airstrip in Shell Lake. He said he would be there at 4, so we go to pick him up, and we saw him walking down the street to a little ice cream store. He was so happy and was reminiscing.

We stayed in these little cabins, and we all went canoeing. He walked out to the canoe, pulled up his shorts and had the whitest legs. There he was, standing in the river. We had a great time.

Other fond memories center on the four of us - JR, Bob, Linda and I - going to Washington, D.C. each May for the American Import Auto Dealers meetings, and we would have an opportunity to meet with Sen. Richard Lugar of Indiana. That was really fun to sit in Senator Lugar's office and visit with him.

Bob always has a good time, but he is successful because he is such a hard worker. He eats, sleeps and loves the car business. He is very competitive.

And it doesn't matter what time it is. When we were in Lafayette, he would call at midnight and say, "How many did you get out today?"

He would make those calls during his midnight run to Chicago. That is "Rohr Time." He has his own clock.

I love Bob so much and have so much respect for him. Now to see my sons working for him is so much fun. And they love and respect their grandpa and work hard for him. I know that he loves me.

Some of our family members were in Spooner, WI, recently vacationing on Little Casey Lake. Bob has left a legacy of memories of the Rohrman Family's history while living in Spooner. Every time we're in the area, we see the schools in the middle of nowhere full of rolling hills, noting that "Dad walked through the deep snow in those fields and woods to go to that school." Oh, and 20 degrees.

Bob's parents settled on Little Casey Lake in Spooner, and each of their eleven children were given a parcel of land of about two acres. Over the years, those parcels have been sold to the next generation of family and to the public. But, for the most part, half of it is still owned by family. When our family goes on vacation there, we always run into extended family members; Aunts and Uncles, cousins and second cousins. Maybe 2-12 of us can be there randomly, and we see each other on the lake or catch a bite at Pair O Lakes Resort or McKenzie's Landing.

Grandpa and Grandma Rohrman's house, where Bob lived for a while, is still standing on Little Casey. It's amazing to me how that small, humble gray house could have held so many, and boy, does it get cold up there. I guess body heat could come in handy.

There are several family members who still own property. This area of Wisconsin is so special to my family, as it's a legacy of my Father-in-Law that has been established. Now, our sons and their wives, and our grandchildren can enjoy the north woods of Spooner.

I can't leave out Christmas Day at Bob and Linda's. Christmas has always been a fun, crazy, busy day with everyone in attendance. The dealerships are closed. Yea!!!

Years ago, Bob and Linda would put a sheet up across the living room so nobody could peek and see the piles of gifts for each family member. The mounting excitement was more than some could handle.

I don't want to mention names, but a couple of our sons and a couple of Rhonda and Vic's daughters could not withstand the temptation to peek. We would have to eat brunch that Linda slaved to make for all of us before we could open presents.

This was to torture the parents, I'm sure of this!!! There were a couple of years when Grandpa Bob would go to the last stores open on Christmas Eve to take advantage of the sales. He loved this. I remember our sons asking, "Do you think Grandpa did his Christmas Eve 'extra shopping' tonight?" With great expectation that he did.

55. Ryan Rohrman

General Manager of Schaumburg Honda

Some of my fondest memories of my grandfather are from when I was young. He always was driving a different car. He was going through this great expansion when our family lived in Lafayette, and I would go see him at his office in the parts and collision center.

From Day 1, he always was testing my math skills. To this day, he still does it. He does not like it when someone picks up a calculator. His brain is like a computer. He would say, "Ryan, if we sold 200 cars last month, and then we sold 300 cars this month, how many cars is that?" If I took more than two seconds to give him an answer, he would say, "Oh, babe, I had that answer almost two seconds before you did."

I also remember him coming to my basketball games. He loves sports, but he never would get there on time. I would look up into the stands to see if he was there yet. He would get there at halftime, and he would bring his own popcorn. I would look into this popcorn bag, and it wasn't just popcorn. He would have candies and chocolates, and peppermint patties are his favorite.

I liked to spend the night at his house on Saturday night, and he knew that, so at halftime of my games, he would say, "If you score ten points in the second half, you can spend the night at my house." He always was instilling that competitive edge in me.

He saw a lot of games, because I played for YMCA and AAU teams and for my team at Highland Christian School.

If I got to go home with him, sometimes he would take me to his office and show me around, or we would go back to his house and watch sports on TV. Then after I spent the night on Saturday, he would prepare this huge breakfast on Sunday.

Before he got into the car business, at some point in his crazy life, he was a chef. To this day, he loves cooking. And every time he cooks something, it is a Rohrman special. At first, he would cook at least one pound of bacon, and sometimes, two pounds. He would have all that bacon grease in the pan, and he would make pancakes.

He would put the pancake batter into the bacon grease, and they would just float in there. He would get his spatula, and there would be grease all over the place. He would get it on his shirt, and this is before we would go to church. He would be ready to go to church, but after cooking, he would have to go change clothes.

He would baste the pancakes in the bacon grease. He would flip the pancakes, and they would come out perfectly. They were crispy on the outside, but so soft on the inside. They were so good.

Then, he would prepare what he called mush. When I would go to other people's houses for breakfast, I would ask for mush, and they would ask me what I was talking about. Grandpa said it is called mush and that you can buy it in stores. Actually, it is called polenta. He would get that roll of polenta and chop it very thin.

He would cook it in the bacon grease, and it would turn dark on one side. Then, he would put jam or preserves on it. Last but not least, he would crack eggs and have them floating in the bacon grease. They were sunny-side up for sure. There would be at least three inches of bacon grease in that pan.

Years later, during my summer breaks in college - after my sophomore and junior years - I lived with him in Downer's Grove, IL. We picked up the breakfast tradition again some 10 years later. I sold cars at Schaumburg Honda for him during those summer breaks.

I now make those breakfasts for my son, and he loves them. I have not introduced him to pancakes cooked in bacon grease yet, but I will do the eggs in the bacon grease, and he loves that.

Living with my grandpa and selling cars for him, I was super nervous. I went to college with a goal of being pre-med. I loved biology and was majoring in it at Bethel College in St. Paul, MN. I had a very small scholarship that was for academics, even though I played soccer. They have a great biology program at Bethel.

My grandfather would call and ask me if I wanted to sell cars. I told him that I really was into the pre-med thing. I would think most grandfathers would want their grandsons to be doctors, but he kept telling me that if I wanted to sell cars, he has thirty stores, and that he could make something work.

He kept calling me almost every other day for stints. It got to a point where I stopped answering my phone. I knew what he wanted. In every dorm room, there was a phone that hangs on the wall with a cord in it. No one knows the number to that phone. But one night at 10, that phone started ringing. My friend answered the phone, and it was my grandpa.

I had no idea how he got that number, but he did. He wanted to know if my cell phone was broken. I told him I was sorry, and he asked again if I wanted to come sell cars for him that summer. Finally, I told him that I would come sell cars that summer and see how it goes.

He said OK, and then I didn't hear from him for the rest of the summer. He won, once again proving that he is the ultimate salesman. He got what he wanted by getting me to say OK. He knew that if I did it and liked it and was good at it, that is what I would do, and if I didn't like it, I could go back and be Dr. Rohrman or whatever I wanted.

At that time, I had no family in Chicago. My parents and brothers were in Eau Claire, WI. So, grandpa tells me that I can live with him. He has a pretty big house, and at that time, he was married to Ronda, and her two daughters were living there, too.

That was the summer of 2005, and I was 21. Ronda's daughters were in high school and middle school at the time. I lived in the basement, and it was crazy.

The first day I sold cars, I was nervous, but I knew something about the car business, because my dad had four car lots and I had helped him. When we still were in Lafayette, I wasn't doing any selling, but I would clean cars. In Wisconsin, I ended up running the gas station for him.

The main money maker at the Spur gas station was oil changes, and I did as many as twenty of those a day.

I knew cars pretty well and could even do small repairs. I would go to auto auctions with my dad when I was in high school and sold a few cars in high school. I had a natural love for cars.

But I never had done new cars. It always had been used cars. On my first day at Schaumburg Honda - June 1, 2005 - grandpa could sense I was a little bit nervous, and I thought he would give me a few tips.

On our way there, he said, "All you have to do to sell cars is get the customer to fall in love with you. If you can do that, you can do anything."

At the time, that didn't help me a whole lot. He told me they knew I was coming, but when I got to Schaumburg Honda, no one knew I was coming. All the guys at Schaumburg Honda told me that I would be fine because selling cars is in my blood. No one trained me.

I basically spent the first two days reading. I learned everything I could about a Honda in a two-day crash course. Then, I started selling. The first day, I was the first salesperson there. I got there at about 8 in the morning and pulled into his house at 6:30. He said, "What are you doing home?" He told me maybe this car thing was not for me. He told me my hours needed to be into the dark.

For the rest of the summer, I worked every day. He said my hours were the hours that were on the door of the dealership. But I sold cars. My first month, I sold fourteen, and after that, I never sold less than eighteen in any single month.

The first week, the learning curve was through the roof. After that, it became an addictive business. Getting someone to say yes to you is fun. My first car sale was to a Korean gentleman, whose name was Bullet. He told me what he wanted, and I did the whole process with him.

But when we ran his credit, his score was 300, which means he is not buying a car. I didn't know that, so I kept pressing.

The guy was a factory worker, so it was hard to get him back into the store. I would wait at night for him, and he would come at 10 p.m. I finally sold him a car, a Honda Odyssey. It was very satisfying. I wanted the respect of all the sales managers, and in a situation like that, half the salesmen would have given up.

His credit score was not good, but in almost all of them, you can find a ray of sunshine. You just have to work it. I think I sold that car four days after I started. The whole process of selling a car is a numbers game. You are not going to close on everyone, but if you are really good, you can close 30 percent. If you want to sell twenty cars, and it is 30 percent, that is like visiting with sixty-six people. There is an up and down curve.

The store record is seven cars in one day. I once did four, and that was a 10-hour day. The best compliment a customer can give you is when he or she says they were not planning to buy a car for months, and they buy the car the same day.

Anyone can sell a car to the person who has spotted a car on your lot and wants it, then says to write it up. The hard one is when they say they are looking, but they are not going to buy for two months. Then, in an hour, you are selling it to the customer.

That summer was interesting. Ronda's two girls are nice, but they like to have fun. Grandpa would tell me that when he was not there, I was the man of the house. He wanted me to make sure everything was OK. There were times I would be in bed at 11:30, and they would have loud music playing.

At that time, my grandpa and Ronda got along well and seemed to me to have a great relationship. We often would go to Pepe's for dinner, and I remember that while he doesn't drink much, he would order a pitcher of margaritas. The only other thing he really drinks that has alcohol is German sweet wine, Smidt and Sohne. It is an $8 bottle of wine.

After the summer of 2005, I went back to school and changed my major to business with a concentration in marketing with an accounting minor.

My parents really never pushed their children in any direction. But from the time I was in high school, they insisted that I have a job. My freshman year in high school, I had a car, but my dad told me the first day of summer not to come home until I had a job. I ended up getting a job at McDonald's. I worked at the Eau Claire McDonald's for about a year.

I had to pay for my car and my own insurance and my gas. I got paid twice a month. By the time I made my car payment, paid for my insurance and put gas in the car, I had about $20 left for the next two weeks, so I started refereeing youth soccer games to make extra money.

Again, they never pushed me into a certain job. They just insisted that I work in the summer. I worked all four years in high school and all four in college, too.

It was interesting timing when I went to Chicago for that first time, because it was about two weeks after I found out that my mom had breast cancer. It was hard on me. I was planning to go to Chicago, but I was concerned, yet they told me not to put my life on hold.

I cried my eyes out during that 5 1/2-hour drive from Eau Claire to Chicago. I did not know what was going to happen. She is fine now.

After my first month at Schaumburg Honda, I never was less than a Top 5 salesman. One of the sales promotions I won was a trip to a Wrigley Field rooftop skybox for a Cubs game. Grandpa actually sent his plane to Bethel to pick me and my brother Chase up and fly us to Chicago for the package I won.

After the first summer I worked at Schaumburg Honda selling cars for grandpa, I had $15,000. I had never had so much money in my life. I put all the money in the bank. I didn't even know what to buy. It was exciting, because my grandpa had told me I had to earn everything.

He said, "If you can do it, I will help you get to it. If you can't do it, you are out." That has been the way it always has been. My parents are the same way. I got my first paycheck and it was for more than $1,000, and I just looked at it and said wow, that is a lot of money. That is part of the addiction to the car business. At the time, I was 21 and had two years of college.

The cool thing about the car business is that anyone can do it if you really want to do it. The amount of money you can make really is endless, even at my store. My top guy makes $160,000 a year, and our lowest guy is like $30,000 or $40,000. It is crazy. It turns out not to be work, which is the crazy thing about it.

The summer, after my junior year in college, I came back to Schaumburg Honda and lived at his house again. That was a great summer. My first month selling, I sold eighteen and never dropped below eighteen. I just rolled with it. Grandpa and I continued to have fun. Again, he would make the big Sunday breakfasts, and while I am not Catholic, I would go to Sunday mass with him.

Then, we would play golf about every other Sunday. During the week, we would play in an occasional golf outing that was staged by those with which he advertised. And we would win so much stuff. I was not as good as my brother Trey, but at the time, I was a pretty good golfer.

At this point, I was going into my last year of college and was going to graduate the following summer, so I had that conversation with grandpa that centered on, "What is your plan for me?"

I wanted to know, because I did not want to come out of college selling cars. I had proved to everyone I needed to prove it to that I could do it, and I could do it well.

He told me he would make me a sales manager at Schaumburg Honda, and I said, "OK." I finished college the next May, and it worked perfectly, because there actually was a position open. In 2007, I became the sales manager at Schaumburg Honda.

In the fall of 2007, I started to National Automobile Dealers Association school in Washington, D.C. and was there every other month for a year. On my graduation day, grandpa asked me to come to Arlington Acura and be the new car manager. I said yes, and he told me to report to work the next morning at 8.

I was there for a short time and then returned to Schaumburg Honda as the used car manager. I was in that position for about two years ad enjoyed it. There is where I got my feet wet. John Barrett was my used car manager at the time, and then he asked me to be his general sales manager. I did that job for John for a year.

A year later, John was promoted to director of operations, and I took over in 2011 as the general manager of Schaumburg Honda.

I am happy with my decision and have no regrets.

Now that I have worked with my grandfather, I think the core of his success comes down to three or four things. First, timing is everything. Second, he is dedicated. So many people ask me when he is going to retire, and to answer their question, there really is no such thing as retiring, because he is not working.

Instead, he has been able to turn his life into what he does so that it is just who he is. That is why he is so successful. One of the reasons he and I get along so well is because we both share a love of cars.

One of the things I have learned is that the grandfather I knew as a kid - funny, hilarious, famous man - is really very smart. He really is a genius. He still is fun and loving, but he is my boss now. Our relationship is very much that, along with the fact he loves family.

He has very deep connections to his kids and grandkids. He doesn't wake up to go to work. He is just doing it. It is natural.

And he is a naturally lucky person. I will sit at a golf event with a raffle ticket and never win anything. My grandfather will sit there and win everything. People get tired of how often he wins. He is a winner. He has turned me into a winner.

If you want to be a ten, you have to put yourself around 10s. He might be a twelve. To be around him, you naturally are going to be elevated.

And being around him is tons of fun.

In 2010, he won a trip from Lexus to go to Peru in South America. I am really into traveling, so he asked me to go to Peru. There were lots of activities we could choose to do, and so I picked white water rafting for he and I to do down this sacred river.

Bob and Ryan rafting in Peru, 2010

He can't swim, but even though he was in his 70s at the time, I knew he would be fine. The highest rapid at the very end was ranked a 4, so he was OK. The other thing about Peru is that once you leave Lima, you can get to an elevation of 12,500 feet.

In our hotel, they were pumping oxygen into the rooms. We go, but I can tell that he is not happy about the white water rafting thing. I kept trying to reinforce that he would be OK. He tried to back out, but I told him he was going.

Finally, we get there and get him into the raft, and he loves it. He thought it was the greatest thing since sliced bread. Everyone got a kick out of him because he was laughing. We would go down a two foot rapid, and he would yell. At the end, where the big rapid was, he started shuffling his feet, and as we took the final rapid, he somehow got himself wedged down in between the seats in the middle of the raft and was stuck.

He couldn't get out, but he was loving it, and it took three of us to pull him from the center of the boat. We were there for seven days, and that was the second day we were there.

The other funny part of that trip was that we were there during the NBA Finals when the Lakers were at the height of their glory. The very last day, there was a concern that we might have too little oxygen in our blood.

He wasn't feeling that well, so we called a doctor. They basically told him his oxygen to blood ratio was like 82 percent, which at any given time, you should be in the mid to high 90s. We had to get him to the hospital, and my grandfather hates hospitals.

I told him he had to go. We got there, and the place was like a bunker. White concrete walls with white concrete ceilings. He started flirting with the Peruvian nurses. The doctor told him he had a choice - he could be hospitalized for 24 hours, or go into an oxygen chamber for one hour.

We sat in the oxygen chamber for an hour and watched the Lakers win the last game of the NBA Finals. They had him on a speaker phone, and he was super loud while he was in there watching the game on TV that was set up on a ceiling above him.

There he was, 12,500 feet about sea level, in Peru, in an oxygen chamber watching the Lakers win an NBA title. It was a great trip for two guys who have the same initials - RVR. The oldest born son has those initials.

His name is Robert Vincent Rohrman. My dad is Robert Vincent Rohrman, JR, and I am Ryan Vincent Rohrman. My son is Ryan Vincent Rohrman, Jr. Now, there are four generations of RVRs.

The four RVRs - from left, JR Rohrman, (Robert Vincent Rohrman, Jr.,)
Robert Vincent Rohrman, Sr. holding Ryan Vincent Rohrman, Jr.,
Ryan Vincent Rohrman, Sr.

56. Chase Rohrman

Used Car Manager at Arlington Acura

When we were younger, my grandpa took each grandson on our own little vacation. I think the purpose was to spend some one on one time with each of us.

We were living in Lafayette at the time, and I always wanted to snowboard. It was my dream. I was 13 when I told my grandfather that I wanted to go snowboarding. I never had been snowboarding, but I wanted to go to a big mountain and go snowboarding.

That winter, my grandfather told me to pack my bags and that he and I were going to Colorado to go snowboarding for four days. He was 67 when we went on this trip. We arrive in Aspen, CO, and neither of us knew how to snowboard and neither of us had a snowboard.

This was in December, so we visited the local snowboard shop and got all geared out. When he bought a snowboard, I am thinking, "So, he is going to learn how to snowboard with me. This is awesome."

We go up 10,000 feet in elevation into the Rocky Mountains and meet our personal instructor, who was with us for three days. The instructor is a former professional snowboarder who is awesome. We both are starting to learn how to snowboard, and we are falling down like crazy. We were on the bunny hill, but we are everywhere.

That day alone, we each probably fell down 100 times. That night, after we returned to our hotel, grandpa was really, really sore. I was worried about him, but I was so young that it really didn't click.

I did not look at him like he was 67. Rather, I just recalled that he is active and that is cool. Now, if we were attempting this, I would just recommend that he just get a pair of skis. That night, he hands me this big bottle of Ben Gay. He tells me I have to rub this stuff over his entire back. I'm 13, and I am smothering this all over his back.

He was super, super sore, and the next day, I think he just kind of chilled and watched me. The best part was our last day. I had learned to snowboard a little bit, but I told him I wanted to go down the entire mountain. He told me he would wait for me at the bottom.

I take the multiple chairlifts that it takes to get to the top, and whatever slope was in front of me was the slope I was taking. It literally took me an hour and a half to get down. It should take an average person 15 minutes. It took me forever, because I was super slow.

When I finally got to the bottom near where we were staying, my grandpa says, "Oh, man, Chaser, I didn't think you were going to make it. I didn't think you were coming down." I told him I didn't think I was going to make it either. I was OK, but it took me a really long time.

The funny thing looking back on it now is that when I talk about it with my wife, she asks, "He was how old when you did this?" it is unbelievable that he even tried. To strap on a snowboard and learn is incredible. For a while, it was mind boggling that he would even try to do something that he never has done. People usually don't start learning to snowboard or to ski at 67.

That is one of my fondest memories, because we got a lot of alone time. We both were trying something new and experimenting with it, so it was fun. But is amazes me that he would even try.

We talked a lot and bonded on that trip, and I remember we talked a lot about what my interests were at that time. A lot of the questions he asked me were about sports. In Lafayette, I was really good in soccer, baseball and basketball.

It is impressive even today how closely he follows all sports. People will ask him how he manages all of his stores and still have time to get to every store and talk to every manager. There are only 24 hours in a day. How does one person even do all that stuff? That alone is amazing and how he manages his time. Still, a neat thing to me is that he never procrastinates. Whatever he wants to do, he will do it at that time.

If he wants to talk to a certain general manager or service manager or parts manager, he will do it right then and there. That is just the way he is wired and the way he runs his stores. Yet he also has the ability to do other stuff, too.

The nice thing about the car business, especially in the Chicago area, is that it blends well with sports. He advertises with all the different franchises, Cubs, White Sox, Bulls, Bears and Blackhawks. So, he has a vested interest in them on a monetary level, plus he follows all of them just because of his love of sports. They kind of go hand in hand for him, so it makes it easier for him to follow a team and to really fall in love with those teams.

In terms of my grandfather and business, there has been very little luck. If anything, you create your own luck. He has created his own luck, and the way he has done that is by taking on different manufacturers that maybe someone else did not want to take on because they thought the risk was too great.

He really saw ahead of his time. His vision was bigger than just the here and now. It was decades in planning. At the time when he started all of his stores, domestic cars were the thing. His vision was to take a Toyota franchise, which nobody knew about. Then, he moved on into Honda and Suzuki and all of these other brands that were a little bit newer.

When those cars came out, people were not jumping on the bandwagon. He is a visionary in that he can see something when it is small but that it could get much bigger.

I think my grandfather also is very street smart. It sums him up perfectly. He barely got through high school and didn't do any college, but he was in the military and then started selling cars. I would say he is the most street smart person that I know.

He is brilliant, but part of street smarts is how you interact with people in relationships. He just knows how to read people and with whom you need to create a relationship. He knows where you need to be and who you need to talk to and what the next step is.

You can't really teach that in college. That is something you just learn as you go. He is one of the best at that.

Now, I really am enjoying working for him. It is funny when he wants me to take on more responsibility, he will say, "Hey, do you want to do this?" I will say yes, definitely, and he will ask if I am sure.

He will then remind me that I didn't always want to join the car business. He will remind me that I wanted to be a school teacher. I graduated from college with a social studies education degree. My original mindset was not to go into teaching right away.

I love history and I love teaching, and those things go hand in hand. The worst case scenario was that if the car business or whatever else was out, I would have seen myself teaching and really falling in love with it.

But I really expected that I always would end up in the car business. I did the teaching as the backup plan, knowing that I would enjoy it.

Just like Ryan, I started selling cars in college at Schaumburg Honda. But I did not do it until after my junior year in college. I am a little more adventurous and wasn't sure that I wanted to start my professional career after my sophomore year in college.

After my sophomore year in college, I worked for Life Action Ministries in the South Bend area. When I started working at Schaumburg Honda, I definitely was nervous. My last name is Rohrman, so expectations were there right away.

I wanted to sell a lot of cars and make my grandpa proud, my parents proud and also make some money. I also knew that the eyes of all the management and sales people were on me. As I got to know the guys and developed relationships, the pressure went down. For the first two weeks, I was nervous, because for the first time in my life, I was learning how to sell.

In a way, because of my grandfather and father, I was around the car business my whole life, but I never had sold anything. I had done some oil changes at my dad's gas station, but all I really knew about the business then was getting to know people and telling them about the cars.

After two or three weeks, I realized it wasn't that hard and that you just started by saying hello to people on the lot. As long as you know your product, it is a pretty simple process.

I graduated from Bethel University in May, 2009 and started on July 1 at Schaumburg Honda. I moved in with Ryan at grandpa's condo in Schaumburg. I sold cars there, attended NADA school in Washington, D.C. and then went to the Ford store in Schaumburg.

I was sales manager and general manager at Ford for a total of three years. Then I went to Arlington Acura on Dec. 1, 2013. The more I learn and am involved in this business, the more I like it. Some people, the more they get into it, they want to get out. The car business is so competitive that it is a sport in its own right. You have all these manufacturers trying to reach the same customers. It is a lot of fun.

The way I view my grandfather's success in the car business is how I viewed going snowboarding. At the time, I didn't think anything of it. I thought it was crazy that he would try something like that at his age, but now that I have been in the car business for six years, it is just unbelievable what he has created. It is phenomenal.

Everyone who works for him has the utmost respect for him.

When I am 82, I would have to say probably not if someone asked me if I could work at his pace as an 82 year old. You never know, but thinking about it, I would be hard pressed to think I will be working 60 to 62 hours a week, which he does. He always is on the move.

I would think I would slow down and turn those responsibilities over to someone else. Yet he always is driving. When Ryan and Trey and I were selling cars at Schaumburg Honda, he would ask how many cars we had sold last month. If we would tell him like fifteen, he would remind us that those numbers would not put us at the top of the leader board.

After a bad week, he will tell you about it, but in his own way, he will get you going again.

When I first started, it was not what I thought it would be, but now, this is more than I ever thought it would be. I love it.

57. Trey Rohrman

General Manager of Bob Rohrman Toyota in Lafayette

What is unique about my grandfather - and what I think makes him successful - is his focus and his attention to the people in all of his stores.

Typically, an individual owner with that many employees and that many locations spread out by miles is not in touch. Typically, you will have people in place who make ownership decisions through you.

He has made sacrifices that most would not make to be able to be in touch with salespeople and with cleanup guys. He knows what is going on in the smallest store he has and in the stores he doesn't have to look at because he knows they are profitable. He is just very in tune with the overall atmosphere.

Just because I am his grandson, it doesn't mean I can just do what I want, work when I want or just show up. He holds me accountable almost more than others. He wants to make sure that I am where I am not just because of who I am. I appreciate that. I would not want to be the typical car dealer's family member who is running a store.

If you sit in my office as family members have done and friends have done, the thing that they say afterwards is, "How do you get anything done with employees constantly coming in and asking for your opinion or asking you to approve something?"

I love that. I come in, and sometimes I don't know what time it is. Sometimes, I don't know what day it is. My grandfather is very in tune with what is going on in a huge business. He knows that people matter, specifically in the sales business where your results are directly from the people and their success.

When I interview or hire sales associates, I tell them that Mr. Rohrman provides the inventory and the advertising, but they are no different than a real estate agent. When you work for Bob

Rohrman, you have to brand yourself, find clients and take care of the customer.

For the majority of people, they have to work hard at it, and that scares a lot of people away after a couple of years. He provides things to his stores that most dealers aren't able to provide. He provides unbelievable advertising, branding, inventory and facilities.

Business is people, places and product. He has great places, and he has a knack for knowing that something that is in front of him now is going to be a gold mine down the road.

I go on trips with him - maybe the National Automobile Dealers Association conference in San Francisco or trips that he has won - and that is the best time, because these dealers he has known for 30 and 40 years tell me things about my grandfather from a dealer's perspective.

It's not a family member or a salesperson, it is another dealer who has known him. They all say that my grandfather has that knack for being in the right place at the right time.

They love to tell Schaumburg Honda stories - that it was a cornfield, and now it is the hub and the centerpiece for automotive selling in Chicago.

That store is by far his golden gem dealership. It is his most profitable store and his highest volume store. Now, he has multiple dealerships on that same road. They sell a ton of cars and provide a great experience for customers.

Customers ask, "How big is he?" Well, he has 30-plus dealerships. He is all over, now including Wisconsin. Those are some things that make him so unique.

It's a lot of things, and leadership can be learned, but that knack for knowing potential and for taking risks, most business people measure risk by worse case scenario. I don't think he takes that into consideration like most people do.

It goes back to the days in Lafayette when he took Toyota when nobody wanted it. He said, bring them on down. Now look. We are sitting in the nicest dealership in the state.

A lot of little towns have Ford and Chevy dealerships, but he took the risks with an ability to see potential, coupled with his hard work, you never can take that from him.

The other thing is that people can't believe that in 2015, he is 82. I recently was talking with some representatives of Chase Bank, and the asked how my dad was doing. They thought my grandfather was my father. They could not believe he is in his 80s. It does not seem possible.

Nobody thinks he is as old as he is. I have never seen anyone with the passion for what he does or what he loves.

Bob Rohrman with a collection of his grandchildren.

One of the other things that is hilarious is what he calls "Rohr Time."

He will call me at 2 or 3 in the morning and tell me he has an idea. He will tell me his idea in a voice mail that is two or three minutes long. He calls those moments "Rohr Time."

He says that if you believe that 9 p.m. is when you should start winding down, then you will lose an opportunity for success. He does not expect to be in bed at any certain time.

He tells me that if he has a good idea and says he is going to do it in the morning and he does not do it right now, everybody else who has good ideas will do it then.

One of my first uncomfortable times working for him occurred during my first six months. It was almost midnight, and he calls. I am sitting in bed with my wife, so I don't answer it, but I listen to the voice mail in case it is an emergency.

His message was that he had gotten a call from a lady who was not happy with her experience with a salesman and doesn't really understand the features of her car. He tells me to call her. But my wife, Cathryn, agrees with me that because it is almost midnight, I should wait until the next morning.

I call grandpa, and he tells me that if I don't call her back right then, he will call her. He did not care that it was 11 p.m. or so. He told me to return the call. He put me in an uncomfortable position. So I called her, and she definitely was not in bed. She was so happy I called her. She was so thrilled that I had called right then.

One of the things I am driven by is my grandfather's approval. I have a lot of employees who tell me they are working hard, but hard isn't always the right thing. Smart sometimes is better.

I began working for my grandfather after my freshman year at Indiana Weslyan. My mother, Kathy, told me that I was going to work the rest of my life and that I should come home and that I didn't have to work.

But I was so excited to begin working in the Bob Rohrman Auto Group. I always had wanted to be in sales. Everyone told me I am a natural salesman, and I wanted to see if I was.

That summer was the only time I was able to work with both older brothers, Ryan and Chase, in the same dealership. We all worked at Schaumburg Honda in 2009 and lived in grandpa's condo in Schaumburg. That I will never forget. It was fun. Ryan was the sales manager, and Chase and I were selling.

I never questioned going into sales for him. I have no idea what I would do if I could not continue doing what I am doing. I obviously enjoy it and I love what I do.

I graduated from college in 2012 and began working at Lafayette Toyota in May, 2012.

After 30 days here and a week at NADA academy, Craig Gipson, our director of operations, comes to me and says that my grandfather wanted to talk to me. I wondered, "What did I do?"

I found out that our general manager had put in his two week notice. My grandfather asked me if I thought I could handle being the general sales manager of the Lafayette Toyota dealership.

He knew I enjoy getting in front of customers and being with customers. In many ways, he and I are a lot alike. He sees that.

What he has done and built, I don't think it could be done again. I would put my life on that, because the only public figures who are threatening to become big players like my grandfather is are people like Warren Buffet.

Warren Buffet has more money than anybody knows what to do with, and there are dealers he is buying because of the cash that he has. That is the only way anybody could ever do it. To accumulate inventory amounts like Mr. Rohrman has, along with dealerships and properties, takes Warren Buffet money.

My grandfather built it from the ground up. Warren Buffet might write a check, but he never is going to step foot in all of his stores.

Bob Rohrman is in touch with everyone at all of his stores. Obviously, Bob Rohrman is an amazing story.

58. Luke Rohrman

Sales Associate for the Bob Rohrman Auto Group's
Lafayette Honda

Growing up, sports was a huge part of my life, and because the hours in the auto business are long, I always appreciated when my grandpa would come to my sporting events.

I knew he was taking some time out of his busy schedule getting out there. When I was a freshman in high school at Granger Christian near South Bend, my brother, Trey, was a high school senior. We were members of the varsity basketball team. We were participating in a tournament at Faith Christian in Lafayette. I was a point guard, and Trey was a forward.

We had moved to Wisconsin from Lafayette when I was 7 and Trey was 9 1/2, so it was kind of interesting to come back here to Lafayette for a tournament. We had attended Highland Christian in Lafayette, and we knew that some of the guys we would be playing from Faith Christian had attended Highland Christian with us.

It was cool, because not only would we see some old friends, grandpa has a home in Lafayette and would be able to attend. We advanced to the tournament's championship game, and grandpa was able to attend. Before the game, he arrived and made his presence known.

He is so funny and was able to make everybody laugh, which calms the nerves. It is just a trait and a talent that he has. He came over to say hi to Trey and I before the game and wished us good luck.

The championship game was a good one, and the score was close at halftime. We were in the locker room huddled around our coach, who had the clip board. We were paying close attention to his halftime instructions. All of a sudden, there was a knock at the locker room door.

We wondered what the heck was going on. This does not happen. No one interrupts halftime during a tournament game. Sure enough, the person at the locker room door is Bob Rohrman himself.

My teammates don't know Bob. But they knew who he was once we got to the tournament. His commercials don't reach over to the Granger/South Bend area. He comes into our locker room, and our coach says, "Can I help you?" He told our coach that he wanted to say some words to our team.

When he had said hi to Trey and I before the game, our coach then knew who he was. It was so funny, because something like that is not supposed to happen. It was out of the norm, but Bob does abnormal things. He takes risks.

So, he begins to speak to the team and is cracking jokes, telling us that we are doing well. Because it was the last game of the tournament, we had been nervous, but he gives us a great pep talk. He left, and everyone was kind of laughing and ready to go.

It was the most absurd, wild thing that ever happened, but he did a good job. We weren't embarrassed, but Trey and I were like, "What's up gramps?" We went back out on the court, played well in the second half and actually won the tournament. His speech didn't hurt. That is a story now that all of the guys on that team like to tell.

After that speech, the confidence was there and the stress level was gone. He has that trait to him that he is so good at. Just relating that to sales, you have to be able to take away that wall that is there naturally with some people who come into a store.

One of the reasons he has been so successful is that he can tear down that wall. Our wall in that tournament was stress and anxiety. He tore that wall down, and we went out there and won the tournament championship.

I played basketball and soccer throughout high school, and whenever my grandpa would come to a game, there might be an opportunity to receive a nice watch from him. If his stores did well, he would win a nice watch. Considering how many stores my grandpa owns, you can imagine he has quite a watch collection. He would keep some watches in his trunk.

So, when he would come to one of my games, before it started he would tell me that if I did well, he had a couple of watches I might like. It was awesome. There were multiple times he would hand me a watch. I have a couple of those watches.

Another favorite story centers on a trip to Disney World with grandpa and grandma Linda when I was 6. My grandma had told me that once I turned 6, she was going to take me to Disney World in Orlando, FL. I wasn't going to let her forget that promise. It is every youngster's dream to go there.

She kept her word, and we scheduled it around grandpa's work schedule. It was a new and fun experience, because I wasn't traveling with my parents. At that age, you usually don't go anywhere without your parents. I wasn't just going to my grandparents' house, I was going to Florida.

We got to the hotel, and I remember looking at all the maps with the various rides we could take. It was so much fun, because it was nice to see my grandpa in a different environment. I would visit him in his office at work, but this was in a completely different setting. He was relaxed.

Trey and I had a good time. Grandpa went on a couple of rides with us, but nothing really crazy. He would pretty much just watch us. I think he enjoyed experiencing Disney World. We were there for four or five days.

It definitely is unique to have a grandfather in that role of popularity and so much success. Comparing it to my grandparents on the other side of the family, it is just a totally different situation. Especially when I was younger, I really didn't understand what he had achieved and how much success he had. It is just mega.

When I got a little older, I began to understand. When I got into seventh and eighth grade, I began to understand what an entrepreneur he is and what a successful businessman he is.

At that point, entering my eighth grade year just after we had moved from Eau Claire, WI, to the South Bend area, I started thinking about what I might do with my future. I had my eyes on Ryan and Chase, seeing what they were doing. I always have been a very observant person.

It gave me an idea about the possibility of the car business. I like the fact that my grandfather has this charisma, just the way he is around people in the dealerships, at a restaurant or at a sporting event.

It is catching. It really is. The way he is is so relatable to sales. If you are having a bad day, and you are dealing with a customer, it is going to transfer over. You have to be sure that you are going to be ready for that. The energy level has to be there, and it transfers. My grandpa always has done such a good job with that. Over the years, it is something I continue to strive for.

At one point in high school, I saw what my brothers were doing, but I had a desire to carve my own niche and a new path for myself. When I hit college at Hope in Holland, MI, I wanted to go into exercise science, maybe pursuing a career as a personal trainer or opening my own fitness center. Health always has been something that interests me, like how to make the body stronger. I read a lot and became very knowledgeable in that field.

When I turned 18, my grandpa said it would be nice to see me in the car business. He told me he thought I had what it takes to be successful in the car business. He encouraged me to follow suit with what my brothers had done.

He encouraged me to start selling cars during the summer while I was attending college. Every one of us began selling cars at Schaumburg Honda. When he would send me birthday cards, he would write that he would be excited to see me in the car business. I absolutely sensed that grandpa wanted me in the car business.

He wants his legacy to move on. I ended up majoring in business management so that, hopefully, I can move into the management side of the business. When I got into the core classes in college, it seemed that everything I would learn were the processes of how you deal with certain situations. I would always relate them to the car business.

I started in the car business as far back as when my dad owned his own lots in Lafayette. I would wash cars and pick up cigarette butts in the lot. Trey and I would receive a penny each from our dad for every cigarette butt we picked up. I was 6 or 7 and still have vivid memories of doing that.

After my freshman year at Hope, I worked in the parts and service department of Schaumburg Honda. That was good for me. As far as dealerships go, there is so much more to it than just selling. There is so much going on in service.

I knew going in after my sophomore year at Hope that I was going to begin selling cars. It was totally different than parts and service. It was different in sales in that no two days are alike. As the summer went along, I really began to enjoy it. Talking to people and interacting just became that much easier.

Between my junior and senior year at Hope, I sold again at Schaumburg Honda, and it was so much easier. I started realizing that I actually am pretty good at this. That is when I really began enjoying it. That also was the first time I really started making good money. I had some good weeks, and I hit some bonuses the dealership had set up for me.

In high school, I worked at Four Lakes Country Club golf course in Edwardsburg, MI, and was making $7.24 an hour. In high school, that was pretty good, but when I was selling at Schaumburg Honda, that was something special.

After graduating from college in May, 2015, I was ready to go all in. Grandpa and I talked about which location I would work, and I really felt like I should try Lafayette. It was a very good decision.

As far as making decisions, I admire that my grandpa is not afraid to take risks. He is a high risk, high reward guy, which carries over into business. He always is ready to try something new. Even if he doesn't like it, he can't say he didn't try it.

If you are too timid, you are going to miss out on opportunities. It is something he has taken advantage of. Considering where he is, he has climbed that hill of opportunity.

From what I have seen of my grandpa, there are multiple things that combine to make him what he is. You don't deny the hard work ethic he has. He is so successful, but to this day, he doesn't want to take vacation. He always has a goal in mind. That is super important in the car business. It keeps you going, even when things are not going well. If you reach a goal, you can set a higher goal.

Another thing is not being satisfied with just reaching your goal. In the car business, someone might sell 10 or 12 cars in a month and be satisfied. Again, it is about setting that goal higher and stretching yourself. That is something he definitely has done. He never gets comfortable. That is when things start to go downhill. Things can get scary, especially in an ever changing business environment. You have to be ever changing and willing to change.

That is something my grandpa has done a great job with.

Once he got a couple of stores and began to have some wealth, he realized that some stores are going to make more profit than others. As an owner, you can take as much profit as you want from that store. But I know a big role in his success is pouring his money back into the dealerships, even when the economy was so poor in 2008.

You can pay yourself as much as you want, but if the dealership is not running well, you are not getting paid more. If one store is doing better than another, that is OK, because you can continue to help the other store.

There also is the notion that you never are too old to learn. He is wise. When it comes to new things, especially with technology, he doesn't understand it too well. But he realizes that Internet shopping is huge now, and we are seeing that at Honda in Lafayette. I have seen dealers who have said they won't spend money on Internet advertising.

If you don't do it, you are missing out on a huge opportunity. My grandpa could have said that he doesn't want to mess with this kind of stuff. But he understood that times change and that he needed to change with those times.

At 82, he works more hours than the average person. He has no plans to stop any time soon. You don't see an 82 year old working all those hours and walking on his lots. Once the average American gets to 55 or 60, he or she is starting to think about retirement. My grandpa doesn't want to retire until he is 112.

His is a rags to riches kind of story.

59. Laura Fleischer

Partner in Orange Media Group
and Bob Rohrman's granddaughter

My grandfather was a huge part of my childhood. My sisters and I spent a lot of time with him and my grandma Linda when we were young. I always remember being so excited when we would stay with them for the weekend, which we often did.

I remember my grandfather coming home Saturday evenings with Arni's pizzas, and then we would spend the evening playing dress up, singing karaoke or playing games. Every Sunday morning we stayed with them, my grandpa made us a BIG brunch.

It was an event of sorts as he went all out-- sausage, eggs, pancakes, grits- which he called 'mush', etc. We loved those mornings and I think he did, too.

Besides spending weekends together, he took me and my older sister, Christina, on many trips-- Disney World, London, Washington D.C., etc. Many of them were work trips, but he still managed to spend time with us.

One of my favorite memories is when Christina and I went with my grandpa and grandma Linda to Door County, Wisconsin. We set off for Wisconsin in my grandfather's motor home. It was older and it was a nasty light green color, hence its name—The Green Weenie.

We loved going on trips in the Green Weenie! We got about an hour or so out of town when the Green Weenie broke down on the side of the road. My grandfather made a few phone calls and somehow we got into another (newer/better) motor home to get us to our destination.

We were off. Until this motorhome broke down on the side of the road as well. Now that I'm thinking of it... what are the chances? Maybe it was user error? I remember my grandpa trying to physically push the motor home on the side of the interstate towards a gas station.

It was then that we decided to give up on motor homes all together. We ended up finishing the drive in a limousine, with my grandpa driving it! He even wore a chauffer's hat—he knew how to make light out of stressful situations.

Holidays, family reunions, company picnics-- all are fantastic childhood memories that include my grandfather. He never missed a graduation, or big event. He was always there.

I would describe my grandfather as extremely loving, goofy, generous and kind. I remember him always singing to Frank Sinatra and Dean Martin in the car, and even inside restaurants we would go to. I would get so embarrassed when he sang in public but secretly loved it.

I always knew there was something a little different about my grandpa. People knew him wherever we went. I remember one of the first memories of this was when he was asked for an autograph when we went to pick up pizza one evening. He signed the guy's pizza box. I thought that was pretty funny.

After college (I am the family traitor that went to Indiana University, despite our strong family ties to Purdue University), I went to work in "corporate America" for a few years. My grandfather always encouraged me to consider to come work for him.

I had some hesitation but finally did in 2010. I spent a month or two in each department of the dealership learning the ropes. I changed oil in the service department, sold cars, worked in the billing office, finance office, parts department and at the advertising agency.

It was the most eye opening experience, being able to see the organization my grandfather built from within. I was lucky to be able to meet and learn from some really fantastic people within the company. I went on to graduate from National Automobile Dealer Association Academy in 2011. Soon after, I decided that I wanted to focus on the advertising side of the business and have been doing that since. It has been a privilege to be able to work alongside my grandfather.

He certainly is not easy to work for, but he is fair, and I've learned a lot from watching him work. He started from nothing and has built an incredible company. He is the most diligent, hardworking individual, and I am grateful for everything he has done for our family!

60. John Barrett

Director of Operations for the Bob Rohrman Illinois Auto Group

As of 2015, I had known Bob for 41 years, first meeting him in 1974 after being laid off work from Ray Magnet Wire in Lafayette. That was the third time I had been laid off from that company.

At that point, I knew I had to seek employment that would be a little steadier. In the factory, you get paid by the hour, which in 1974 was not a whole lot of money. Of course, things didn't cost as much at that time, either.

I was married with two children in 1974. I had gotten out of the Marine Corps in 1971 and couldn't find a job to save my life. When I was in the Marine Corps, I was in aircraft fire and rescue and had visions of being a firefighter when I got out. I applied in Indianapolis and Lafayette.

At that time, being a firefighter was a pretty good job, because you worked eleven days a month and were off the rest of the time.

I had been laid off from the factory and literally walked into Bob's store on Sagamore Parkway. At that time, we had only a one-car showroom. He had Toyota and AMC Jeep. When I walked in, I met a young man by the name of Chico Jensen. I told Chico I was looking for a job.

Unbeknown to Mr. Rohrman, my father had been in real estate in Lafayette and had owned Key Realty, and my mother worked for Lafayette National Bank. She was the first female vice president they had appointed. I graduated from Lafayette Jefferson High School in 1967, where I played for a 10-0 football team.

I filled out an application, and Chico gave it to Mr. Rohrman, who came out and interviewed me. I also had walked in with John Davis, who worked at the factory with me. We were tired of working and getting laid off. We also had worked swing shifts, which were 4-12, 12-8 or 8-4.

Mr. Rohrman gave each of us an opportunity, so at that time, there was a total of six of us. I started on Feb. 10, 1974 and sold eighteen cars from the 10th through Feb. 28.

Then in the middle of March, the factory called and said my job had opened and would I like to come back. I had gotten my check from the previous month from Mr. Rohrman and told the factory I did not want to go back.

I did that until 1981 when I became the Honda manager. In 1977, we had taken on Honda. Also in 1981, we bought Lincoln Mercury and then got Subaru. As things were starting to grow, I took advantage of Mr. Rohrman needing help. I didn't wait for him to ask me to do things. I just did them.

The first month I was at the Toyota store, we sold one hundred cars. You would have thought we hit the lottery. It was a great feeling. We had a gentleman by the name of Bob Brown who was our finance manager and was ornery as could be.

That also was back in the day when people smoked indoors. Mr. Rohrman smoked, but I never was a smoker. Every morning, we would go over the used car sheet in his office and list our trade ins and remove the ones we had sold. Guys would be in there smoking. As time went by, the smoking kind of went to the wayside.

It was at that time Bob married Linda, who is one of the nicest people I have ever met. Bob and I don't talk about it much, because we both have been married a couple of times, but leaving Linda is one of the few mistakes he has made. The difference between Bob and I is that my divorces never cost me as much as his cost him.

Because I watched him go through it, it was not what Linda wanted it to be, and it wasn't what he wanted it to be. She did everything humanly possible to avoid having that happen. But when he gets in his head to do something, he is going to do it whether it is right or wrong.

He started working the Schaumburg Honda deal in 1982. Jerry Resnick, who owned Schaumburg Toyota, told Bob he should get the Honda store.

He got the franchise for free, but with it comes the building and everything else that comes with that. That one turned out to be the store that essentially printed money and always has.

I made a mistake at that time in that I hadn't trained anyone to be the general manager at either Honda or Toyota in Lafayette. JR Rohrman was running the Lincoln Mercury store. So, I couldn't take a position at Schaumburg Honda when we opened.

During the time Schaumburg Honda was being built, there was a lot of stress on Mr. Rohrman, because it was our first venture outside Lafayette. It was a huge investment. At that time, we would get paid a flat dollar amount for each car sold - $50 for a Toyota and $75 for a Corona. There was no commission structure at that time. When we got Honda, it was $50 for a Civic and $75 for an Accord. We didn't discount, so everything else went to Mr. Rohrman.

Then, there was a meeting, and the guys wanted to be paid percentage commission. At that meeting, he told all of us that we could leave. This was upstairs where the old Toyota store was in Lafayette. I remember him saying I will get somebody else to do this. He was about to blow a gasket. He knew it was time to change. He just didn't want to let it happen. He thought about it for two weeks and realized he had good guys. He put us on a 20 percent commission.

I liked the car business as long as I was selling. There was one period when I went four weeks without selling a car. Over my first year, I averaged eighteen cars a month, but in that one period, maybe I was pressing too hard. I thought about getting out of the business, but I just got off the couch and got back in there. That Saturday, I sold five cars and was right back in the race.

It is more than just selling an automobile. It is a relationship. Mr. Rohrman has said for years that you have to love the customer. When you get that customer's trust and they believe in you, they always are going to call you for the next car or just for general advice.

It really was a natural thing for me, although until I started selling cars, I never had sold anything in my life.

Finally, I was able to move to Schaumburg Honda as the general manager, which basically is what I was doing in Lafayette. He finally told me that I had to get up there, because we weren't selling the cars like he wanted. And we weren't selling used cars. They had him believing they could sell only 20 used cars a month. That just didn't sound right.

I got up there in November after Schaumburg Honda opened in May, and we kind of never looked back. He had made a promise to me that if I would go to Schaumburg and make things work, if an opportunity would come along, he would help me get a dealership. That is all I needed to hear.

That opportunity came along in Fort Wayne. When the time came for him to write the check for his 49 percent, he gave me the check and said, "Good luck." We opened Fort Wayne Acura in 1988. Because we had a great relationship with Toyota, we went after the Toyota point in Fort Wayne and got it.

I wanted part of Toyota, and he said he would give me 25 percent of Toyota if I would give him 26 percent of Acura back. It seemed like the right thing to do at the time. But it wasn't an automatic, because Fort Wayne is an extremely rough market. It is very GM.

But unfortunately, being partners with Mr. Rohrman is like being the highest paid employee. Things were a little tough with Acura, and things weren't going the way I would hope for it to. It really wasn't worth it - mentally as much as financially - so I left and went to Florida for a time.

I went to Naples and worked for a Toyota store. I was there two years, and then I came back when Mr. Rohrman kept calling me.

In 1993, he called, and I agreed to come to Chicago and be his director of operations. When the day came for me to come up from Florida, he said he had the Indianapolis Honda store and had gone through thirteen general managers and was not making any money there. In fact, he said they really weren't even paying the rent.

The more I thought about it, I told him I would go to Indy Honda. I loved Indy, plus it was close to my family in Lafayette. In 1993, I went there in November, and by January, we were making money.

I briefly went back to Florida, but after six months in 1999, I came back to Mr. Rohrman as the Oakbrook Toyota general manager. It was a mess at the time I got there. There was a bad GM, and they weren't making any money. I spent a lot of time and energy getting it going.

It took off and it just rocked. In 2002, I told Mr. Rohrman that if an opportunity ever came to go back to Schaumburg Honda, I would.

In 2003, the general manager at Schaumburg Honda passed away. He had liver cancer. Brad Mugg came to Schaumburg from Lafayette as the general manager in 2003. In 2005, Brad got a deal with the largest Honda store in the country, one based in California, and he moved.

Bob asked if I still wanted to go to Schaumburg Honda, and he said he would think about it. Two weeks went by, and he came and picked me up, and I went to Schaumburg Honda in 2005.

I was the general manager from 2005 until 2011, when Bob's grandson, Ryan, took over after college.

In 2011, I became director of operations for all fifteen Chicago area stores.

He obviously has been my mentor, and you obviously learn something from him every day. Being around him is interesting to see how he operates. He is one of the smartest men I ever have been around. He is brilliant and could have been whatever he wanted to be. He could have been a great attorney.

It is interesting to see some of the factory people come in and try to muscle him to do something, and it doesn't work out. You don't hit the wrong button with him.

Working with Bob is like a marriage in that it has its ups and downs, but I think over the years he has appreciated that I am very truthful with him. He asks me a question, and I give him the answer. I never have BSd him.

It has been a phenomenal career. I worked six days a week for forty years but only because I love it. If I take a vacation, I wish I hadn't. I really have enjoyed mentoring people, and that is the part I like. Mr. Rohrman appreciates that. I always have wanted guys to want my job. I want them to learn my job, because that makes my job easier.

I have always said, come get it.

61. Pam Bockwinkel

Comptroller for the Rohrman Auto Group in Chicago

I had the pleasure of working for Bob as the comptroller from 1998 until I retired in 2013, but I began working for him in 1992 as the office manager at the Saturn Store in Waukegan, IL with Bob's son, Randy.

I interviewed with Randy and my predecessor, Kathy Roubas, who worked for Bob for 13 years. Unfortunately, Kathy passed away. From 1992 until 1998, I worked with Randy. Then in 1998, I became comptroller for eight stores in the greater Chicagoland area.

I grew with Bob from eight stores to fifteen, back to thirteen and then back to fifteen. There were lots of negotiations going on. I learned an awful lot from Bob.

I talked to Bob many times on the phone before I met him and actually had more interaction with Randy than with Bob during the first few years. My first real interaction with Bob was when Kathy was retiring. I got a call from Bob, who asked if I could come to the Lexus store and meet him.

I drove to Lexus, I met Bob face to face and we talked about the job. He offered me a salary, and I said that I needed to think about it. I knew the offer was about half of what Kathy Roubas was making. About three weeks later, I got a call from Bob, and he said, "Wink, are you going to take this job or not?"

I said absolutely not. He asked why I wouldn't take the job, and I said, "Because you won't pay me." So, he asked me to come back to Lexus for a second meeting. We negotiated. We discussed maybe me doing four stores and that he would hire somebody else to do four stores.

We finally agreed that I would do it all, but he was going to pay me this amount. We settled on a price and then an amount if he added stores.

So, my first interaction with him was that I was not taking the job unless he was willing to pay me.

Before I met him, I thought he was a crazy man. An absolute crazy man. My interactions with him were comprised of monthly meetings, and it was all business. There really wasn't much personal one on one.

I saw him as a very demanding person. Sometimes, I thought he was fair with the office managers, and sometimes, I didn't think he was fair with the managers. What I did see from the man from the day I met him until the day I left was a man of his word and that his integrity is second to none.

One funny story is that once I was hiring the office managers, Bob came to me one day and said, "You know, Pam, you don't have to hire these women by the pound." I said, really. I told him, "I do that so that you don't try to take them home with you."

That is him, up one side and down the other. With all due respect to him, he is not real good with those women. He is just a man of the 1930s. He is 82, and he believes that women should be home, barefoot and pregnant. Even for me to be in the position I was in was unique. Everybody asked me how I got along with him.

I got along with him fine, but remember, I am from Kentucky and am not taking any BS from Bob Rohrman or anybody else. Bob and I got along well. He would tell me to go to hell, and I would tell him to go to hell. He respects people that will challenge him.

We had a very good relationship. When I left, I wasn't on the greatest terms with him, but we remain friends and I have continued to help him through the summers. I still help him today if he needs anything.

I have done a lot of things for him and with him. We were kind of a team. I would negotiate a lot of the contracts and get them down as low as I could get them, and then I always knew Bob would do better, come hell or high water. He always closed the deal.

The funniest story about a new store was maybe the second one after I came in. He was buying a store in Libertyville, and I usually didn't know exactly what was going on until the morning of the transaction.

I would know, because he would call and say, "Hey, Pam, I need a million dollars today."

He would tell me to meet him at the destination at 1 p.m. and that he was going to buy a store.

I would get on the phone, get money and get everything set. I went to the bank, got the money and met him in Libertyville. We are sitting in the dealership, and I have my computer. I can see a gentleman meeting with Bob. I can't see Bob. I can see only the back of Bob's chair. They are talking, and all of a sudden, I hear pieces of paper - the contract - being ripped apart. The man with whom Bob is meeting, well, his eyes are getting bigger and bigger and bigger. With every rip, the eyes were getting bigger.

All of a sudden, Bob stands up, walks out the door and says, "Come on, babe, we are leaving. We are not buying this store." And away we go. It took about 15 minutes, and we were out the door. They wanted Bob to take on a liability for some warranty, and he wasn't going to do it.

Bob absolutely got up and left this little man with eyes as big as half dollars. The man was bewildered as Bob and his entourage walked out the door. That absolutely is Bob.

They were not going to intimidate him. It is Bob's way or the highway. He has done it long enough and is financially sound enough that he doesn't have to do it any other way.

It would be impossible now for anyone to put together what Bob has, because today, the manufacturers want everybody to have millions of dollars available to them and want them to build $30 million or $40 million facilities. People can't do that today. Bob is very lucky that when he did it, manufacturers still let you sell from a small building on a gravel lot.

Bob got Toyota right off the bat. He got Dodge and gave it back to them. He got Honda because he was doing so well with Toyota. Then he got Schaumburg Honda, which at the time, was in the middle of nowhere. He has turned that into a gold mine. Today, it is one of the most successful Honda stores in the country.

That was in 1985, and then he got Lexus and Acura and the Nissan store. In 1992, it really started rolling. He has been wise and is especially street wise.

Yet when Bob would call me at 11 at night to discuss something business related, he would be home fixing a grilled cheese sandwich and a can of Campbell's Tomato Soup, which he loves. He is extremely frugal with the dollar, but he can be very generous.

I am very fortunate to have known Bob.

62. Craig Gipson

Director of Operations, Bob Rohrman Auto Group

I met Bob in 1979 while I was employed at The Sportsman sporting goods store in downtown Lafayette.

I came in to purchase an automobile - a Honda Civic - and began talking to a couple of Bob's employees in the finance office. I began talking to Chico Jensen, who was doing the financing at that time.

Chico explained the business, because I had questions about it. I wanted to see if it would be something that I would be interested in. At that time, I was 28.

I enjoyed automobiles. In high school, I actually had a Corvette. My father also enjoyed automobiles.

I went through the process of buying the Honda Civic, and Chico asked me if I would be interested in coming here and working. I told him I would be interested.

When I started, I worked for Bob's Toyota/Honda/AMC Jeep together on the Sagamore Parkway. I started selling Toyotas and Hondas and AMC and jeeps.

Obviously, Bob has been so successful because it is his life. It is what puts a smile on his face every day. He comes in, and he works it. This is what he loves doing. He has had some vision, and how he has it, I don't know.

I come from a hard-working family, too. My father worked two jobs, but this man, it is not stressful to him. It is fun for him. To a lot of us, sometimes it is a grind. But with him, it is a life. I have been blessed to be around him this long and see what he has been able to do.

To be a part of that and to help him a little bit from a business standpoint has been the best business relationship I could have asked for. He has been more than fair to me. To watch this thing proceed the way it has has been amazing.

For him to take the business to the level he has is surprising. It has been fun.

This is a people business, there is no question about that. It is kind of like retail is everywhere, but not only must you like the customers, you must like your employees as well. It is the people. Period.

It doesn't matter if it is a farmer, a doctor or a lawyer. In this part of the business, everybody contributes. Bob looks at everything. I have learned a lot along with him.

His story is almost like it is not reality. It is such a dream. He started from nothing. Just to be alive is something else. To have the mind and the vision and the energy, which he still has, is amazing. I am so happy about that.

Still working like he does carries over to his employees. We wonder how he does it. I hear from customers and employees, "Why does he still do this?" They don't understand why he still does this. It is because of the drive that he has and the love that he has for this business.

They don't understand why a person with the money that he has would want to keep working at his age. For he and I, it's not working. I tell people that I am going to my office, not going to work. And it really is not work to him.

If he tells you he is going to work until he is going to be 112, he really means that he is going to be in this business until he is 112.

If he stopped, he would be bored out of his mind.

When I first started, we had these little books in which everybody kept track of sales. Everything was written down. He wanted us to keep track of our people, as well as the numbers that we were selling.

Back when I started, not only did he own the place, he was the general manager, CEO and treasurer. He did it all. That is who we reported to. Writing things down and keeping track on a daily basis and knowing all the programs comes from him having an amazing mind.

He has a gift. It's a big corporation, and he runs it by himself. He keeps it fun, and he keeps it rolling. I hope it keeps going forever.

63. *Nate Barrett*

President, Twin City Dodge-Chrysler-Jeep-Ram

The first thing that helps me identify with Mr. Rohrman is that my grandfather, Don Trout, who started our dealership and was my mentor, came from a similar background as Mr. Rohrman.

Each came from really humble circumstances, both economically challenged. From my grandfather to Mr. Rohrman - in the same town - to have earned their opportunity the hard way, has made me always admire him, and it was something my grandfather admired about Mr. Rohrman.

My grandfather knew what that meant and what Mr. Rohrman had to do to get to that point. It was all the hours and the commitment and the willingness to do things that involved making the extra phone call. At times, they had to make sacrifices to do that and to build a business from the ground up.

Everyone who has built a business from the ground up knows what that is about. Instantly, as a child, I heard the grandfather I admired talking about his relationship with Mr. Rohrman. Hearing those stories, I gained admiration for Mr. Rohrman.

That was reinforced over the years as I learned more about Mr. Rohrman and heard more stories about how hard he works. Now at a point when he doesn't have to work as hard, he still chooses to at age 82 because of his love of the business and because of the people he can help as a result of that work.

There is much about that to be admired and to give people who have a dream hope that it still can be accomplished.

His fun commercials are part of the persona. No child grows up in the Lafayette community not knowing who he is. Everyone knows who Bob Rohrman is. That now is for several generations. He would appreciate that my children get a kick out of his commercials. They know his slogan as well as anything we are saying at our dealership.

He looks like he is having fun with the commercials, and that makes people identify with it. You can sense that no one is having more fun doing them than he is. That, coupled with the jingles that he has had over the years, particularly "Old Bob Rohrman is a good friend of mine, he traded my way."

Everyone from age 75 down to 35 knows that jingle. It has become iconic in Lafayette.

One thing we try to be with our commercials is authentic. Mr. Rohrman always has been authentic, particularly in his radio ads, when he is able to talk a little more. In television, an ad is 30 seconds. In radio, it usually is a 60-second spot. He can banter more, and you see his personality come out more.

The man you hear on those radio ads is what he is like in person. So, he is authentic. When people sense that you are authentic, it all works. You can smell a phony, and they know that what you are trying to be on television and radio is not who you really are.

He always is authentic. I have a now deceased uncle who lived in Virginia but who is a Lafayette Jeff grad and knew Mr. Rohrman in high school, and he told us that what he is like in television and in business is what he was like in high school.

The personality that we see now was there when Mr. Rohrman was at Jeff High School in the early 1950s.

If you look at business books and biographies, nearly every successful business person on any large scale has been willing to take risks. Mr. Rohrman was willing to take risks at a time when others wanted nothing to do with Toyota or Honda.

Like everything else in life, whether that is sports, politics or business, it also is timing. He had the right product at the right time with the right promotion to make it all work together. It is hard for people now to look and say, "Oh, lucky him."

There always is that piece that takes more than luck. It is a combination of factors coming together. It is a vision, and he had a vision. You talk to anyone who knows him, and no one saw a deviation from that vision. He knew what he wanted to do, and he has not turned away from it.

What also cannot be discounted in his story is that when he first acquired Toyota and Honda automobiles - those manufactured by the Japanese - some older citizens still were angry about what happened with World War II. That was a piece of the risk of taking on those lines at that time, especially among older potential purchasers. No question about it.

He continued that pattern with some of the Korean lines with KIA. He took some brands that some domestic dealers at that time would have passed on. He was willing to make that work. Now, car dealers would love to have those brands.

The quality is there, and it has been proven over time. As World War II and Korean War generation adults move more from the scene, their grandchildren think more about a quality car, a quality warranty and what is my car payment.

In our community, which has such a large international population at Purdue, people realize that the generation that is here now had nothing to do with those wars. It is like the children who grew up here had nothing to do with those conflicts.

Napoleon Hill, who did the "Think and Grow Rich" books years ago, wrote about how some people just may be put on this earth to show the rest of us what is possible. I kind of think of Mr. Rohrman in that vain as a reminder of what is possible among people and what they can achieve.

The best lesson I have learned from Mr. Rohrman was one he shared with me during a charity luncheon. I was asking him about deals that maybe did not go the way he wanted or opportunities that he did not get.

He stopped me very quickly and said "Don't look back. Just keep going." For me, that was a great lesson.

Another element in which Mr. Rohrman excels is selling the event of the car dealership very well. He sells the fact that every day is a big deal in a car dealership. Every day is a great sale. Those who would kid about Mr. Rohrman would say, "Every sale or every theme he ever has had is the greatest of all time."

But, what is the alternative to that? Low enthusiasm? Let's take this month off? When you set up advertising, you always want to give a customer a reason why now is the right time to purchase a car. He never has deviated from that. It always has been full steam ahead.

Having watched my grandfather age, it is fun for them and just part of life to want to leave something to those who come after you in what you put into the hearts of other people and also into their minds. That is a piece of your legacy.

As long as someone is imparting the principles you taught, there is a piece of you that is living on well beyond your years. He now is entering that phase where his grandson, Trey, and the rest of the family can soak in his vast wealth of knowledge to set them up for success.

Something about him that is noticeable to me when I see him at a charity function or at a sporting event, most of the time he is still in a coat and tie. How many in this day and age dress in a coat and tie every day? Particularly those who do not have to. Yet, he chooses to carry himself that way, which is very impressive to me. It sets the tone for everything else that follows.

When I see him walk into a room, heads turn. He is a tall man in an elegant suit and tie, and people take notice. His presence in a room changes a room. I have seen that happen.

His passion is infectious, and he asks the critical questions. He wants to know who he is talking to today and what does he have out today? Those are questions that have to be asked in any business. He is focused on the bottom line. He is working even if he is at a ball game or at a restaurant.

I watch him at the Purdue games, and he will eat popcorn, just like any other fan in the stands. He sits in the bleachers and enjoys the games, yet you can't help but wonder what he is thinking about. What opportunities is he looking at for the future?

He really likes people, and the people make it fun for him. He likes the comradery. But in one of his sales meetings, from what I understand, your information better be accurate and you better be ready to explain what you are doing in your store. Yet at the same time, he knows how to laugh at himself. That is very important and very humanizing.

One story I want to share is that one of my most prized possessions is a WGN Chicago Cubs bat and ball set that he gave to my grandfather to give to me when I was 4. I still have that. It was so thoughtful of him to come to an automotive competitor and give that to that competitor's grandson. It shows the thoughtfulness that no one ever would know about.

It always has meant a lot to me to have that.

The iconic image about Bob includes the fact every child knows of Santa Bob and Count Bobulla, but his work is his hobby. When you speak of an individual whose work is his hobby, it is a difficult combination to beat.

Now as he brings his grandchildren into the business, it has to be one of the most satisfying parts of his career.

It would be difficult to ever create what Bob has amassed, simply because of the sheer capital for one of these places. It has grown significantly in the past 20 years. New vehicles are so expensive that it is a very capital intensive business.

His rags to riches story is still there in this country, but how he did it in this business, it was the right man at the right moment with the right vision and a belief in himself. He has a unique place in the history of Indiana business.

64. *Dave Piercefield*

Dealer Manager at Bob Rohrman's Indy Honda

I am from Martinsville, IN, and have been working for Mr. Rohrman for almost 22 years as of 2015.

I was selling pharmaceutical supplies for Bunzl for three years in the early 1990s and was on the road all the time, driving 40,000 miles a year. I just got burned out on doing that. One day, I was driving south on U.S. 31 and saw the Honda dealership.

I thought that I should apply for a job there. I pulled in, applied and was interviewed on the spot by John Barrett. I then was interviewed by the new car manager at the time. Five minutes later, they offered me a job.

It literally was welcome to the car business. When they offered me a job on the spot, I said sure. This was December of 1993. I gave my company two weeks' notice and started Jan. 4 of 1994.

I was a salesman, and John Barrett took me under his wing. He saw something in me. Six months later, I was moved up to sales manager. From having never sold a car before, I was the sales manager in six months. I was just trying to learn and soak it all in.

Two years later, I was the new car manager. That is when I really was introduced to Bob Rohrman. Mr. Rohrman came to Indy Honda, and I met him. I sat in on a couple meetings with him.

My first true interaction with him was while we were trying to solve a situation that was going on at the dealership at the time. I get a phone call from Mr. Rohrman, who says to pick him up at the Greenwood Airport.

I drove to the Greenwood Airport and picked him up. As we are driving back to the dealership in my demo car, he says, "Whose demo is this? You've got a really nice demo." He had his meetings, and he had his pilot with him. He told me to let the pilot take my car and go get something to eat.

I had seen his commercials, but until I got into the management side of the business, I did not know what a stern dealer he was, although I had heard stories. He required a lot, and it was not beyond him to fire an entire management staff all in one fell swoop.

That kind of puts that fear into you. My initial thoughts of him were, "Oh, gosh." But once he learns that you are loyal and that you work hard, a lot of that goes away. I always felt my success with him was that he knows I am loyal to him and will bust my butt to do everything I can for him and for his dealership.

You have to earn his trust. He used to call daily and want to know our daily sales count. It might be the 23rd of the month, and he would tell me to go back to the 10th of the month and want to know the daily sales from the 10th through the 23rd. You might say, "Today, we sold four new and two used."

He might say, "Oh, that day wasn't good." Or, he might say, "That was a good day." You always hope you have to go through only a few days. At some point, he would tell me I wasn't doing my job and that we were not selling enough cars.

You always wanted to be sure that when he called, you had had a good day before that day. That always motivates guys. The thing about Mr. Rohrman is that he motivates without ever being around the dealership. There is a motivational factor just from working for him.

I figured out a long time ago that I have to motivate myself every single day, because if not, he is going to come down and motivate me. If I stay motivated, I know I am doing the right thing. Internally, I am triggered by his motivation. I want to make him happy and proud, because I want him to say good things about me.

When I took over running the dealership in April of 2002, Mr. Rohrman and I sat at a desk in my office and went over a pay plan. Then, he added a bonus plan for the end of the year. He told me that if I met certain goals between April and December, I would receive a specific bonus.

And he told me what Indy Honda should be making every month.

The first month, I far exceeded what the store was supposed to do. He was pretty happy with that. Leading into that first month, he tested me more than I ever wanted to be tested. I got so many calls from him, but it was Mr. Rohrman wanting to make sure he had made the right decision by putting me in the general manager's spot.

He wanted to make sure that I could handle the pressure of running the dealership, which basically is answering to him and running his dealership for him. He put me into so many awkward positions that first month that I convinced myself there was no way I could handle this, but I did. We had a great month.

At the end of the year, I drilled him for a huge bonus. I had just gotten paid on that bonus and was headed to a charity function with my wife when my office manager called me and told me not to cash that check. Mr. Rohrman thought the amount was incorrect.

I said the amount was not wrong and that it was my check. He double and triple checked that amount and finally approved it. I hit a mark that he never thought I would hit during the first eight months of running his Indy Honda store.

After that, my year-end bonus structure changed quite a bit, but that was OK. Working for him and being successful makes him successful. That makes me feel really good.

Now, I have gotten to know Mr. Rohrman really well and have several favorite stories.

I few years ago, I was sitting at our sales desk, and the Indiana Pacers were playing the Chicago Bulls in the NBA playoffs.

At 4 in the afternoon, Mr. Rohrman calls me. He instructs me to meet him at St. Elmo's restaurant in downtown Indianapolis at 5 p.m. He tells me were are going to have dinner with two gentlemen from Comcast Sports out of Chicago and then go to the game with them.

I was a bit nervous, because at that time, I had not been his GM for a long time. We go to St. Elmo's, and I had had St. Elmo's shrimp cocktail many times. Mr. Rohrman and I are seated on one side of the table, and the two men from Comcast Sports are sitting across from us.

I am drinking a beer, and when I took a bite of my shrimp cocktail, that horseradish in the shrimp cocktail sauce hit me, and I accidentally spit a mouthful of sauce and beer across the table onto one of the guys from Comcast Sports.

Mr. Rohrman slaps his own leg about ten times and is laughing as loud as you can imagine. It was hysterical laughter. At that second, I am thinking that I am about to be fired. But Mr. Rohrman continued to laugh and was slapping me on the back asking if I was OK.

I could not have been more embarrassed, but Mr. Rohrman treated it as if it was the funniest thing in the world. I loved him for that. That probably still is my most embarrassing moment, but he made the situation feel like it was a comedy. The guy from Comcast Sports was so cool about it because Mr. Rohrman was laughing so hard that he had to laugh with Mr. Rohrman.

He blew it off like it was the funniest thing in the world, and that is just him. He never would have looked at me and said I was fired or called me a dummy.

We went to the game, walked out together, shook hands and parted ways for the evening.

Another good story centers on a time when we had advertising meetings set up, and he arrived an hour late. He comes in, and we had ad reps lined up waiting on us. He looks at me and asks if I am hungry.

I reminded him that we had people waiting on us, but he insisted we go down the street to the China Buffet and eat. We had lunch for an hour, and everybody was waiting on us. But we were on his time. We were on "Rohr Time."

I had a lot of fun that day because it was just he and I in a casual environment. During lunch, people would say hello to him, and he was very courteous and polite. I sneaked away and paid the bill. When I got back to the table, he said we had to pay the bill, but I told him it was taken care of. He didn't want me to pay, but I told him that now I can tell everyone I have bought a multi-millionaire lunch. He started laughing. Seven hours later, we had our meetings done.

Probably the most interesting story of mine with him and learned from him centers on a meeting we had with some advertising people who were trying to raise our rates on us without us knowing. It was a renewal meeting.

There was a young, attractive female and her boss, and the attractive woman ponied up to Mr. Rohrman and handed him a couple of gifts. He took all of that in stride. They were in the meeting for about five minutes, and he flips right to the back page of their proposal. He didn't want to see the first eight pages. He just wanted to get directly to the bottom line.

They weren't past Page 1, and he looked at them and told them to get out of the office. The ad people kind of blew it off, but he insisted that they leave and told them that he was not going to do business with them.

He told them that they were not coming into Indy Honda and raising his rates. Finally, he ordered them out of the office. I looked at him and knew that he was serious. The female still did not want to leave, but he told her that if she did not leave the office, he would put her out of this office.

That was the first time I ever saw Mr. Rohrman really impose his power on somebody. He was so mad that they were attempting to undercut him and raise his rates without him knowing. You don't think a guy like that is going to notice?

As soon as they were gone, it was as if the switch was flipped, and he was right back to being the fun loving guy that we all know and love. He said, "Piercy, who is up next?"

I learned that day that you do not take stuff from people. You have to stand up for yourself, and if you have to kick someone out, you kick them out and move on.

Yet when he cares about someone - and he cares greatly about people - he is the best. I have a parts manager who has been at Indy Honda since the store opened in 1990, and Mr. Rohrman always speaks so fondly of parts manager Tim Woodall.

Any time we are in meetings and parts comes up, he always mentions Tim and Tim's dedication to the dealership. That says a lot for a man who has as many employees as Mr. Rohrman, because it is easy to forget people. It is easy just to deal with your GMs. He takes it a step further.

I have a salesman - Bob Hagy - who was our salesman of the year three years in a row, and at a Christmas party, I made a point to introduce him to Mr. Rohrman, who made the time to stand there and talk to him for ten minutes, thanking him for what he does. You often don't get that.

Mr. Rohrman loves to engage with people who have put blood, sweat and tears into it and made Mr. Rohrman what he is.

Let's face it. Without all 1,500 of his employees, Mr. Rohrman still would be successful, but not at the level he is now.

It absolutely is proof that the American dream can happen. In our used car building, we have six photos of back when he had his gravel lot in Lafayette with his used cars. You look at those pictures from 50 years ago, and then you look at the magnitude of what he has now.

Just look at the Lexus building in Arlington Heights, IL, and the Toyota building in Lafayette, and it is just unbelievable.

Some people say he was lucky. He wasn't lucky. This man is smart and knew what he was doing when he started. He is smart to this day. People ask how old he is, and I tell them that in 2015, he celebrated his 82nd birthday.

People ask why he doesn't stop. But he is not going to stop. This is what he knows and loves.

His formula of liking people and being a good listener works. We won a President's Award three years in a row, and I think we are the only Honda store to win the President's Award.

The year I am most proud of is the year we finished in the top one percent of all Honda stores in the country, and that is for customer satisfaction scores and overall sales. I got even more involved at that point, because I wanted that award so badly.

I learned that you need to greet a lot of customers and say hi to customers in the middle of negotiations. I thank them for their business. Being out there all the time is still something Mr. Rohrman does today.

He doesn't have to stop and talk to customers, but he still does it. That proves to me that I always need to continue to do that. You have to continue to love people, which he does. We have more than twenty customers who have bought at least fifteen cars from us at Indy Honda.

That is all about knowing and loving people.

What I have been able to have by working for more than 21 years for Bob Rohrman and what I have been able to give and provide for my family, it is something I never would have imagined when I started, thinking I was just going to do this for a short time as a quick fix.

Cars and Mr. Rohrman got in my blood. I would not change anything.

65. *Larry Kruse*

General Manager of Fort Wayne Lexus, Toyota and KIA

I grew up in an area just outside Fort Wayne called Leo, graduated from high school there and went to IPFW, where I studied business and marketing.

I graduated from college during the Reagan era when there was kind of a recession in the early 1980s. My dad had polio as a kid and raised a family of five, always using crutches with braces on his legs. I wanted to stick around the Fort Wayne area to be there for my parents.

I took a job with a pest and weed Control Company and did sales for them for about two years.

I had a friend, Tom Shears, who was in the car business and actually now is my Lexus sales manager. At the time, Tom was working for Whitley County Motors, which was a GM store just outside Fort Wayne near Columbia City. Tom was the used car manager there, and he and I were golfing buddies. He told me I should get into the car business and give it a shot.

He told me he thought I could make good money. So, I ended up taking a job for a local Ford dealer, whose name is Bob Jackson. He had a Ford and Mercedes store in New Haven, IN. In February of 1984, I went to work there selling cars. I worked for Bob Jackson at that location until he opened his other location on Coliseum Blvd in October of 1984.

I sold cars for a few more months and did pretty well. The first six months, I averaged selling about twelve a month, and then, I kind of took off and found the technique, really getting it down pat. He was using a system called Automotive Profit Builders, and I really just followed their training method. During the next six months, I averaged twenty units a month.

In January of 1985, they put me into management. I went in initially as a closing manager and then worked in the finance office for a period of time, then as a new car manager and as a used car manager. I then moved back into the role of finance director.

Bob Jackson's philosophy was that his managers needed to learn every position within the sales side. A guy might prefer one position to another, but he was cross trained. That proved to be a really good learning ground for me.

In late 1988, he decided to bring in one of his Ford buddies from the outside, because he really wanted to try to gear things up. We were doing pretty well, but he wanted to take things to the next level. The guy he brought in from the outside believed in management by intimidation and was not real customer oriented. His belief was to squeeze every dollar you could out of the customer.

My beliefs are different than that. I just didn't want to operate that way. I quit working for him on March 31, 1989 and got married the next day. I had some money saved and decided to take some time off and then find another opportunity, whether it was in the car business or not.

I just didn't want to work in that kind of environment any longer. I looked at different opportunities, mainly in the car business, and looked at some opportunities in St. Louis. I finally accepted a position with a Ford Dealership in Chicago for a store called Lynch Ford as a finance manager.

When I took the job, I did not realize the dealership was in a community comprised primarily of Polish people, who when it comes to buying cars are pretty much cash only. As a finance manager, I really couldn't communicate very well with them because they all wanted to pay cash for their cars. After a couple of days, I decided that situation was not for me. I picked up my stuff and went back to Fort Wayne.

At that point, I heard a guy named Bob Rohrman was going to open a Toyota store in Fort Wayne. I heard this man was doing well in Lafayette and had Schaumburg Honda. He was expanding into Fort Wayne and had the Acura store in Fort Wayne. I decided that was the kind of guy I wanted to go to work for and is going to have some opportunities to grow with the company.

I went in and interviewed with John Barrett at the Acura store on Lima Road on the north end of town. Now, it is on Illinois Road on the southwest side of Fort Wayne. I wanted to come in as a finance manager, but John had that position filled. I was kind of persistent with John and followed up with a cover letter and a couple of phone calls. He didn't get back to me right away, but I was persistent.

Finally, he said he wanted me to come to work for him as the used car manager. He said there wouldn't be any used cars right away at the new Toyota store, but you can get a cut from the new cars too and that I would be working with a guy named George Lopez. George was a new car manager at the time. John was a partner with Mr. Rohrman and was overseeing the Toyota store and the Acura store.

I began to work at the Toyota store in October of 1989. I really didn't know Bob at the time and didn't meet Bob right away. He would come in for our monthly manager meetings, so I got to know him through that.

He would come in and discuss the goals and discuss the results from the previous month. I always wanted to make sure that I knew my numbers and that I knew my inventory. With used cars, you pay particular attention to your inventory, because it depreciates. When Bob came to those meetings, my numbers were pretty good.

He knew that when he asked me a question, I always knew the answer. I tried to anticipate the questions he was going to ask. If I didn't know the answer, I would say I didn't know but that I would find out right away.

I was always straightforward with him. In January of 1991, John left Fort Wayne to accept a position in Florida, so Mr. Rohrman plugged me in as general manager. I didn't know anything about being a general manager other than John had told me a couple of times that he was grooming me to be a general manager.

I always paid close attention to what John said. I had studied business and marketing and always made a point to read motivational books and anything I could about business. When

I started as general manager, there certainly was a learning curve, but I knew the Fort Wayne market and had a pretty good understanding of Fort Wayne.

I also always have been a strong used car operator, knowing that if you run a strong used car department, it will help your new car department. It also will help you on the finance side and on the service side. It helps you all the way around.

My foundation was a good understanding of the used car market and I paid a lot of attention to it. I paid close attention to the value of vehicles and the reconditioning aspect that you do to used cars to make them sellable. I wanted to offer a better pre owned vehicle to what the other guy could do. Customers certainly have a lot of choices when they get out to look at a vehicle.

I wanted to run a clean business and have clean used vehicles, too. Some guys will trade for a car and maybe clean it up a little bit and do an oil change and not much else.

My belief in pre owned vehicles is to make them as close to new as you can. You have to anticipate what you are going to spend for them before you trade for it. Then, you have to follow through with that. You have to be sure you service it completely and be sure that everything interiorly and exteriorally are standing tall. You do whatever body work it needs along with the detailing. You go a step further than everybody else goes. If your cars look better, people will be willing to pay more because it is a better product.

I know a used car operation is how Bob got started. I think I had a pretty good understanding of that. I also think John Barrett sensed that, even though we were limited in those early years by the inventory we could carry.

We did well with what we had, and there were times I took some cars from the Acura store and got those cars sold. If you don't move your used cars, they depreciate every month.

That was kind of the start of the whole thing, and then we picked up Lexus in the early 1990s. What a great franchise that has turned out to be. It is the luxury car division of Toyota. I also talked Mr. Rohrman into buying a couple of lots along Illinois Road in order to expand the used car division. Initially, he put a Nissan store there, and I had a used car lot in between the two.

Then, he decided to move the KIA point from the north side of Fort Wayne to the southwest side. We really have done well with KIA over the past 10 years. We have had some incredible months with KIA, which redesigned their product and had a very attractive price point. We aggressively promoted that vehicle and did really well. It tied in well with our used car operation, too.

The last 10 years, I not only am the general manager but also the used car manager. I do all of the buying and selling on the wholesale side. I do most of the appraising on the used cars and control the reconditioning. We work that end of it really hard and sell between 150 and 200 used cars a month. In May of 2015, we sold 190 used cars, and the next month, we sold 175.

There have been a couple of times over the years when Mr. Rohrman has asked me to step in when he has had to make a change in general managers. He had some struggles getting the Acura store to work in Fort Wayne. Recently, he asked if I wanted to be involved in Acura again, but I told him I am really happy doing what I am doing. It is tough for me to be a general manager and do more than what I do now without losing attention to something. I am involved with the manufacturers, advertisers and then buying about one hundred used cars a month.

It is a lot of work, but I enjoy it, and I have enjoyed working for Mr. Rohrman over the years. He is the kind of guy who just gives you the ball and lets you run with it as long as you can do the job. He gives you a lot of leeway. That has been great. He has given me a lot of latitude to be successful. I report to him about once a week with my numbers.

He doesn't come to Fort Wayne too often. The word used to be that if he was coming to Fort Wayne, he might be coming to fire someone.

Fort Wayne is kind of a different market, because it is a strong GM town. The domestics always have been real strong. But I never have limited myself on the used car side. We sell more than Toyota, Lexus and KIA.

Mr. Rohrman is always positive, and failure is not an option for him. He has very high expectations. I also have been a person who always has had higher expectations. I have done well, but I always feel like I can do better. I think Mr. Rohrman feels that way. As well as he has done, he still thinks he can do better. He believes we still can increase our numbers and provide more opportunities for people.

Knowing Mr. Rohrman, I know he enjoys providing opportunities for people to grow their careers and take care of their families. I look at things the same way. One of the things that drives me is going in and leading my people and seeing them do well. If they do well, I will do well. If you have good people, you will do well.

Mr. Rohrman has told me that it is about getting good people and then developing those people. He says you never can provide enough training. As a general manager, you really are a teacher. You have to hold your people accountable, which Mr. Rohrman does. We all set goals at the beginning of the month, and while we don't always get there, we get close.

If you have accountability procedures within the dealership, you are going to do much better. When general managers don't put a structure in place, they usually end up floundering. He always is energetic and positive. He can scold me, but five minutes later, it all is behind us and it comes out in a positive way.

He is firm but never has a bad attitude. He just wants to get the most out of his people.

I have enjoyed attending some dealer meetings with him, and he has been nice enough to have me attend some sporting events with him. He has had my son and I join him for a couple of Purdue football games and a basketball game. A couple of years ago, he gave my son and I his Ross-Ade Stadium suite tickets for a Purdue-Notre Dame game. That was special. He took the regular seats in the stands and let us have the suite tickets.

In the early years with Lexus, there would be a spring meeting for the dealers in Florida, and we would have a couple of days of golf. It was nice to unwind and have fun. Once in Naples, we were paired together with a dealer from Evansville named Vern

Gash and Gene Kowalis, a Lexus dealer from Chicago and a good friend of Mr. Rohrman. Gene was like Rodney Dangerfield, and to see the two of them having fun going at it was fun. They would just rip on each other.

I didn't play very well that day, because I was having more fun watching them than I was playing golf. Mr. Rohrman likes to laugh and have fun, but he also is very driven while at the same time having a big heart and being very generous.

He has been a good leader to me and probably is why I never went out with anything on my own. I do enjoy working for him, and he always has been very fair with me.

66. Mark Battista

Director of Governmental Affairs for the
Rohrman Automotive Group

In 1984, I was having lunch at Copperfield's, right across the street from Schaumburg Honda, which was Bob's first store in Illinois. I was sitting with Jerry Resnick, who was a Toyota and Lexus dealer and a friend of Bob's for several years.

As we were eating lunch, this bag that Jerry had on the table began to shake and ring. Jerry told me that it was a new phone. He unzips the bag and answers the phone. It was Bob Rohrman. Jerry told Bob that he and I were sitting across the street watching his Honda store being built.

Jerry told Bob that he was sitting at lunch with a guy Bob needed to meet.

I was the secretary of state representative who would be giving Bob his license. Jerry also told Bob that I would be governor someday. Jerry told Bob he needed to talk to me and handed me the phone.

Bob said hello and said he needed a license. I told him I would get the information for him. Subsequently, I went back into my office, and about a week later, one of the sargeants walks into my office and tells me that there is a guy in Schaumburg selling cars without a license and that we needed to get down there and shut him down.

He told me the dealership was on the corner of Plum Grove and Golf. The guy told me that was my district. I told him that I know the guy - Bob - and that he is from Indiana. I said I would go see him.

I went to see Bob and told him that I had gotten a complaint at the office that he was selling cars without a license. Bob said that was not entirely true. I asked what he meant, and Bob told me the cars already were sold. Bob said he didn't have any more to sell at that time.

That is how I met Bob. I signed him up with his dealer license on the first day we met. From 1985 on, when he opened Schaumburg Honda, I was moving up the ranks, and Bob was buying more stores.

In the early 1990s, Bob's secretary was talking to my secretary, and I became the director with 1,650 employees reporting to me. Bob had about the same number of employees. Bob and I remained friends. We would participate in golf outings, go to dinner and attend sporting events.

In 1999, I retired as the director of licensing and enforcement for the state of Illinois and came to work for Bob. At that point, I had known Bob for 14 years.

As of 2015, I have been working for Bob for 16 years.

I think the reason, in part, that Bob and I get along so well is because my father was a businessman and also a politician in Illinois. He was just a few years older than Bob. They both were depression era babies and grew up in the same kind of atmosphere in which they had nothing.

They started with zero, and each built a business. They realized the values and the traditions of valuing a dollar. They came from very humble beginnings and knew responsibility. I understand that, and I understand Mr. Rohrman, who is a carbon copy of my dad, who died in June of 1985.

I understand Mr. Rohrman, while a lot of his employees do not. I know what is coming out of his mouth before he even says it.

I have been in thousands of meetings with him and have spent a lot of time with him during work and during afterhours. I have a clear understanding of how he thinks personally and business wise. He has taught me a lot, kind of where my dad left off.

I think the best asset I have is that I understand Bob Rohrman more than most people do. I grew up with him, and we think along the same lines. Our values are the same.

I think the thing that brought us the closest together was his divorce from Ronda. It was a very difficult time for him. I was with him every step of the way. I had done the investigation for about a year on that whole case. It broke his spirit for a short period of time.

But he never let it affect business. It did take time away from the business, but it did not take his character or drive. He didn't let anyone see how much it really bothered him. I could see that it was taking a toll on him. I did whatever I could to make that time in his life easier.

There were a lot of different things that I had to discuss with him that were not easy for him. It wasn't easy for me, because I kind of looked at him as a father. It really bothered me that I had to tell him certain things and show him certain things.

But he got through it.

One of the many great things about Mr. Rohrman is that he compensates people that work for him very high if they work extremely high. If you do not work hard, there is no room for you in this business, particularly in management. At the lower levels where they do not have personal contact with Mr. Rohrman at all or maybe once a month, he doesn't see them as much, and they can squeak by not doing long days.

A general manager has constant contact with Mr. Rohrman and is expected to work a lot of hours, but they are compensated for that. So, he is very demanding.

I have lots of stories about Mr. Rohrman, who is a guy who makes lemonade out of lemons. He is very positive and upbeat, even during frustrating times.

For example, the construction of the new Lexus store in Arlington Heights has taken a lot longer than Mr. Rohrman had thought, but the end result certainly paid off. It is the showpiece and the palace of the fruits he has worked so hard to achieve. I don't know that there ever will be a store he will build like this.

It probably is the most beautiful store, coast to coast. It is elegant. It will be remembered as the Coliseum in Rome.

I don't have a lot of hilarious stories, because my job is enforcement.

Nobody comes to me with jokes. They call me The Oncologist, because usually when I am in a store, it's never good news.

I am a very serious person, and I am the guy that has to let people go or arrest people and indict people.

We have done indictments when people who work for us have been less than truthful. We have prosecuted people who still are in jail.

Away from work, Bob and I have had lots of fun. He knows my family and my brothers, who run my family's business, which is funeral homes and cemeteries. There are only three of us left, my two brothers and I. I am an owner, but I am not involved in the daily business.

I am a people person, and I am not afraid of the enforcement end of this. I am not here to make friends. I am here to make sure I have Mr. Rohrman's back. That is my job. He knows that when I make a decision, it is based on what is good for the company.

With Bob, it is about the deal. It is not about how much the deal is or how big it is. I run deals past him that we have negotiated for five, six or eight million dollars. He would just sign off on it and have me read the contract.

But if I tell him I am going to an auction, and I am going to buy some used equipment for construction or for the stores, he will get all excited about it because it is an auction. He loves to get in the car and go buy some stuff.

We might run down to an equipment sale, and he would get out in the rain and walk through a muddy, 10 acre lot, looking at bulldozers, dump trucks and sky jacks. He would be in a suit and dress shoes. He would pick out equipment and bid on it at the auction.

He has a great time and loves that stuff. Here is a guy who would rather push an $8 million deal aside, and go buy a sky jack for $1,100 because he knows that new, it costs about $10,000. That is a deal for him.

He would also teach me how to buy stuff, such as chairs, at an auction. Two and three years later, he would ask me what we paid for the chairs for, say, the Toyota store. He would test me to see if I knew what we had paid. He would ask how many we bought and where did we put them.

Bob would do that until he knew that I knew where everything was. I would watch him test me, and then I finally realized what he was doing.

He has been amazingly successful in part because he has been willing to take a chance. This is a guy who jumped on the back of a motorcycle in Lafayette, IN, drove to Chicago and lost his clothes off the back of that cycle to wash dishes at the Midlothian Country Club.

Very similar to my dad, who jumped on a train with one of his buddies with a piece of luggage and went to California at 14 years old.

They each went to see what the world was all about. Then, when Bob went into the military, it was a turning point. He went from a boy to a man. When he came out of the service, his values had not changed, but his responsibilities changed.

He has a passion for people and is a people person. He also has a passion for discipline and work ethic. He always installs that in everyone. He always was an overachiever and never has settled for less.

Still today, he always is willing to learn, which is amazing. He reads and studies a lot and always has the TV on in the background. He watches sports, the stocks and always knows what is going on in current events.

What fascinates me is that he knows the president or CEO of a company in which he invests. He will read everything about that company before he invests. He sleeps very little and says the only guy who works more than him and sleeps less than him is Mark Battista. We are a lot alike in that respect.

He taught me that if you love your work, you will work more, and you will make more money.

His other claim to fame is that he is very, very humble. He may go to a restaurant and find it more interesting to sit at a table with a bunch of truck drivers and find out what is on their mind than sitting at the next table with a bunch of bank executives, who would be boring to him.

The truck driver is interesting to him because they are six pack, blue collar Joes who also are very humble and came from the beginnings he did.

I look at him as a boss, a mentor and a father figure. I get to spend a lot of time with him away from the office. Years after I was working for him, I found out that the very day he opened his first dealership - Feb. 3, 1963 - was the day I was born. That was almost chilling. But that is just Bob's life, because he is involved with so many things and so many people. He is just a legacy. I am so proud to be his friend.

And I must share one funny story in closing.

When I was the director, I put together a group of car dealers, which we called the Illinois Dealer Advisory Board for the governor and the secretary of state. Bob was on that board, and I staged a golf outing for the secretary of state, who later became governor.

There were 1,400 golfers playing five courses at one time. Bob flew into Midway Airport, a car picked him up and drove him to Cog Hill. He was running late, but I was holding his tee time. I could hear him laughing when he comes to me and says, "I am ready to go, but I have to run into the pro shop and get a pair of pants."

Just then, the governor and secretary of state walk up and want to meet Bob Rohrman. As Bob turns around, he had split his pants from the top of his belt to his groin, and his pants were wide open.

He turned around to the governor and said, "I am going to have to play golf in my underwear today."

I told Bob to come with me, and I took him to the pro shop and got him a pair of pants. He played golf, stayed for dinner and had a great time.

That's Bob.

67. Sheila Klinker

Indiana State Representative

I became aware of Bob Rohrman at Lafayette Jefferson High School basketball games, because my husband, Vic, played for Jeff in the 1956 state finals, and Bob was a Jeff fan and a Jeff grad.

As an educator, I always was fascinated by the story Bob has shared many times about how he wasn't making it to high school on time because he was working 3-11 at Brown Rubber and how an administrator at the high school insisted that Bob work 11 p.m. to 7 a.m. and then could come right to school. Then, he would still be awake.

Bob credited that Jeff administrator for being able to graduate from high school.

As time went on, I watched Bob with his cars and all of his ads, which I got such a kick out of. Those commercials are amazing. Having been a teacher and having fun in a classroom, I would sometimes sing, and Bob loved music. For a time, I sang with an orchestra in Lafayette, and Bob would watch us perform at The Elks or at the Lafayette Country Club.

Living in Lafayette after graduating from Purdue, I watched Bob's career grow. When I first began driving, I was a Dodge and Plymouth fan, but when the Subaru factory came to Lafayette, many of us in the Indiana State Legislature helped with that.

Bob and former Lafayette mayor James Riehle were an integral part of that. We all worked together. We gave Subaru some tax breaks in order to come here. I thought it was very exciting.

I bought the third car - a Legacy - manufactured off that Subaru assembly line in Lafayette. It was majestic blue. I loved that car and drove it and drove it and drove it.

After that car was showing some wear, I bought the car Bob was driving, which had a sun roof, and that was different for Subaru. It was a black Subaru Legacy.

My next car was a larger Legacy. Then the Outback came out, and I love the Outback. As a politician with all the things I have to carry, the Outback is very convenient.

I am sold on Subarus, and the people at Rohrman's are very good about making sure that you fill out the form about how you were treated in the customer experience. It is excellent, and I have told Bob that.

When I go in, they are very kind. I appreciate the fact they all are very kind people. Car dealers sometimes get a bad rap, but Bob is a wonderful dealer. Driving back and forth between Lafayette and Indianapolis as frequently as I do - especially with the ice and snow in January and February - I feel safe in my Outback.

Not only am I a fan of Bob and the people who work for him, I am a fan of Subaru.

Bob has been wonderful to me in allowing me to put a large Sheila Klinker political sign on Farabee Drive across from Bob Rohrman, which is a new lot. I know Bob Rohrman is not particularly a Democrat, but Bob liked Jim Riehle, who also was a Democrat. Bob supports Ron Alting, a Republican state senator, so Bob is bi-partisan.

He also let me put up a sign on the grounds of his dealership on Creasy Lane. The great thing about Bob is that he can look at a candidate personally rather than just politically and then be willing and able to make that commitment. I never have forgotten that.

He also has contributed to my campaigns, which also is greatly appreciated.

Bob's story is one almost everyone would categorize as rags to riches. It is a story not only for a book, but also for a movie. Bob has been through a lot in his life.

As an elementary school sixth-grade teacher at Miami Elementary in Lafayette, I had the pleasure of teaching Bob's youngest son, Rick. Most of Bob's other children attended parochial elementary schools in Lafayette, but something happened where Rick didn't get along with either the nuns or the principal at his former school.

Bob wanted Rick to attend Miami, and he was in my class. At that time, Rick was a very rambunctious child who liked to do a lot of things, but he was a great kid. Years later at the dedication of his dad's performing arts center at Lafayette Jeff, Rick was so nice and sweet to me. I reminded him that I had him sit right in front of me in my sixth-grade class.

Rick never was a behavior problem for me. He simply was a sixth-grade boy and went on to be a good student.

I also had the pleasure of having Bob's third child, Randy, as a cadet teacher at Miami from the program at Jefferson High School. Randy was a great baseball player who went on to play in college at Indiana State.

Randy was one of the best cadet teachers I ever had in that program. He was quiet yet very involved with the kids. He was an excellent listener and always asked me what he could do to help me. He graded papers and helped me put up bulletin boards. He was tall, and that helped.

Then, he would go out at recess and relate with the students. He would play ball with them. I told my students that Randy was an excellent baseball player at Jeff, and so the children all looked up to him. It is good for children to have sort of a mentor and hero from a high school setting.

I always thought Randy missed his calling by not becoming a high school teacher and coach or a college baseball coach.

But when you have a large, successful family business such as the one the Rohrman family has built, it is difficult not to be a large part of that. I know Randy was a large part of the opening of the Schaumburg Honda store in the 1980s.

I don't blame Randy for the decision he made. Certainly, teaching is tremendously rewarding, but not monetarily speaking. Randy saw an opportunity and took advantage.

I know Randy taught briefly in an inner-city elementary school in Chicago, and while it was rewarding, it wasn't something he wanted to continue doing.

I knew all of the Rohrman children, and each of them is a great person.

In terms of what Bob has meant to the state of Indiana, I have served on the state budget committee for years, traveling to Richmond, Fort Wayne, Jeffersonville, Evansville and Gary, and everyone knows who Bob Rohrman is.

They always like to have fun and say, "Bob Roarrrrrrman!"

The northwest Indiana folks now know him just like the rest of the state knows Bob. He is not just state wide, but Bob is now everywhere in the Midwest. It is amazing.

Bob is responsible for many people making a very good living, not just in our state, but also in the surrounding states. That is very important, making a difference in a lot of people's lives.

He has assembled a lot of people who not only buy his cars, but who have become part of his family. I even feel like I am part of Bob's family. He loves people, and it warms my heart that Bob has been so supportive of education.

Even though he didn't have an opportunity to attend college, he certainly has acquired several degrees in several areas. In my mind, Bob Rohrman has a PhD.

68. Ron Alting

Indiana State Senator

I have known Bob Rohrman and his family - I was 59 in 2015 - since the early 1970s and attended Lafayette Jefferson High School with his two oldest children, JR and Rhonda.

In knowing them when we were young kids, I also got to know their parents. Bob always has had kind of an icon or movie star image my whole life.

If someone were to ask me, "Tell me about Bob Rohrman and what you think," it would be that not only am I proud of what he has done in his life and professional life, but I look more to how he has influenced hundreds and hundreds and hundreds of kids. He probably does not even know it.

When I was a sophomore or junior at Jefferson High School, one of the great mentors in my life was my basketball coach, Joe Heath. He headed the Fellowship of Christian Athletes, and Joe asked me to get involved in that organization.

Like many young males at that time, I was kind of uncertain what direction I was going. I probably was more prepared to make poor choices than I was to make good choices. So, I joined the FCA, and in doing that, I had an opportunity in the summer before by junior year to go to Rome, GA, for a one-week FCA camp.

The camp included speakers who were great athletes, some from the Olympics, some from the college ranks and some from the professional ranks. All were motivational speakers who spoke about how Jesus Christ had helped them achieve what was significant in their lives.

They talked about how God helped them become a better, well-rounded person. Joe said, "Why don't you come to this, because I think it will be good for you." I agreed.

I asked how all of us were going to get to Rome, GA, from Lafayette, IN. We took five cars, and coach Heath's golfing partners volunteered to drive. Joe went to Bob Rohrman and told Bob that he needed five or six cars.

He told Bob that those cars were going to be driven a couple of thousand miles each with a bunch of sweaty kids traveling a long distance in those cars. Bob Rohrman always donated those cars.

The meat of the story is that it was nice that I got to experience a week of FCA camp and swim and listen to those motivational speakers. But what Bob Rohrman has done for not just Ron Atling but for many athletes I know is that because of that trip, we found Jesus Christ and were saved.

That was a turning point in our lives. Some of them - 40 years later - put their arms around me and ask if I still remember FCA. I always say absolutely.

Without Bob Rohrman and his behind the scenes assistance, many Ron Altings would be looking at a different life today. He reached out to help middle and low income families. Until that FCA camp, I never had been out of Tippecanoe County, much less out of the state.

When I left Rome, GA, I had gone as Ron Alting but left as a different boy and am a different man today because of that. It was one of the greatest things that has happened in my life. I give credit to my God, Joe Heath and Bob Rohrman for giving me the opportunity to do that.

It helped shape who I am today. I would not have had that if not for Bob Rohrman.

In terms of business, he has been an asset to each community in which he has an automobile dealership. What he personally does for charity - and all that his dealerships do for animal rights, diabetes and cancer walks - is amazing. He does not just take from a community. Instead, his philosophy is to give back to the community.

He always has understood that he is a kid from Lafayette who attended Jeff High School and acquired great values coming out of that school. We are who we are because of the people who have touched our lives.

You need some smarts and some good luck along the way to achieve what he has achieved, but you also need a lot of hard work. Bob is not a taker. He is a giver. He understands that in order to give, there have to be people there who are there for you. Then you can reap the rewards, because people do not forget that.

Bob and I have very similar backgrounds. My parents lived on the old Toe Path along Wabash Avenue and then finally moved to a home on South Fourth Street. That is where I was raised.

The other thing I learned from Bob - and I preach this to kids today - is that you can go to higher education from a father standpoint and as a senator's standpoint, but if you are afraid of hard work, that higher education is meaningless.

Working hard is the key to everything in success.

When I got elected to the Indiana Senate, I thought of Bob Rohrman, because I got onto the computer and studied the people with whom I would be serving. There were graduates from Harvard and Yale and other Ivy League institutions who were some of the smartest men and women in the country.

And here I was, a kid from South Fourth Street in Lafayette with a physical education degree from Purdue University. I looked into the mirror and asked myself, "Are you really going to be able,to go down to Indianapolis and be a player in the senate and do well?"

It was what I learned from Bob Rohrman - outwork people - that sustained me, a C student who was a 5-foot-9 guard on a high school Final Four basketball team.

When others go home at 5, I go home at 7 or 8. If they go home at 6, I go home at 8 or 9. That is how Bob got to where he is, and it is how you must continue to live your life if you plan to achieve and move forward.

For example, I played golf with Bob one Saturday last summer, and we played early in the morning. When we finished our round, I asked him if he planned to stay for lunch. He said no, because he was on his way to visit five or six of his dealerships that afternoon and early evening.

He said he has done that his whole career on Saturdays. He is an absolute workaholic.

He is a wonderful example for all of us who want to achieve great things in our lives.

Education, intelligence, people skills, being open minded, believing in diversity and being a person of faith all help, but to go along with all of that is hard work. Bob Rohrman is the epitome of that.

I am also very flattered that he says at one time when we were in high school, he wanted his daughter, Rhonda, to date me. I hope her husband - Mr. Isbell - doesn't read that, because he could beat the tar out of me.

But in all seriousness, Rhonda is one of the sweetest girls I ever have had the honor of knowing. We were very close. We were buddies. We were friends more than anything. You always have girls or women in your life who are like sisters.

We hung out together and laughed and joked. We had great talks like a brother and sister. That was during the time Bob and Rhonda's mother were getting a divorce. Rhonda and I became very close.

That fall, I took her to my uncle's house for Thanksgiving dinner. I took her as my friend, almost like my sister, so to speak. I now know I am getting old, because I see her children in Bob's television commercials and being a part of dealerships.

When I think of those times with Rhonda, I am very humbled that Bob would say nice things about me as a person. The real winner there was me, because Rhonda was - and still is to this day - a very sweet person. She has a great family, and I am very proud to know her.

Obviously, I am very proud to also know her father.

69. *Michael Malone*

Account Executive for WGN-TV, Chicago

In 2006, I first put together WGN-TV's and CLTV's advertising package for Mr. Rohrman. At that time, he was a very big print advertiser with the Chicago Tribune.

So, I had my first meeting with him in December of 2006. While I did not know exactly how much the Bob Rohrman Auto Group was spending in TV advertising at that time, but decided to put our best foot forward.

We are sitting in front of him and are presenting. He was just so matter of fact, I never felt intimidated by him. Maybe I should have, but I never did. To me, he was kind of that lovable grandpa type. I knew him through his TV commercials and how silly he was in those.

He did buy a fair amount of television advertising, back then and when you see so much of him, it's like you know him already.

We did our pitch to him, and I thought it went well. As it turned out, his advertising agency called me a month later and told me that I had gotten the annual package, which was awesome. It was pretty substantial, because he was going with one or two stations for the annual. That started it. His commercial schedule would be on both stations in the Tribune Group, WGN-TV, and CLTV.

About a year later, we started doing something pretty cool, when product placement in shows became popular. CLTV produced a show called "metromix," which was an entertainment show. We would visit restaurants and clubs, review music, videos, and tell viewers all the hot spots. We came up with the idea of placing a car in the show, with the host driving around every week. It would be a great promotion for The Bob Rohrman Group, seeing their cars on TV but not just in commercial slots.

The guys in Mr. Rohrman's ad agency were just so forward thinking. They were not worried about ratings. They just wanted to do something different. They were very open to different advertising ideas. This was all new to us…we were making it up as we were going along, but we did have some talented Tribune producers, so I knew the quality would be good. We rotated in Lexus and Honda and a lot of brands and did it for a couple of years.

It made for great television, and it gave Bob Rohrman something different in the market that he did not have. It really was fun, and we got to meet Mr. Rohrman, when we did a segment with him in it. There were so many things we started doing with Mr. Rohrman and the Auto group. He became so engrained in the station. It's years later now, and today, from the general manager to the newsroom to the promotion department and the sales department, Mr. Rohrman has become not just a fixture, but a friend.

I am so lucky, but I would have no problem introducing them (The Bob Rohrman Group) to different advertising things. Some things aren't going to fit for them, but I learned not to make that decision. I let them make that decision. More times than not, Stephen at Orange Media Group will say, "That sounds good."

One of the biggest things they have done in recent years is with weatherman Tom Skilling, who is one of the most popular people at the Tribune Company and on Chicago TV. The Skilling 7-Day Forecast sponsorship on air became available. It is the Holy Grail for the station. People trust Skilling, and he has an enormous viewership. Mr. Rohrman along with his agency thought it to be a wonderful opportunity and aligned with it. As of 2015, they are in their fourth year of the sponsorship - and are seen in virtually every newscast on WGN-TV; with weather being such a big deal in this market. Then, a couple of years ago, we asked if Mr. Rohrman would like to be a part of the station's annual toy drive for kids during December.

Channel 9 does its annual toy drive for kids every December. The Bob Rohrman Auto Group decided to use their dealerships to collect toys in the fall, then Mr. Rohrman, I mean Santa Bob and his elves show up every year at the crack of dawn on WGN-TV's morning show with literally a truckload of new toys. The morning show begins at 4 a.m., but we try to be a little considerate to Santa Bob's sleep schedule, so he and his elves make their appearance usually around 6:30 or 7, which is when the viewership is its highest, anyway. He always says, "I'll be there."

We do the Toy drop off, live on air outside the station. Santa Bob shows up on a shiny red pick-up, sitting on the tailgate and his elves soon begins unloading their goods. Year in and year out, He cannot be any more gracious, generous and fun at 6 in the morning. Every year, it is a given that he is going to do it.

WGN-TV's morning news is silly, silly and silly. We are not the New York Times. We have a lot of fun. You get your news, and you get your headlines, but we have a ton of fun in doing so. A few years back we did an Olympic spoof featuring Mr. Rohrman and a few other local celebrities. That was funny as heck. We had another silly spoof with former Blackhawks hockey star Bobby Hull and Mr. Rohrman. It was so funny.

Again, he has become such a part of the station, I have the news producers asking me, "Do you think Mr. Rohrman would be willing to do this?" They know how he is in the market. Truthfully, they want funny television. And they get it with him. Is it good for sales and promotion? Of course it is.

We are in our second year of doing live commercials once a month at Channel 9, with Mr. Rohrman . We do them in the last hour of our morning news. He will come in at 9 am and we will go over the script. Our goal is to sell cars and have fun in about sixty seconds. He and the announcer have developed a really nice relationship. When we first pitched the live commercial idea to Mr. Rohrman, he instantly liked it.

Each month, before and after production, I have the pleasure of talking to him person to person and relating to him. I have developed such respect for him. Now, we have a couple of other auto dealers that do them, but Mr. Rohrman does them the best. He told us that he was doing live commercials 50 years ago in Lafayette. Now, 50 years later, he still knows how to sell a car better than anyone

Sometimes he'll go off script, but you get the idea because he is so funny. Sometimes we hit a home run with it, and sometimes we hit a double. But it's OK, because at least we're in the game.

He is not just putting spots on WGN. He is engrained in WGN.

This past November, we also got involved in a car giveaway as the result of a deer falling off an overpass onto a family car. The news story broke after this deer fell on the vehicle, and the lady had four or five kids. Thank goodness nobody was hurt.

When we contacted Mr. Rohrman if his dealer group would be able to turn this story around and generate a happy ending…he said yes, and donated a comparable family van to help this family. He was not into it for the news coverage or publicity. He doesn't need that. Then, Mr. Rohrman wanted to continue that type of giving for other worthwhile charities.

This year we developed a program called "WGN's Helping Hand." The Bob Rohrman Auto Group is our premier sponsor this year. We solicit applications from needy charities, and then there is an awarding process. They all are deserving, but we pick one charity per quarter, and they receive a van, courtesy of The Bob Rohrman Auto Group.

He also is so generous in sharing projects he has working. In our last negotiation, he asked me if I wanted to come over and look at the new Lexus store on Dundee Road. I told him I would love to, because we have been talking about this forever. He was gracious. I got to see him as a negotiator and as a business man. It was a privilege for me to do that. He is tough, but funny and fair at the same time. He gets it done. He can ask very stern questions in a mild way. He commands respect in every situation, I've seen him in. You don't question him. This is a man who has a commitment to marketing his company. I get it, and I respect it and I totally appreciate it. That is a smart, smart man.

I think what really helped Mr. Rohrman - and this is just my perspective - is his humble beginnings. You can go to Harvard or another Ivy League school and find success…but he has a basic desire to succeed. I've said this to my kids….I don't want you to be a success, but rather I want you to want to be a success. He wanted to be a success. That really is what it is. It's that simple. Isn't it funny how people in business can make things so complicated? He just gets it done.

70. Mary Hart

Automotive Sales Manager at Comcast Spotlight

I met Bob Rohrman in 2001 when I was new to the Chicago market. I was new to sales management and was managing a team that was selling Cars.com. The Internet was very new to Mr. Rohrman and to myself.

I was scared to death. I had a meeting with this man, who was very, very important to the Chicago Tribune. You had to put your best foot forward with this guy. It is intimidating. He is a multi-millionaire with huge buying power and a big customer within our organization. I thought I was going to be extremely intimidated.

I waited for several hours for the meeting, because he was on Rohrman Time. Now, 15 years later, you can plan for that. When we finally met, I sensed his genuineness. Obviously, I was relieved. I remember going home and talking to my husband and telling him that Bob is so down to earth and hilarious.

We started the meeting, and I had an agenda, but when we began talking, it was more about getting to know each other. Over the years now, I have negotiated millions of dollars of advertising with Mr. Rohrman, and the majority of the time during our conversations was not spent discussing advertising.

I always felt he was a fun person to introduce a new opportunity to, because he wanted to be on the cutting edge and wanted to be our house in the market. We brought him an idea to be on the front page of the Chicago Tribune, and we came at him with our best price offer.

He said to me, "That's too much, babe." It was always that. He always knew he could get a little bit more, and we always would be willing to negotiate. One of my favorite things he ever said to me was during one of our annual contract negotiations.

And boy is he a master negotiator. We got down to where we almost were going to make a deal, and he said to me, "Mary, you are a good guy, right?" I said I am a good guy. And he said he is a good guy. He said, "Do you know what good guys do, Mary? They meet in the middle."

I told him that made perfect sense, and we got the deal done. We did a handshake and a hug, and then we got a cup of Dunkin Donuts Coffee. He didn't want any fancy stuff.

I loved to meet with him when we weren't in the midst of a negotiation. I would bring him pens or a calculator, and this multi million dollar advertiser acted like I just gave him a Rolex watch. He would keep the gift and remind me two years later that I had given him that gift. He genuinely is grateful for anything anyone ever has given him.

He definitely is thrifty, and so many people who have achieved what he has achieved just forget where they came from. I remember one time he was doing some sort of promotion in the paper in which he was going to give away gas cards for every test drive.

We were talking about how we were going to execute the plan, and I asked him if I should just go get the gas cards. He said, "Honey, don't worry. I will get these gas cards, because I want to buy them on my Speedway Card so I can get the points."

I said, "Your Speedway card?" He told me that every hundred dollars he spends, he gets free cups of coffee. It told me just how conscientious he is about the dollar. No matter how much he has, he is grateful for every penny.

When he took his trips to China, he loved to negotiate for his fake Rolex watches. He always is fun to entertain, but he always enjoyed talking about the advertising business as well as the automobile business. To get his perspective and his knowledge is great, because he shares the trends.

In 2008, the economy was poor, but Mr. Rohrman understood the ups and downs of his business, unlike other dealers, which is why he is who he is. He would stay the course, and when the going got tough, he got going.

At the time other advertisers were not spending, he was willing to jump in. We brought him a good idea, which we were really excited about, because our business was struggling. His business was soft as well, so we decided to help each other.

We got to that meeting, and we talked more about the stock market and about what the manufacturers were doing. I remember getting a hot stock market tip from Bob, and it was like picking the winner in the Kentucky Derby.

He was telling me that he was buying Ford, because it was in such bad shape but he knew they were going to turn it around. I told our sales rep that even if Bob doesn't buy the idea we were presenting him, we were going to buy some Ford stock. We did.

I went home and bought like 1,000 shares. That day, it was at like $2. Now, every time I am with him, I ask him what I should buy.

He also has been interesting in his adaption to technology, even 10 years ago when people were using palm pilots. He had his little flip phone and his little book in his pocket. Here is a man of his stature who relies on a pen and paper. Actually, I think all of that information is in his head. He is a steel trap.

For a man in the automotive business, he understands the media like no other. Clearly, it has made him a celebrity. I know he is in Indiana, but in Chicago, anyone who knows what I do for a living asks me, "Do you know Bob Roooohrman?" He really has put a stake in the ground in Chicago.

He has done in television and radio something that had been unheard of in the Chicago market. Some people may think his commercials are goofy, he resonates through his personality and people love the way he is.

When he opened Arlington Nissan, I told him I was going to do something for him, even though I know he gets so many perks for being in this business. In the grand opening, for the man who has everything, I had a Rohrman cake made for him and congratulated him. You would have thought I paid for half the store. That is how excited he was. He was elated with the creativity and the thoughtfulness behind it. That is what I love about doing business with him.

He is a very smart and shrewd negotiator, and usually, he wins. He gets a very good deal, and he should. You don't mind giving

Bob more, because you have a personal relationship with him on top of it, and you know he is committed to a partnership with you long term.

You would rather deal with someone who you trust and who is committed than with someone who is not. At the Tribune, every year as part of his car deal, we would get a skybox for a Cubs game so that he could take and entertain his general managers.

This speaks to true local celebrity. We are at the game, and to get to the skybox, you are walking and the crowd below can see you. The people in the stands saw him and started yelling, "Bob Rohrman, Bob Rohrman." The crowd went crazy and created a total distraction from the game.

At the seventh-inning stretch, he left the skybox and sang to the crowd. It was the greatest thing ever.

Whoever the person was that was singing the seventh inning stretch officially lost all attention, because there was Bob Rohrman singing, "Take me out the ballgame" from the skybox.

I felt thrilled and proud to be with him that day. He really has fun. The man has so much energy.

Personally, I have learned that while business is important, it is also important to have relationships as part of doing business. It solidifies that. It is an honor to meet and know a man who went from nothing to everything and yet is still humble. It is very unusual. There also are very few who give back the way he does to his community in Lafayette and to his family and extended family. He also gives to Chicago.

But I will tell you he still is getting free cable from Comcast. But it is just basic Cable.

We laugh and he doesn't take me seriously when I tell him I want to be his granddaughter, wife, daughter or extended cousin or business partner.

I have been so lucky to have gotten to know him over the years, even when he asks me to buy 800 hoola hoops for the company picnic, which we fund.

71. Pat Joyce

Sales Executive for Comcast Sports Network Television, Chicago

I met Bob Rohrman in a United Center sky box in 1995 for a Chicago Bulls basketball game. The first thing Bob wanted to know was when the dessert cart was going to arrive at our suite.

I thought that Bob would want a drink or something more substantial, but his interest was in the dessert cart. He walked over and looked at the dessert cart, and his eyes got real big. I will never forget that he was like a kid in a candy store.

I was right behind him when I heard him say, "I think I will take this." I told him that he could take anything that he wanted. It was classic. I hit it off with him right from the very start. He got a dessert, we watched the game, and he turned to me and asked if the dessert cart was coming back at all.

It was like he cared more about the dessert cart than the game, although he really didn't. That is Bob.

This is the guy whose commercials are legendary throughout the Midwest. It is like a comic series. Each time, he comes up with a new persona, either as Count Bobula, the Hulk or Santa Bob. He is so iconic. People watch and say, "Oh my gosh, look at him."

We watch his commercials in our office, where everybody knows Bob. You can't believe this grown man is acting like Count Dracula or the Mummy. But the great thing about the commercials is that they reach out and grab you, and you don't forget.

He is masterful at getting his name out there constantly. He entertains people, too. It absolutely has worked remarkably well for him. In most other car commercials, they show you a pretty car and tell you they give you the best service and are very much standard. They don't really jump. They all sort of look alike.

Bob adds a comical element that makes his commercials entertaining and worth watching. With Bob Rohrman, they won't forget that name. He has done a remarkable job of cutting through the clutter of a lot of different ads. He does them in a way that they really are good.

He has charisma, and when you hear that voice, you know it right away. The face fills the screen. Others are like a standard operation. Most dealers do that because it is the easiest way out. You don't pay attention, and that is the difference.

We are glad to be aligned with Bob. It is great. When you advertise with sports, it is a good endorsement, because the teams or the broadcasters are those you believe in. Viewers identify the ads as good places. It is that implied endorsement.

It may sound ridiculous that the mind works that way, but it does. People can't get enough of those big institutions - the teams - that they love. You tie it all together, and it is a nice endorsement.

It is implied - there is no Cub player telling you to go to Bob Rohrman - but the association makes Bob a legitimate guy among Cubs fans. We do a lot of auto ads, because the dealers like to identify with sports teams.

And it is fun to identify with Bob.

One time, we are going to a Purdue basketball game in West Lafayette, and I meet him at his old Toyota store. We go pick up another guy, and the three of us are going to go to dinner before the game.

Bob turns to us and asks what we feel like eating. I told Bob that Comcast was paying, so pick the best place Lafayette has. He says, "We've got Olive Garden over here, and TGI Friday's over there."

I told him to pick something really good. He picks the Golden Corral, which is a very reasonably priced buffet. I didn't know the Golden Corral. He pulls into what looks like a shopping center, and I see all these people walk into what is a smorgasbord.

He said, "Hey, babe, don't worry, the prices are good here." We sat down with these trays after I thought we were going to have a fancy steak. Bob says, "Hey, this is some really good macaroni and cheese."

Then all of a sudden, I look over, and there is Bob's son, Rick, and his family eating dinner there. I figured the Golden Corral must be the hot spot before a Purdue game. It blew me away that Bob is such a regular guy.

Another time, Bob and I were headed to a meeting at Comcast Sports, and he wanted to stop for lunch. He starts to get hungry and pulls into an area that has a KFC, a Taco Bell, a McDonald's and a Burger King.

He says, "Which one do you want, they all are here." I picked McDonald's, and he said he was hoping that was what I would pick. I told him that the new Angus Burger is pretty good. He has the Angus Burger, and about ten minutes later, he tells me, "You know, you are right. This is one heck of a burger."

Only Bob would appreciate the finer cuisine of McDonald's. He was excited that Comcast again was picking up the check. When I turned in the receipt, the guy who does our expenses said, "Are you really turning in a $9 receipt from McDonald's?"

We went to the Master's in Augusta, GA, with a bunch of guys, and we went to Wendy's for lunch. Bob said, "Let me tell you guys something about Wendy's. Don't get the large chilli. Get two mediums. It is about a dollar less that way, and you get more."

Everybody wondered how in the heck he knew that. Everybody got two medium chilli's.

On another trip to the Master's, Bob and I go to Easter Sunday mass. The collection basket is going around. I looked in my wallet, and I had a hundred dollar bill, a fifty and a ten. I am thinking Bob will think I am the biggest cheapskate in the world if I throw in only $10 on Easter Sunday.

I throw in the $10, and when the basket gets to Bob, he has a pocket full of pennies and puts it in. I told Bob he was a guy after my own heart. It was unbelievable.

He comes from humble beginnings, and it shows. He has stayed with it. I respect him so much. Like him, I always was trying to save a buck.

He doesn't try to be flashy when a lot of his counterparts are that way. He has them all outfoxed.

And he knows sports. He always knows the baseball standings and if a certain team is six games out of first place. I work in the business, and I don't even know that. He knows a player's agent and when the player's contract is up. He has an insight into all of these teams.

He has a trap door mind for sports statistics and how teams are doing.

The year the Indianapolis Colts played the New Orleans Saints in the Super Bowl, he called and asked if I wanted to go with him. A sports outlet in Indianapolis invited Bob, and he took me. He and I both are Drew Brees fans, so we wanted the Saints to win.

I bet on New Orleans, and while we are sitting there watching the game, I am having a few drinks and am pretty excited, because the Saints are winning. I won a few hundred bucks, which was fun.

So, this husband and wife wearing Colts jerseys get up to leave because the Colts have lost, and I say, "Better luck next time, you should have bet on the Saints."

The host snarls at me and says, "That is our biggest client." Bob turned to me and said, "Oh, you really got us into it now." But then Bob burst out laughing and could not stop laughing. I was like the idiot on the trip. Bob and I shared a suite, and I remember his big thing was going out to get some hair spray.

He always invites me on these trips, which is great. We have a great time together.

72. Norman Hull

Retail Division Manager for the Chicago Tribune

I was a sales rep at the time I met Bob and was assigned the Rohrman auto group. I was at Oakbrook Toyota, and when I walked in, they were shooting a commercial. While they were doing the commercial, I recognized my agency guys, but I did not see Bob.

But when I came around the corner, Bob was wearing this outfit for the commercial. It was a Halloween theme, and he was made up as Count Dracula, which he is known as Count Bobula.

I meet him for the first time, and I am thinking, "Oh, my God, what am I into here?" I just had the greatest time watching this unfold. He is naturally funny. Eventually, he had a break, and I was able to get in there and introduce myself.

He said, "Oh, gosh, don't get used to me putting these outfits on all the time." This roughly was 2000. The only time I really would see him was at a grand opening, a dedication or just at one of his stores, which he frequents all the time.

Every time I would see him, he could not have been nicer to me. I am not just saying that. It is true. I always said that he always treated me with total respect. As a sales rep, I never lied to Bob, who was our No. 1 guy. My feeling always was that this was going to be a win-win. He was a wonderful negotiator. He asked for everything, because every year, he did a little bit more.

He got what he wanted, and we did, too, which is great. He pretty much is a man who is a creature of habit, because he wants things a certain way. Once you learn that, it is a good thing.

As long as we did not deviate from that, we were fine. He has a passion for advertising, and everybody knows his jingle. Each time I would see him at a dealership, someone would say, "Oh, there is Bob Roooooohhrrman!" That is all I ever would hear.

Because of his personality and friendliness and longevity of looking the same, people always enjoy being around him. I will say that because he is as sharp as he is and active as he is, it keeps him sharp. When most people give that up, they don't charge or energize their mind. He always has something going on.

If he asks you a question, he knows the answer before he asks the question. You better give him the right answer, or otherwise, you are out of here. If you lie about that, you are lying about something else. He has very few core people around him that he has had for a number of years - John Barrett, Mark Battista and a handful of others. That is his inner circle and something he can trust.

I am not part of that inner circle, but I was with him for 12 years. I felt like that if I ever needed him, he gave me the time of day, which he really didn't have to do. I felt good about that. In time, he learned that I was trustworthy and wanted to do what was right for both of us. I also knew that if I did what was right for him and his organization, we would win, too.

In some of our chats, he would give me some of his fascinating history about growing up in a log cabin with a dirt floor and then taking care of everybody around him. He is a self made guy and has been very savvy. He made it with his first used car lot because people could trust him. He just did what was right and knew how to treat a customer.

One of the magical things throughout his life has been his gift of gab and the fact he is a trustworthy guy. He trusts that whatever he asks you to do, you are going to fulfill it. He is very much a handshake kind of a guy. If we have to sign a contract, we will do that, but his word is good.

From me, he always wanted new ideas and was willing to try them, although he is not a person to throw money at something that he did not think would work. If it works out, he will continue to do it.

We developed a section for him in our auto portion. He tried it, and it was awesome. He continues to do it today. He sees the big picture and likes all of those guys in his dealerships being together. He is on the front of our auto section. There are three strips on the front of our Saturday auto mart, and he bought the right hand rail. He insisted on that position. He wanted it because then readers had to touch his ad to turn that paper to get it open. It was a wonderful idea. That is just Bob.

And with Bob, there always are fun stories. I fondly recall when he donated money to Lafayette Jefferson High School to build a new performing arts center for the music department. They dedicated the new building on a Sunday, and I told my boss that I was going to drive from Chicago to Lafayette and attend.

I was doing it for him, but I also was fascinated and thought it was a great opportunity to support Bob. It was like a 1 p.m. dedication, and I arrived hungry. So I pulled into Culver's and ordered a jumbo patty melt with French fries.

I got back into the car after finishing lunch and drove to the high school. I got out of the car and realized I smelled of onions from the patty melt. I didn't have gum or mints, so there was no way to get rid of this smell.

I saw Bob and knew I had to say congratulations to him. He looked at me, and said, "Oh my gosh, you stink." He wanted to know where in the heck I had been. I told him I went to Culver's, and he said he loves Culver's.

I was mortified, so when I got into the auditorium, most people congregated in the middle, but I sat all the way to my left by myself. I thought how stupid of me to come all this way, and then smell like onions. But he appreciated that I came.

He had 1,000 people to say something to that day, but it was nice he was able to spend a couple of minutes with me.

I love that while Bob always thinks he is right, he also can laugh at himself, which is such an endearing quality. He always has been a true gentleman and a great guy. He never is on time, which we would laugh about, and when he would build a new store, we would ask when he would have his grand opening.

He would say, "The third of the month, we are doing that." But the third of the month could be May, August or November. That became a fun joke with Bob. Whenever it gets done, it gets done.

73. Stephen Allsteadt

Part Owner of Orange Media Group

My very first job my first day out of college, I started working on the Rohrman account at Western International Media, which was the largest media management company in the United States. That was right after Memorial Day weekend in 1991.

While we had talked on the phone many times, the day I met Bob Rohrman was the same day O.J. Simpson was being driven in his Bronco in Los Angeles. That was June of 1994. We were sitting in the WAZY radio studios in Lafayette with Mike Wild, who worked for WAZY.

Mr. Rohrman, me, Mike Wild and my former business partner were watching the whole O.J. drama unfold. The song "Jealousy" was playing on the radio station. I remember thinking that this was really weird. O.J. probably did it out of jealousy. It left that kind of mark in my brain.

That was the day that I put a face with a voice that I had known for three years. People ask me all the time, "What is Bob like?" I tell them that he is exactly what you see on TV.

I honestly believe that he is out looking to have a great time and enjoy himself. Laughing is something that is second nature and something that he wants to do. One day I was with him when he was dressed as Santa Bob, and we were doing the Rotary Club Run in Arlington Heights, IL. We drove Santa Bob around in a Nissan convertible, and he sat in the back and waved to the crowd.

After that 5K race, I told him that he was incredible. He said, "We probably sold fifty cars today." I told him that he easily had sold fifty cars just by smiling and waving to people. People were even singing the "Old Bob Rohrman" song to him. He told me that he is just a big ham.

He will do anything. I recently wrote a TV commercial that I was not sure how comfortable he would be doing it. In that commercial, we asked Bob to cross dress. It was an Oscar's theme, and there was a female actress up for an award. We had him put on a blonde wig. I had a backup plan if he did not want to do it, where he would be the MC giving the award. It would have been an easy switch with no problem.

He took the wig and said, "I usually have a nicer wig." He had no concern about doing it. He will take a chance on anything. I don't even have to ask twice.

I do agree with those who say there is an actor inside Bob Rohrman. I would bet that nobody has done or been in more TV commercials in the past 25 or 30 years than Bob Rohrman. When you think about it, he does 25 or 30 new commercials every single month. Add that up. George Clooney does what, one movie a year?

Bob is incredibly easy to work with in these commercials, but he also is a stickler for the message he puts across. He wants his commercials to be meaningful. He wants them to entertain, create awareness and interact with this very friendly person at his dealerships. It is a strategy that has worked very well for him.

Each month, we present Bob with five or six different ideas for commercials, along with a history of what we have done for the last 20 years. He visualizes that. Then, he sees himself in that role and picks the role based on the same way an actor would.

He does each of the commercial shoots phenomenally quick. He gets the lines in a couple of seconds. He is not seeing the scripts an hour before or a day before. He is seeing the lines for the first time as we are there shooting. We have it down to a system in which some of it is voice over, and some of it is on camera. We try to mix it up.

Sometimes, he comes up with an idea for a commercial. In the fall of 2014, he called me with an idea that he wanted to do a commercial in which he actually is playing football. He wanted a certain group of people in that spot.

More often than not, he is busy off selling cars, so we come to him with ideas. I couldn't see Bob being a professional quarterback in that commercial, but in a pickup football game in the backyard, I totally could see it. It came out a lot of fun.

I think Bob and I have an interesting relationship. At a certain level, he is my boss. He owns part of our advertising agency, so on a certain level, he is my business partner. And he also is a dear friend of mine.

I know for a fact he is a friend. He invites me to go to a Michigan State basketball game knowing that I am a Michigan State graduate. He knows that I am a Chicago Blackhawks fan, so he gives me Blackhawks tickets. We go to major league baseball games occasionally.

He also is my boss in that his stores are my clients. He makes the decisions, and I certainly have to respect him on that level. He also owns five percent of Orange Media, so he is a business partner. It has been great. Every bit has been great because he is a fantastic person on all three of those levels.

In the 20 years we have been business partners, I don't think there has been a single bit of friction. He has been a great friend. His granddaughter Laura knows him on four levels, the same three as me, but then also she is his granddaughter.

Yes, he does have millions of dollars, but I don't think he cares about perception. For the longest time, he wore a fake Rolex with a Timex watch band. He bought the watches on The Great Wall of China and gave them to his kids when he got home. He negotiated with a guy and ended up buying all of these fake watches, but he also wanted the box they came in. He gave them out as presents, because he is a generous guy. He doesn't care if it is a real Rolex or a fake one.

My description of Bob is the down home Indiana guy that you see on TV is Bob Rohrman. There is no act in that TV commercial at all.

I once read a review of Bob Rohrman that someone had written on the Internet, and I thought that it had to be a disgruntled employee, because the writer said that everybody addresses him as Mr. Rohrman. Everybody addresses him as Bob and he is the nicest, down home guy ever.

He also is an incredible business man, but away from the business stuff, he is a great, normal guy.

One of his philosophies for selling cars is that if you fall in love with the customer, the customer will fall in love with you. That makes it real easy to sell a car.

Bob also is such a generous man, giving $3.5 million to Lafayette Jefferson High School, which is his alma mater. It was a great story, for which I wrote a press release. The Indiana news outlets picked it up great, but Chicago, where he has fifteen dealerships, I had to beg for coverage, almost pleading on my hands and knees.

Years later, when the story came out that Bob was suing a doctor who allegedly had an affair with Bob's third wife, I must have had fifty calls from TV stations asking for a photo or video of Bob. It was that old Don Henley song, "Dirty Laundry."

He does an incredible thing for his high school and receives very little news coverage in Chicago, but this kind of controversial thing comes along, and it was nothing but dirty laundry.

To this day, that still bothers me, because it says a lot about the human condition.

Bob now does a car giveaway to someone who is needy because a deer fell off a Chicago overpass and landed on a car and ruined it. Bob's grandson, Ryan, had the idea to give a car to that family whose car had been totaled.

Ryan could not believe the number of calls he got from people thanking him for taking care of that family. Ryan thought it was a good thing to find a way to do this in the future. We gave the idea to WGN, who thought it was a great idea to give away a car each quarter. Within two seconds, Mr. Rohrman agreed that we would do that.

I think one of the keys to his success is that it seems that he has a photographic memory. He will remember things that other people have to look up. He also has an incredible mind for math. I need a calculator to do seven times seven.

It is probably one of things that has helped him negotiate deals nonstop his entire life. In 2013 and 2014, we had spots for the Cubs radio broadcasts on WGN. In 2015, the Cubs moved from WGN to WBBM. The WBBM people came to us and said they would be happy to continue having us as a sponsor for Cubs baseball.

They said whatever deal WGN had given us, they would be happy to do the same deal this year. We sent the details of the deal we had with WGN, and a week later, they came to us and said there is no way WBBM can do this. We were not even close.

I am very sure we had negotiated one of the best Cubs baseball deals ever. So, in 2015, we were not on Cubs baseball on radio. But with Comcast Sports Chicago, we have a TV commercial on every live sporting event, such as the Blackhawks, Cubs, White Sox and Bulls.

Back in the day of Michael Jordan, there were spots going for $20,000, and Bob had spots for about $175. He had negotiated a deal for a spot on every live sporting event. It was something like a 10-year contract. He was in this deal before the Bulls acquired Michael Jordan and Scottie Pippen and built the championship team.

No question, I am blessed and incredibly lucky to have this relationship with Bob Rohrman. And all of this from a guy who took two years off after graduating from high school to attempt to become a professional golfer.

Then, I applied to Michigan State University for their school of business. They accepted me to the university but said they could not put me in the school of business because I did not have the prerequisite math class.

So, I decided to go into the school of communications with a concentration in advertising. I liked it and decided that is what I wanted to do. It has served me well, although it all happened on a whim.

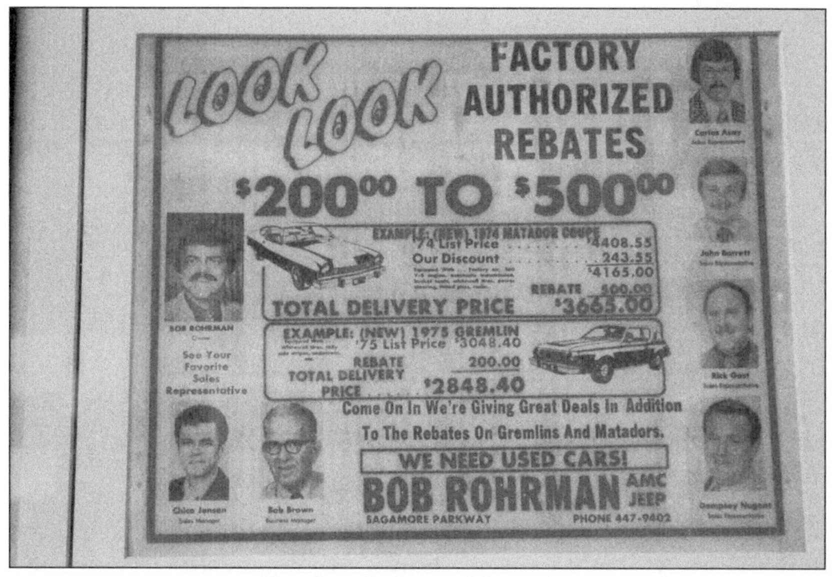

A typical Bob Rohrman ad from the 1970s,
this one featuring AMC cars.

74. Don Whipple

Former Pastor at Lafayette's Kossuth Street Baptist Church

It has been said that trouble introduces a man to himself. When I first met Bob he was busy meeting himself.

I met Bob through JR and Kathy Rohrman, who were members of Kossuth Street Baptist Church. At the time I met Bob, he and Linda were going through some marital difficulties. Through the suggestion of JR and Kathy, they recommended to Linda that Bob and Linda could give me a call and that I could give them some help in their marital struggle.

The first time I actually talked with Bob was with Linda in a room at the Kossuth Street Baptist Church. We began some counseling to restore and reconcile their marriage. Bob and I have often joked years later that either I was not a very good counselor or he was not a very good counselee given the results of our marriage counseling. I think I know the answer but for the record, Bob may not agree.

At that point, I really didn't make any connections with the public Bob. I just saw a man who was in enough of a jam that he would even meet with a Baptist pastor who he did not know. At that time, I really didn't understand who he was from a business standpoint. I didn't keep track of auto group size and was not aware of the extent of Bob's business success.

As a matter of fact, from time to time I would hear family or others talk about things he could afford, and I would think that they must really be exaggerating. I really didn't connect the public persona. I just saw a man and a woman who were in a crisis stage in their lives.

In these early weeks of meeting regularly to talk about their lives and teach them principles from the Bible is when my heart really began to embrace both Bob and Linda. While not always a model student, Bob was for a period of time open to listen and learn.

In those days we read the Bible together, participated in Bible studies and he even came to hear me preach a few times. Back when it was ok for churches to have Super Bowl parties, he showed up at ours and fit in like he had been a lifelong member.

Ultimately what I saw in Bob was the contrast between a guy who can be so outrageously successful in public life, yet so unsuccessful in some basic personal and relational choices. I never have really seen Bob as this intimidating successful man. Rather, I have just tried to be a friend to him, like a normal guy and help him see life from another perspective.

The delight to me, and the reason I can honestly say I love Bob Rohrman, is more along those lines. I think we actually enjoy each other's company and have fun. We would go to football games together or basketball games and we would take trips together. We just talked about all kinds of stuff. When we were just sitting around, I loved to hear his stories about the business and what he was building. He would even laugh at my stories once in a while.

While I deeply respect Bob, I am not really in awe of him in any way. As a matter of fact, I really would not want to change places with him. I have a lot of fun when we are at a football game, basketball game or just out in public. People will come up and say, "Can I have your picture?" or "Can I have my picture taken with you?"

Before he can answer, Bob will start with a little giggle or chuckle, because he is so delighted that he has been noticed. Before he can say something, I have learned to say, "Sure, you can take my picture, but do you want Bob in it, too?" That gets him laughing, and by the time some of these college kids look at me like I am from outer space, Bob and I are laughing, and then they tell me that they just want a picture of Mr. Rohrman. I tell them that it is their loss.

It was not unusual for Bob to get the celebrity treatment when we were out together. He and I used to have breakfast at the restaurant that was located at the corner of 26th and 52nd in Lafayette. One day, we were eating breakfast, and a guy that I had never met walks up to the table, looks at Bob and asks Bob if he knows who he is eating breakfast with.

Bob says yes, that is Pastor Whipple. The guy says, "You better watch your wallet. Don't you know he is a pastor?" Bob just about lost it. I'm certain the guy didn't understand our enjoyment.

Bob has an incredible family. My wife Sue and I have a great friendship with Kathy and JR and know the other children and their families well enough to say that Bob has a wonderful family. His family does an amazing job of loving him, tracking him and staying in touch with him.

The last year Purdue played in the Rose Bowl, which was close to the time of his divorce from Linda, Bob called me and asked me to go with him. The five children and families were all traveling out to the game with Linda.

On the flight to Los Angeles, Bob had a briefcase full of gift certificates and had me help fill in each grandchild's name while he signed and sealed each card. I remember Bob walking off the plane with all of his family Christmas gifts ready.

When we got to the motel, and they gave us our room it had only one bed. The first thing out of Bob's mouth was, "Oh, no, this won't work." We walked back down to the front desk and he told the person there, "You have to understand, I am a Catholic, and he is a Baptist. We need two beds."

On that trip he also did a big family dinner on the Queen Mary, and I was invited. All the children and grandchildren were there. I sat at the end of the table with a couple of the grand kids and just watched. This was when everything was pretty raw, because Bob was leaving Linda. It was interesting watching the family dynamics. Bob's children have consistently shown in my presence an amazing capacity to love their Dad in an understanding way even when they may disagree with him or at times been hurt by his behavior.

Bob's first wife Shirley is a special lady. She and Sue struck up a friendship through the chiropractor office where Sue worked. Shirley's occasional commentary on Bob was helpful and kind. Shirley impressed us with her love for her children and for Bob after obviously going through some real life challenges. Shirley has a great sense of humor and warmth that we thoroughly enjoyed.

I entered Bob's life after he had been married to Linda for more than 20 years. I don't know how to score these kinds of things, but if Bob says the biggest mistake he ever made was ending his marriage with Linda, it would be hard for me to argue with that. There were several frustrating meetings, conversations and letters in those days trying to sort out his commitment to being a one woman man. Linda demonstrated an amazing strength of character and dignity in the swirling challenges of Bob's poor choices.

I remember Linda used to say, "I am absolutely convinced that Bob does not know what love is." I think I know what she meant. The kind of love that is sacrificial and generous. The kind of commitment to a person that will give and change for the other's best interests. Bob struggled with that kind of relational depth but as he has gotten older I think he recognizes the loneliness of not loving someone in that manner.

While Bob has a wonderful family, I think he would take a few mulligans and do-overs if he could. Wouldn't we all? Many times I have heard him tell stories about his children and grandchildren as people would often stop him and ask how they were doing. He is very proud of them. In my world I understand the challenges of growing up as the pastor's kid. My grown sons still tell stories of growing up with the public expectations and challenges of Dad being up front all the time. I think Bob's kids faced similar challenges. I know Bob is proud of his children and the way they have chosen to raise their families.

I remember during the days before the divorce with Linda was final Bob was describing to me what Linda and her lawyers wanted. I looked at Bob and said, "For what you have put Linda through, how much of a check do you think you would have to write her to make that right?" He said, "Don, I don't have that much money." Years later, he told me that advice I gave him was the most expensive he ever received.

Bob and I have talked many times about relationships. I remember one Sunday afternoon when he picked me up at our house on South 14th Street in Lafayette, and he had a yellow Lexus coup. He wanted to take a ride and threw me the keys. He was in the mood to talk.

We talked all the way to Monticello, IN. to his house on Lake Shafer.

That was the deepest conversation I ever have gotten into with Bob. He seemed just dumbfounded about himself. I asked him a very direct question about why he made the choices that he was making.

He put his head down, then looked at me and said, "I do not know. I just can't help it." I don't know if Bob remembers much of our conversation that day but I feel like it was both a significant opportunity and crossroads for him. I deeply appreciated his trust and transparency that day, it was hard for Bob.

In those counseling days, I made the suggestion that I have some friends on the East Coast who are very successful business people who also have a deep commitment to the Christian faith. Their Christian faith permeates how they do business. I pulled in all the favors I could, and got three of these acquaintances to meet us in Philadelphia. Bob, Linda, JR and Kathy all agreed to go to Philadelphia. We met for a day, and it was interesting to sit there and hear the stories of these people who were Bob's peers in business.

They could talk the same language as Bob. They presented how they conducted their business from a uniquely Christian faith perspective.

We got to the end of that day, and while there were some intense exchanges, Bob seemed to appreciate the day. In my opinion it also was another crossroads. He was exposed to a different way to think, which would allow him to open up more to people and connect the dots between his faith, family and business. He understood some of it, but he just wasn't ready for it.

Bob is a religious man. He has often introduced me to people he knows as the Baptist pastor who wants to become a Catholic priest. I typically reply that I enjoy being married and wouldn't look good in the robes and pointy hats. Our friendship has raised some eyebrows as if some wonder just who is trying to convert who?

I have attended Bob's church services with him a few times. They are quite different than what I am accustomed to so I would ask Bob to explain the various parts of the service to me. Why does the priest do and say this? How do you know when to stand or kneel? Those kinds of questions. His standard response was always pointed at my eventual 'hoped for' conversion – "I don't really know but you'll just have to get used to doing it the right way like we do."

Before going on the Rose Bowl trip we agreed that we would attend church on Sunday morning. Rather than make it difficult, we decided to go to two church services – we each chose one and the other had to go. Bob's choice of church was named St. Thomas of something. It was a beautiful building and fine representation of Bob's religious perspective. I came away with the same questions by the way. My choice was Grace Community church, a large Bible centered church pastored by John MacArthur. John is a well-known preacher and author in evangelical church circles. John tends to preach a lengthy sermon with a clear authoritative tone to it. On the way to our car after that service Bob commented that it was clear around that church who was the boss. I responded – "so you liked him then?" Bob laughed.

Bob has told me that he believes his business success is a blessing from God. I know Bob does and gives a lot to help people that I am guessing not many close to him know about. He has shared stories of how he has helped his church and others in quite generous ways. He had a particular relationship with Father Miller, an older priest that he had known a long time. Father Miller was nearly blind. I have a significant hearing disability. I think it was highly entertaining for Bob to take us both to football games and watch us try to get along. Bob would put his headset on and enjoy the game while I enjoyed explaining what was happening on the field to Father Miller and trying to understand his incredible stories and jokes. He often would point at Bob and shake his head while chuckling. I thoroughly enjoyed those times with father Miller and joining Bob in making a somewhat forgotten man feel loved and appreciated.

Regarding our different religious perspectives, the biggest disagreement we have, if you can call it that, has been about why Jesus was crucified and raised from the dead and what that accomplished. We both believe that he did die for our sins and that he was raised from the dead but we both recognize that we are miles apart in what that means in terms of living out that belief. I think it is a sign of a strong friendship when two people can agree to disagree and continue the friendship. Bob and I have not had a decent conversation about faith in a long time. I am trying to grow in my understanding of Jesus teaching that in order to gain real life, a man has to first lose or give his life up to the lordship and control of Jesus. I really miss those deeper exchanges with Bob and pray that he will grow in his understanding of the only important issue about religion - who Jesus is and why he was crucified.

One of my favorite stories is when Bob and I were getting to know each other we would often have breakfast and Bob would always buy. The check came one morning, and I picked it up. He asked me what I was doing. I told him I thought it was my turn to buy.

I asked him why he thought he had to buy breakfast all the time. He said, "Don, it is as simple as this ... I think I have more money than you. And until you have as much money as I do, I think I will buy."

I am so grateful for Bob's friendship and trust. I say that knowing that there is a public and somewhat complex side to him. He is a brilliant and blessed individual. I appreciate the simplicity of spending time at a game or a meal and just enjoying each other, even if we only get to go deep in conversation once very few years.

75. *Jack Schult*

Retired Teacher and Coach at Lafayette Jefferson High School

I always knew about Bob, but my earliest direct memory is when Bob would come to the Lafayette Jeff basketball games beginning in the late 1960s or early 1970s when I was an assistant to coach Joe Heath and then when I was the head coach.

Bob would sit right behind our bench, and when I would sit down, he said before every game, "If your team is in trouble tonight and you need some (coaching) help, let me know, because I am right behind you and will help you out."

We began talking together a great deal, and in 1975, my boys tennis team won the Indiana High School state tournament. After we won the championship, Bob came to our season-ending banquet. I don't know if he was invited or not, but he came to the banquet.

He told me, "You are going to get a car." Our superintendent and principal, who were at the banquet, did not like the idea of Bob giving me a car, because at that time, I don't think the Indiana High School Athletic Association permitted coaches to receive that kind of gift from a booster or alum.

Bob approached us, and he gave me a car - a small box with a miniature Toyota. Years later, he remembered that gift and asked me what I had done with the toy Toyota car. I told him I think I gave it to our daughter, Jackie, to play with and that eventually, I may have thrown it out.

He said, "Oh, my gosh! That would have been a collector's item today."

Now, he takes me with him to the Purdue and Indianapolis Colts football games. At Purdue, we sit outside if the weather is nice, but if the weather is bad, we sit in the press box. Even though he is able to attend just about anything he wants, he never has forgotten where he came from.

He always is down to earth. For him to want me to go with him to the Colts games and to Purdue games is fascinating, because here is a man who has all the money in the world - he gave Jeff High School $3.5 million for a performing arts center that bears his name - yet he still caters to me in a sense.

He will buy me anything I want to eat when we go to these football games, even though I don't eat that much. He has always been a good friend to me, and I enjoy spending time with him. He always has something interesting to say.

And when we go to sporting events, interesting things seem to happen.

We will go to the games, and as we are approaching the stadium, he always is stopped by fans who know who he is. We almost don't get to the games, because the people want to talk to him, get an autograph and have a picture taken with him.

He probably is the only car dealer in America who would get stopped by football fans and asked for an autograph.

One of my favorite stories about attending football games with Bob is the time that he asked a priest and a minister to go with us. Bob sat the priest on one side of me with the minister sitting on the other side of me.

The minister was hearing impaired, and priest was visually impaired. The priest would ask me what yard line was the ball on, and the minister would ask me what the priest said. That went on all afternoon with me explaining things to them as best I could.

I looked down the row at Bob several times, and he just smiled. I later found out this had taken place several times when Bob had taken the priest and the minister to games. Finally, Bob found a good pigeon - me - to communicate with the visually impaired priest and the hearing impaired minister.

Bob has been successful in life because he likes people, and he has been willing to take chances. Those two ingredients pretty well sum up Bob Rohrman.

I certainly believe it is true that when you think about Bob Rohrman, he is proof that the American dream exists. He is without a doubt the most successful man in Lafayette, IN and Tippecanoe County.

He did it by liking people, working hard and having wonderfully fascinating commercials on TV. He told me once that kids watch his commercials more than the adults. Kids love his bloopers.

I think there is an actor inside Bob Rohrman, and he so much enjoys what he does with those commercials. He is very, very good in his commercials.

He likes to talk about one of the first commercials he ever did - The Mummy - at Lafayette's TV-18. He looked into the camera dressed as a mummy, and said, "Put your hands on a Toyota, and you can't go wrong."

Bob always has wanted to have fun and to give to others, which is what makes his gift to Jefferson High School so special.

When I was still teaching, I asked Bob if he wanted to give any money to the Jeff athletic department. Even though he graduated from Jeff, he said he didn't want to give to the athletic program, because Jeff would be playing other local schools whose players' parents may have bought cars from him or who were considering buying a car from him.

He thought that if Jeff beat those teams, the potential car buyers from those schools might have a sour attitude towards him.

So, instead, we looked at the possibility of him giving some money to the music department. He thought that was a great idea. In the music department, he would not be stepping on anyone's toes from the other local high schools.

He felt that as a Jeff graduate, that would be satisfying to him. So, he gave $3.5 million. On the day the performing arts center was dedicated, Bob attended, got up on stage and sang, "I did it my way," by Frank Sinatra, who is his favorite male vocalist.

He did a pretty good job singing that song. That is the performing ability coming out in him. He received a huge ovation after singing. For those who attended that day, it is something they never will forget.

He mentioned to me that another reason he wanted to create the performing arts center is to provide opportunities for those who have talent in something other than athletics, which Jeff is well known for. He wanted a place where those students could sing or act or dance or play an instrument. It is pretty neat that he wanted to do that, and he did it.

Bob loves Lafayette. For example, each September, we stage the Lafayette Jeff Birdie Bash golf tournament to raise funds for the Jeff athletic department, and Bob always enters his own team, led by his grandson, Trey Rohrman, who is a terrific golfer.

Trey is an ace, and he has me, himself and one of his general managers on his team. The most recent Birdie Bash, our team won. Trey won it for our team. Bob enjoys coming to things like that and being in his community with people he knows.

Bob would do anything for Lafayette. He is a great business man and a wonderful person to be able to say that he is from Lafayette, IN.

I think another element that people like about him is that he is not afraid to poke fun at himself, especially in his commercials. The auto-buying customer likes that and senses that he is a good hearted person.

He also stands behind all of his cars, which is a key to success.

What Bob has accomplished is amazing. I often have told him that if he tells everybody the secrets to his business success, everyone would have the opportunity to do what he has done. He said, "No, they would not work at it like I have and would not do the things that I did. I don't care if they know the secrets or not."

I don't know if anyone could start at the point he started and accomplish what he has accomplished in any venture. He truly is a miracle man. He has been great for me to know.

76. *Dan Keen*

FAA Aviation Safety Inspector and Bob Rohrman's pilot

I started flying for Bob in 1984 when he purchased a brand new Piper Saratoga, which showed up at Aretz Airport in Lafayette.

Bob had a couple of pilots flying for him, and one of them couldn't make it one day. I was a member of the Lafayette Police Department and was able to get some time off. He asked me if I would be willing to fly the plane. I said absolutely and have been doing it ever since.

I got my pilot's license right after graduating from Lafayette Jefferson High School in 1974. I also am a musician and was very fortunate to earn some money playing throughout school. I took that money and started taking flying lessons.

Flying was always a hobby, as my career was in law enforcement. Flying still is a hobby. After I retired from the Lafayette Police Department in 2000, I went to work for the Federal Aviation Administration. I also taught aviation at Purdue for four years. Anything related to aviation safety, that is what I do now. I also do pilot certification and investigate accidents in Indiana.

I owned my own plane for about 35 years, and I used it quite a bit for travel, including musical gigs. My band - The Keen Sounds - was a variety band that could play anything from Glenn Miller music to whatever was on the current charts. We were very successful and usually were booked a year in advance. We had a blast doing it.

But as a detective the last few years on the police department, I was on call all the time, so the band kind of went to the wayside. Even with the FAA now, I am on call. Plus, the music scene in Lafayette now is not what it was. I still play solo trumpet, although I played the drums through school. One hobby kind of paid for the other.

As his pilot, I have always loved Bob, who always has treated me right. We always have a good time, from putting trips together, or flying back and forth to Chicago. I could not ask for a better passenger than Bob.

Plus, the guy knows how to fly himself, although he won't tell you. He actually soloed years ago. Deep down, I think Bob always has had a real interest in aviation. The guy knows that airplane better than I do.

We fly all over the Midwest, mostly to Chicago and back to Lafayette and to Fort Wayne and back to Lafayette. We also have flown to Tennessee and to Wisconsin and Minnesota - wherever he wants to go.

It absolutely makes me feel good that I can help Bob, and I do it for fun. I don't think I have charged Bob for more than 20 years. I enjoy doing it for him.

We have enjoyed some funny or interesting experiences together. One of my favorites involves a flight from Chicago back to Lafayette, but the weather in Lafayette was horrible, and we had to end up landing in Kankakee, IL. I had the Lafayette chief of police riding along with me.

I never will forget landing in Kankakee, and as we walked into the airport, I heard over the loud speaker that Bob had a phone call. I had secured the plane, and Bob already was on the phone. He arranged with an auto dealer over there to get a car and drive back to Lafayette that night.

The chief of police and I spent the night in a hotel and flew back the next day. Because we don't have deicing on that plane, it won't fly in all kinds of weather. We basically fly on good weather days, which is the way Bob likes it. But he is a great passenger.

The thing I really appreciate about Bob has the personality and the fact he always is in a good mood. He always is smiling, and he treats me fantastic. Sometimes he will take me to a ballgame, and I get to go right into the suites with him. I have gone into some meetings with him, and he always introduces me. Being out on the golf course with him is fun, too.

It's fun to hear all the people yell to him when he walks into a sporting event. He will sign as many autographs as people want or have pictures taken with him. At restaurants, I have seen children lined up to have a picture taken with him. It really is a neat thing to see.

Bob is successful because he definitely understands it. In all the dealings I have had with him, he really cares about all of his customers. The guy will take phone calls from wherever. He is demanding on his employees to be sure that all customers are treated right.

In his commercials, he is not afraid to make fun of himself. We all need cars, and not only does he give people a good deal, he also makes buying a car fun.

Each of his dealerships is built first class all the way. He honored me by being able to take my band in and play the grand openings for most of his dealerships, including Schaumburg Honda. I also have played for a lot of his Christmas parties.

When he was building Schaumburg Honda, I would fly him there and get as low as I could get so that he could circle fields and take pictures. He would have maps in the back of the plane with Monopoly like buildings so he could move those pieces around to see how it looked. He would ask me about where I thought he should put a building.

He would ask if I could fly even lower so he could get a better picture, and I would remind him we were only five miles from O'Hare Airport and that I couldn't get much lower. I had the honor of looking at the field when he was deciding where to build Schaumburg Honda, and then the honor of playing at its grand opening.

He is a really humble man who enjoys being around someone like me versus being around the President of the United States.

77. Lew Neuman

Praxis Construction, Engineering and Architecture

Everyone calls us everything in reference to Mr. Rohrman. They call us his architect and his builder, but I call myself his coffee maker. We do a lot of his construction and design work, especially for his larger facilities.

I have been doing work for Mr. Rohrman for approximately 15 years and have been involved in maybe 15 or 20 dealerships, doing everything from small remodels to new builds.

The Arlington Lexus store, which opened in the summer of 2015, was a project he sent me a book about a long time ago. Lexus puts out a best of the best book of Lexus dealerships across the nation, and when I got the book, I asked him what he wanted me to do with it.

That book had very, very nice dealerships in it. These were the best Lexus has. I asked him, "Am I to use this for the new Lexus dealership?" He said, "Yeah, babe." I told him OK. We were going to go that route.

I kept that book, because every time I come back to Arlington Lexus, people say it is over the top. I tell them no, not compared to the stores in the book he sent me. Arlington Lexus is the biggest store we ever have done for him.

It is 145,000 square feet with a $40 million price tag and growing. It is one of a kind. We have never undertaken anything this large, but it is nice.

It has been a long journey since I met Mr. Rohrman at Gurnee Saturn, and I was working for John Espenes. I never had spoken to Mr. Rohrman. Everything always was through John. I was in the hallway of that Saturn store measuring something at the same time the furniture guy - a guy named Buddy Broadway - was installing furniture in an office.

There was a water cooler in this office that had been on the plan since Day 1. And the guy's furniture was conflicting with the water cooler. His opinion was that the water cooler should be moved, and my opinion was that the water cooler should not be moved, because it had been there since Day 1. I felt the furniture, which came long after the fact, should be moved.

The interior of the Arlington Lexus dealership, which was completed in 2015.

I forget how Mr. Rohrman addressed me, but he asked if I was with Espenes. I turned, and there was Mr. Rohrman and Pam Bockwinkel. Mr. Rohrman asked me why the water cooler was in the way of the furniture. That was his first attack on me.

I told him the water cooler has been there the whole time. He said it was in the way of the furniture, I told him it was not in the way of the furniture. I said the furniture was measured after the fact. I told him he had signed off on the water cooler being there.

He said nothing more and walked away. I stood my ground with him, and generally, if you stand your ground with him, there is a tolerance for you. I wasn't BSing him or lying to him. At that point, it probably all clicked for him and it all made sense to him.

That was my first encounter with the man.

Now, everyone who comes to see the new buildings we have done more recently asks, and I tell them he really is the driving force. We have some of the creative ideas, but we couldn't do it without him. To us, he is like a philanthropist. He supports us. He could say he is not going to do these crazy things we come up with.

In the end, when the customer sees the facility, I think he really appreciates it. He has an appreciation for the things we design that maybe some other people who are paying for things do not have.

He also is a pretty diverse person. On the one hand, he is pretty pragmatic, but when you sit down with him to do the Lafayette Toyota store or the Arlington Lexus store, we present the basic ideas, but we lean on him. His review is not just some cursory review. He asks questions. He wants to know specific dimensions. He asks why we use a certain material, or why did we do that?

He spends the time to try and understand the most diverse things. He is real involved in the process. He asks how one space will lead to another. He gets down to the very detail of it. He thinks the way we do creatively, but then he can turn it around and say, "What is the number and what is the cost?"

He asks if we can change this or change that. He really understands it, and he is fearless. When we talk about how to achieve something, he has ideas and contributes. He by no means is outside the fire. He is in the middle of it.

With the Lafayette Toyota store, Toyota had two color palets. We asked him what color he wanted, and he said he liked each color, so let's do them both. We did that, and we also knew his history in Lafayette is where he really started.

We wanted the people in Lafayette to know how big he is, because he does not carry himself that way. We wanted Lafayette to really appreciate what he is and how far he has come. That started a whole process of us wanting to do that store with the quality of the stores we do in the Chicago area.

We asked him if it was OK for us to pay homage to his history. We went with that, knowing we had a little more breadth of scale. He told us we could do that. We wanted to create a store in Toyota's image, but let's also reflect on his love for Japanese art.

My staff and I bought books about Japanese art and went to museums to study Japanese art, culture and color. We wanted to get in our own minds what relationships were OK. We put together a color palet for him and made decisions for him.

The night we presented it to him, he came to the office at 9 p.m. and didn't leave until 2:30 a.m. We went through everything from sinks to faucets. I was worried, because it had snowed and there had been an ice storm, and he drove that night from Indianapolis to Lafayette.

He had to chip close to half an inch of ice off his car. But he stayed until we got through it all. Sometimes when he looks at things, he will say, "I don't know," but there is a trust. We never would do something to embarrass him or look bad for the group. He appreciates what we do.

He really is a sink or swim kind of guy. He might give you the pool to swim in, but after that, you are on your own.

Mr. Rohrman has been a success because he is one of those people whose business is his hobby. He loves it. He eats, sleeps and breaths it. And I also don't think he has forgotten where he came from. Somehow, that has been engrained in his mind, and he values hard work.

He understands that hard work is the way to succeed. He doesn't quit.

78. Jon Espenes

Senior Construction Manager of the Jon Espenes Company

In 1972, Bob was just getting ready to open the Jeep store on the corner of Sagamore Parkway in Lafayette. I got a call, asking if I could give them a price for cleaning up and painting the little used car building that they had been working out of for years.

That was the first job I did for Bob Rohrman. It happened to be the second job ever done by the Espenes Company. From there, things blossomed over the years.

As I was finishing that job, Bob needed a new vent put in his home garage, so I remember getting into his car and going to his house. I wanted to make sure I did a good job for him, because I wanted to do more work for him. He was pleasant and drove me back to the dealership.

Our friendship began to blossom when I was renovating TV18 in Lafayette, and Bob decided he was going to do the commercials for the all-night movies. I had gotten to know everyone at the TV station, and I was told they needed some people willing to be participants in the skits that were Bob's commercials.

My girlfriend at the time and I were in one of his first skits. The first one we were in involved a wet tee shirt. It was pretty funny. Bob was a blossoming actor. The program director was very talented and was writing some great commercials for Bob.

We were in several of those commercials. Over the years, the trombone has kind of been my party instrument, and I used it in some commercials with Bob. In another commercial, the program director and Bob were in a bed, and a live horse was brought in to nudge them and wake them up. That commercial aired during a Western movie.

After the scene, the horse walked down a hallway and used the area as his bathroom. It was too funny.

I probably was destined to end up in the construction business, because my dad was a carpenter and built a lot of school houses. He also built a lot of churches and dormitories.

So, once I got started in Lafayette, I learned that a construction manager for the Tippecanoe County Outdoor Drama project was needed, so I told the organizers that we could do that job. I got the job, and about three quarters of the way through it, Bob came to the site to see what construction management is all about.

I showed Bob what we were doing, so Bob gave us two or three more jobs. I got Bob's first Lexus store in Chicago. I also did the additions to Bob's Schaumburg Honda. We also remodeled Acura.

I enjoy working for Bob, because I know that when I am working, he is working. With him, work does not stop at 4:30 p.m. There were times we would sit for long hours going over plans or color schemes.

You love working for a guy you can call and tell him you have a problem. When we built the Lexus store, I wrote a check for $50,000 out of my own pocket to a lighting company, because we could save some money. I told him the next day, and Bob wrote the check and put it in my bank.

We also flew to projects on what Bob calls "Rohr Air," which is his plane. We would start in Lafayette at 6 a.m. and head to Chicago where they would drop us off and Bob would get a car for us, and we would visit all the dealerships. Then we would head to Fort Wayne and do all of his stores there.

I have done a lot of projects for Bob, who is very hands on, which is good, because I like to have contact with the owner. He always has trusted me to make a good decision. You learn a lot about a person when you work closely with him.

I remember one time we went through a building, and Bob told me he didn't like the towel racks. He likes ones that are automatic or pull downs and don't waste towels. Better yet, he likes the electric hand dryers. You learn and adapt.

We actually have written a Bob Rohrman specs book that includes all the things he likes. Now, somebody could come in and pick up from where we left off.

I also had the pleasure of starting and finishing the Toyota store in Lafayette, but I got fired from the project in the middle. You haven't really worked for Mr. Rohrman until you have been fired once or twice.

I have many fun stories about Bob. I especially like getting on the airplane with him. We may have to be in Chicago at a certain time, but there are two things Mr. Rohrman stops for. One is to go to the bathroom, and the other is to eat. Eating is the biggest one. We can be running 20 minutes late or an hour late, but if he is hungry, we are going to go eat.

Another time, we were at the airport waiting for him so we could take off, and here he comes with a bucket of fried chicken. We would have a picnic on the plane.

Sometimes, we would fly in the winter, and we would ice up coming back from Fort Wayne. We took off and almost hit some deer on the runway. Then, we got iced up, and the pilot was being real quiet up front.

Bob, who always sits in the tail, was looking out at the wings and started singing, "There is one motor gone and we are still carrying on. We're coming in on a wing and a prayer." Then he said, "We have had a pretty good life, haven't we Jon."

We hit the ground, and the ice would shatter off the wings. We had that happen a couple of times.

Then there was the time we were on our way to a meeting with the Lexus people, and Bob ripped his pants. Instead of running in somewhere and buying another pair of slacks, Bob taped the rip with duct tape. And we went to the meeting.

He can have whatever he wants, but he likes the little things. When we flew out of Palatine, IL, he liked to stop at the McDonald's there. The kids would flock to him and say, "It's Bob Rohrman!" He would sign autographs or have pictures taken with him. I never saw him turn down a kid.

He always eats at places where normal people eat. He says, "I want to eat with the people who buy my cars."

I think another way we connect is that he served in the military, and so did I.

I was raised in LaCrosse, WI and always wanted to attend Purdue University. After graduating from high school in 1964, I attended the University of Wisconsin-LaCrosse for a year and then joined the Marine Corps.

In 1968, I went to Vietnam. In 1967, I got a chance to pick up an enlisted commission, and I did that. Until that point, I had gotten up to a buck sergeant. In early 1968, I was commissioned as a second lieutenant. I had my choice of where I wanted to go, and I decided I wanted to go on the ground. I went into Vietnam as a platoon commander. I got to see a lot of action over a short period of time. In early August of 1968, I was in Vietnam.

The third day I was in Vietnam, I saw my first combat. The action lasted from 1 p.m. until 7 the next morning. We lost seven Marines. I ended up in a company with a bunch of Marines who had fought in Hue City.

I was shot on Aug. 15, 1968, and the round went through the back of my flak jacket. It went up through my neck and out through the ear. The flak jacket took everything, even though the shot picked me up and threw me through the mud.

I was lucky. I wanted to keep that flak jacket forever. It just grazed me and drew a little bit of blood.

The bigger injury was Sept. 15, a month later. I went to disarm a booby trap, and it went off. I thought I took most of the brunt, but I found out that several other people were hurt. I took the brunt all the way from my legs to the top of my head.

Again, it was that flak jacket that saved me. I kept it zipped, and only one piece of schrapnal made it to my chest. Most of my left arm was blown off, but they pinched the arteries. I was hospitalized the rest of my military career. I retired from the military in November of 1969.

I had several surgeries early on after the injury and then one later to repair the nerve damage in my left arm.

My older brother, Kenneth, also was in the military and was part of the 40-man patrol that captured Mount Suribachi on the island of Iwo Jima and did the famous flag raising that is a legendary photo from World War II.

After I retired from the military, I wanted to realize my high school dream of going to Purdue. When I was in high school, I wanted to play football for Purdue. I actually came to West Lafayette for a visit in my junior year of high school and visited with athletic director Red Mackey.

Mackey looked at me and told me I was too small to play football at Purdue. I also wanted to run track.

When I finally made it to Purdue, I did so on a full military scholarship. I attended my first class at Purdue in the fall of 1970. By 1972, I had had enough of it. There were a lot massive cheating problems going on in the classrooms at that time, and I wasn't happy. I actually went to the dean of students about it. They fixed the problem.

I was studying to be a veterinarian, and there were great people in that school. But I couldn't use my left arm to perform surgeries. So, I didn't push it.

I was going to go back to Purdue, but I started helping John Smith Construction at the apartment complex at which I was living. I did some roofing and painting. That is how I got started. I learned a little bit about business and how to be a contractor.

I had $60 in my pocket when I started. I went deer hunting in Colorado, and when I came back from that trip, I started my own business, which led to my relationship with Bob Rohrman.

In working with Bob, I have observed several components that explain why this man has been so successful. The reasons are simple.

First is hard work. You have to stay at it, and it is not easy. You have to be focused on a goal and educate your people to achieve that goal. Everybody at these dealerships is undergoing training.

He spends a lot of money training his managers to do the right thing. When an employee comes to work, his shoes should be shined. You come dressed to sell a car.

His dealerships are clean, and he has great customer service. If you call and ask for Bob, they will put you through. His philosophy is that if he has an upset customer, you don't upset the customer any more by asking who it is and what is the nature of your business. He enforces that philosophy of putting the customer through to the person he or she needs to talk to.

The exterior of the Arlington Lexus dealership, which opened in 2015.

He will call his own dealerships just to learn who is answering the phone and how they are answering it. It is annoying to me when I call someone and can't get a real person.

The key is the first impression that a person has over the phone. If Bob doesn't like that impression, he will call the general manager. He does not like to have customer problems. If they do have a problem, he will get it solved.

He has practiced a lot of life lessons that his mother and his family probably taught him.

For a person like me, he has offered so many opportunities that I never would have gotten anywhere else. I would never have had the chance to build a place like Toyota in Lafayette.

When you put a place together for him, everything rings Bob Rohrman. It is part of his story.

79. *Jeff Washburn*

Writer of Bob Rohrman's biography, "A Fantastic Ride"

Washburn spent twelve months interviewing fellow Lafayette, IN, native Bob Rohrman and thirty-five others in the process of writing this authorized biography of one of America's most successful, fascinating and entertaining automobile dealers.

Like Rohrman, and four of his five children, Washburn is a graduate of Lafayette Jefferson High School (1972), and is a 1976 graduate of Purdue University, earning a Bachelor of Arts degree in journalism and radio/TV while minoring in history.

From 1972 until Oct. 1, 2013, Washburn was an award-winning sports writer for the Lafayette (IN) Journal and Courier, covering high school football, boys' basketball, baseball and golf from 1972 until April, 1994, when he accepted the Purdue men's basketball beat, following the Boilermakers for nineteen seasons, eleven with legendary coach Gene Keady and eight with coach Matt Painter.

While at the Journal and Courier, Washburn won seventy-one writing awards and was voted Indiana's Sports Writer of the Year in 1991. He was a frequent columnist and also helped with coverage of Purdue football and baseball, the Lafayette Men's and Women's City Golf Tournaments and PONY Baseball's Colt World Series for 15 and 16-year-olds, staged annually in Lafayette's Loeb Stadium. Washburn covered Rohrman's third child, Randy, when the hard-throwing left-hander pitched for Lafayette in the Colt World Series.

Beginning in October, 2013, Washburn started covering Purdue football and basketball for The Associated Press and the Fort Wayne Journal Gazette and began covering the NFL's Indianapolis Colts and the NBA's Indiana Pacers for The Sports Xchange, the sports wing of Reuter's News Service.

In 2015, he covered the NCAA Men's Basketball Final Four in Indianapolis's Lucas Oil Stadium, and a month later, he covered American Pharaoh's Kentucky Derby triumph, the first leg of the horse's journey to The Triple Crown.

Including 2015, he has covered the Purdue men's basketball team in the NCAA tournament fourteen times, and also covered the Boilermakers in the Maui Invitational twice, the Great Alaska Shootout twice, the Puerto Rico Invitational twice, The Big Island Invitational once in Hawaii and the Virgin Islands-based Paradise Jam once.

He has covered the Purdue football team in bowl games 10 times, including the 2000 Rose Bowl. He also covered John Daly's epic victory in the PGA's 1991 Championship at Crooked Stick in Carmel, IN. He also has covered Major League Baseball playoffs, the NFL playoffs and the NBA Finals and playoffs.

For his countless sports writing efforts, many on tight newspaper deadlines, Washburn has been inducted into the Indiana Basketball Hall of Fame, the Lafayette Jefferson High School Hall of Fame and the PONY Baseball Hall of Fame, which is based in Washington, PA.

"A Fantastic Ride" is Washburn's fourth book. He also wrote *Gene Keady: The Truth and Nothing But The Truth, Tales from Indiana High School Basketball* and *The History of Purdue Sports,* a project that afforded Washburn the opportunity to develop a friendship with legendary UCLA coach and former Purdue basketball All-American John Wooden.

Born Sept. 20, 1954 in Lafayette, Washburn is married to the former Cheryl Lynn Lunsford, a special education teacher and specialist for the Lafayette School Corporation.

Washburn and his wife are the parents of one child, son Jade Ryan Washburn, a 2011 graduate of Lafayette Jefferson High School and a 2015 graduate of the University of Missouri's school of journalism.

In addition to watching and covering sports and writing books, Washburn is a passionate, lifelong fan of the Baltimore Orioles and enjoys Duke Men's basketball, primarily because of coach Mike Krzyzewski.

Washburn enjoys traveling - Las Vegas and Longboat Key, FL are his favorite destinations - watching movies (Casablanca, Animal House and The Long, Hot Summer are his favorite films), barbecue, playing BlackJack and spending time with his wife and son.

Of the Rohrman project, Washburn said, "Listening to Bob's marvelous stories and learning about his path to building an automotive empire has been absolutely one of the most fascinating things I have ever done. Bob is fun-loving, candid, engaging and extremely intelligent. He was a joy with whom to work, as were all of his family members, friends and business associates. His is an amazing story and proves that the American Dream is alive and well. I am honored that Bob selected me to write his life's story."

Jeff Washburn